David Thomson

Scott's Men

Allen Lane

Allen Lane
Penguin Books Ltd,
17 Grosvenor Gardens, London SWIW OBD
First published in 1977
Copyright © David Thomson, 1977
ISBN 0 7139 1034 8
Set in Monotype Garamond
Printed Offset Litho in Great Britain by
Cox & Wyman Ltd
London, Fakenham and Reading

for Mathew

Contents

List of Plates

The author and publishers are grateful to Paul Popper Ltd for permission for photographs 1, 6, 10, 11, 12, 13, 14, 15, 16, 17, 18, 19, 20, 21, 22, 23, 24, 26; to Radio Times Hulton Picture Library for photographs 2, 3, 4, 5, 7, 8, 9, 27, 28; and to the Scott Polar Research Institute for photograph 25.

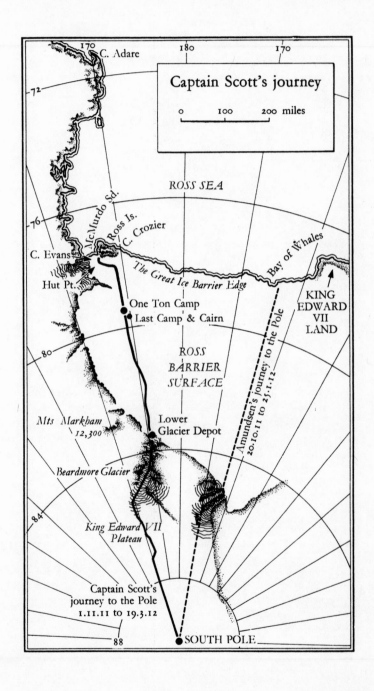

Preface

Between the middle of January and the end of March 1912 five men died in the attempt to return from the South Pole to their base on the edge of Antarctica. Their leader, the last to die and the man whose diary described the pitiful difference between vanished strength and remaining miles, was Robert Falcon Scott. Their journey back began with broken morale in that they had been narrowly beaten to their object, the Pole, by a band of racing Norwegians, led by Roald Amundsen. The Norwegians were hauled along by dogs, while Scott and his men themselves wore harness and pulled their sledge through ice and snow, across ridges and crevasses.

The bodies of the last three to die were found seven months later and, ever since, Scott's men have been British heroes. It is that legend, as much as their ordeal, that is the subject of this book. I have not been to Antarctica, and do not accept all the reasons they gave for going there. But that does not make me a critic of going south, or of exploring wild parts. I only suggest that their journey had few practical purposes, but enough appeal to the imagination to make their story moving and intriguing today.

I have tried to tell that story as clearly as possible, knowing that the brave suffering easily weathers the reality of confused leadership that has often been overlooked. Scott does not strike me as a great man – at least, not until near the end, and I have tried to make this story the biography of a group. Scott's men are at least all those who went with him, humble or famous, and the supporting characters give a fascinating picture of a rather marooned portion of English society in the years before the First World War. Of course there are other individuals that I have felt bound to deal with: Amundsen and Shackleton, his rivals; Clements Markham, his discoverer; and his wife, Kathleen. With all these characters, none more prominent than another, the story of the drama becomes also an illustration of human and social character. And, to the extent that Scott is legendary in England, the book tells something about the English and their attitude to duty.

I

Elderly Men and Young Leaders

Clements Markham was sixty-three, and determined that he was not finished yet. So the snowy-haired veteran of the Royal Geographical Society nagged at British awareness of Antarctica towards the end of the Victorian era. It was always a side-show; nothing illustrates that more than the manner in which Markham initiated and monopolized it. But, as a public performance, chance gave it a form that would first capture and then overwhelm the British people. In the 1920s and 1930s Scott's tragedy seemed the dying fall of a virtuous age, and a belated guarantee that Englishmen had had the stoicism, nobility and uncritical service for four years of warfare by attrition. In retrospect it has epitomized a strain in Edwardian manhood, absurd, admirable and remote. All those blurred notions of England before the Great War, and of a breed of Englishmen that was extinguished or chilled by war, all those myths would refer to Markham, and to Markham's protégé, Robert Falcon Scott, as shining figureheads, men of resolution, patriotism and self-sacrifice.

It was in 1893 that Markham was made President of the Royal Geographical Society. Perhaps, as the British Empire already relaxed its grip on the far world, there was some consolation in the hope that so fine a thing as 'geography' could be royal and best handled by a society of honourable, independent travellers. The several British attempts on the

South Pole spoke with unequivocal earnestness of the need
to stamp a British imprint on the most inaccessible part of
the Earth. There was disappointment, envy and grumbling
at unsportingness when a Norwegian flag was found stuck
in the snow, and there are all manner of flags in the grim
portraits of the British party second at the Pole: flags from
schools and colleges, national flags, pennants given by
queens, flags to honour the wind. Had the British been
there first, with smiles on their burned and shrivelled faces,
the South Pole would have made a pretty scene of chival-
rous bunting, like a fête in an English cathedral city on a
cold June day.

But suppose instead that Scott's men were already past
their time when they perished, that the attempt upon the
South Pole was as much a hangover from the expansiveness
of an earlier time as the busy American treading on the
Moon, and President Nixon's intemperate intrusion upon
that novelty, inset in the live T.V. pictures of first footings.
That master of the pathetic impromptu was heard to claim
that 'This must be the most significant moment in history
since the birth of Christ'. That seems now a foolish thought
about a gross, expensive and tactless exercise. Scott's
expedition was rigorous, modest in cost and immensely
touching, but it was equally marginal to the mood and
needs of 1912.

Markham's shadow hangs over it, and not simply the
influence and patronage of a man who clung to the spirit of
an earlier time, but the aspiration of a boy, ill with mumps
in 1839, thrilled by an account of Parry's Polar voyages.
Scott's journeys were ostensibly geographical, but their
deepest appeal has always been to armchair and sick-bed
explorers, to the imagination of people going about
ordinary, domesticated lives. Eight thousand men volunteered for Scott's second expedition, yet funds for it came
very slowly. How many of those 8,000 were dreamers

yearning to escape smothering realities? What better location for such escapist travels than the aridity of the Moon or the beautiful desolation of Antarctica? One attraction of Antarctica, for the men who marched there and for those who read their journals, has been the emptiness, the calm, the impossible natural beauty unspoiled by the strains and clamour of a built-up society. Antarctica exists most vividly in the mind, as a saucer of wilderness on the bottom of the Earth. To go there is to diminish its purity. It is a never-never land that resists every diligent attempt at justification on the grounds of geological meaning, mineral wealth, strategic value or meteorological forecasting. There was no practical or profitable reason to go there, as many people told Markham and Scott, while many more could not be bothered to reprove the old-fashioned. Scott's Britain was already scornful of the pointless, even if it was only years away from a war in which very few could fathom the origins or the outcome. Even Scott himself had calculated that he would be back in time for whatever conflict it was that Europe was preparing. He could have expected high rank in that war; he might have struggled with command in the confusion of Jutland, or died in that battle. Had he survived, he must have been a national figure in the 1920s and 1930s, not a leading politician perhaps, but a token hero who might have been used by other men. One can see Scott on the angry public platforms of the 1930s, speaking tensely and passionately, unaware of uglier forces beneath whatever hope for regeneration he might be urging.

Those decades could easily have dissipated the glory he won with death. There was a despondent side to Scott that appears to have recognized the destiny of heroic failure on the journey back from the Pole. Perhaps as he waited for blizzards to subside he even had time to realize how far he was the active protagonist of Clements Markham's ambitions. At the very end, among all his last letters, there was nothing written for Markham, only a message for someone else to give him.

Markham was born at Stillingfleet in Yorkshire, in 1830, the son of a clergyman and grandson of an archbishop of York. His mother, Catherine Milner, was from Nun Appleton Hall. It was a comfortable upbringing that led naturally to private education for the child at Cheam and then two years at Westminster before, aged thirteen, he entered the Navy. If that programme limited a boy, it is one we shall see repeated for Scott and many of his colleagues. It is too easy to regret what a boy loses by being taken out of school early; the robust thirteen-year-old boy may be as bumptious and confident a creature as the world permits. The Navy was harsh, but only towards the person and independence of the young teenager. His unfledged, shrill ideas would have accorded very well with the Navy's opinion of what the world was and what a man might make of it. One disturbing characteristic among Scott's men – though notably absent in Scott himself – is their lack of doubt. Perhaps higher education only instills a capacity for scepticism and critical reservation. It is neither unfair nor irrelevant to say that Markham's industry and energy went hand-in-hand with a reluctance to assess evidence critically or impartially. Some of his warm bias helped to kill Scott.

Markham served in his teens on the *Collingwood* and saw whatever of the Pacific and South America a British midshipman was able to comprehend. Then, at the age of twenty, there occurred one of the shaping experiences of his life. On the *Assistance*, in 1850–51, he took part in one of the forlorn searches for Sir John Franklin. In 1845 Franklin had set out to find the north-west passage, one of the legendary attainments that still eluded explorers. Nothing more had been heard of him. In the late 1840s the unexplained loss of Franklin troubled Britain and stimulated several attempts at rescue as well as poetic tributes from Tennyson. It is ironic that Markham should have scanned cold, grey, northern seas for one lost hero in his youth, and that the eventual and fruitless tracing of a north-west passage was made by Roald Amundsen, Scott's surreptitious rival.

For the next forty years Markham led the active, inconsequential life of a Victorian gentleman on his hobby horse. He left the Navy and worked for the East India Company and the India Office. Always travelling, he picked up much diverse knowledge and a reputation as a geographer. His roamings are too extensive to be described here, but he had helped in finding medicines for malaria, he had been to the Andes to collect chinchona trees, he was present at the capture of Magdala during Sir Robert Napier's Abyssinian campaign, he sailed to Greenland in 1875 and he was the author of a spate of travel books, stately, picturesque, complacent and dull. In London he lived in Eccleston Square and belonged to the Royal Geographical Society, of which he was honorary secretary from 1863 to 1888.

The details of Victorian Britain and Empire were administered by men like Markham, and very often they organized their small corner of affairs so that it was a domain in which wisdom and foolishness alike, steadiness or inefficiency, went largely unnoticed by those outside. This is not to suggest that Markham was anything other than a kind, loyal, generous – if fussy and interfering – patron for Scott. But we may question what it was that he was sponsoring and why his choice fell on Scott. At this distance, the title of geographer fits Markham awkwardly in that he seems to have had so definite and clear a preconception of the world he travelled over. In June 1910, the month in which Scott's second expedition left Britain for the south, the eighty-year-old Markham was given an honorary doctorate of science by Leeds University. The address on that occasion is just such a conventional listing of his qualities as Markham may himself have believed in. It seems to regard geography as the study of parts of the world not inhabited by the British: 'he has been for sixty years the inspiration of English geographical science, the leader of the movement which has given the subject a new orientation in the realms of knowledge, and has secured for it an honourable and independent position in the highest courts of learning. It is almost entirely owing to his un-wearied advocacy, combined with an unerring judgement in the choice of men and methods, that England is taking her proud part in the new era of Antarctic discovery.'

There are several questions begged in that tribute. Markham's judgement of men did err, and was often weighed with emotion. As to methods, in the matter of polar travel he was fixedly in the wrong, even when other approaches had proved themselves. And as to the 'proud part' played by England, or Britain, one is quickly drawn into a discussion of pride and its objects. It seems to me more accurate to say that, in old age, Markham success-fully insisted on Antarctic exploration by representatives of his own country.

Some presidents of the Royal Geographical Society have treated that office as an honour and left the running of the society to its other administrators. But Markham announced that the target of his presidency was to pursue south polar research. In May 1893, as soon as he had been elected president, he 'resolved that an Antarctic expedition should be despatched'. He set up a committee of the Geographical Society to investigate prospects and began a personal campaign of lecturing on its behalf. He wrote articles for the popular press and addressed the Council of the British Association, the Imperial Institute, the Royal United Service Institution and the International Geographical Congress.

Markham took it for granted that the expedition should be naval, or that it should be based upon naval discipline and have a regular naval officer as its commander. This indicated the impression that the Navy had left upon the young Markham, and reflects how far British polar voyages in the second half of the nineteenth century had been naval affairs. Not only Franklin, but Admiral Sir George Nares, had contributed to Markham's sense of naval prerogative in such enterprises. It might be added, however, that the first significant sailing into Antarctic waters, by Captain Cook in 1773, led to his matter-of-fact mercantile estimate that the region was so barren and waste as not to be worth bothering about.

There is a note of this gulf between merchant pragmatism and naval dogma in a meeting of the Geographical Society in 1892, at which Fridtjof Nansen was invited to address the Society. Nansen had already made an heroic and innovatory sledging journey across Greenland, and he now proposed a daring and ingenious venture. He had noticed that timber and sea life from eastern Siberia were also found floating off Greenland. Nansen argued that they were brought there in the ice pack that drifted over the Arctic area. His plan was to have a ship and its company frozen in the ice and then carried over the North Pole in the process of drift. He had designed and built a wooden ship that should withstand the crushing power of the ice. When that ship was launched, in October 1892, it was named *Fram*, and in years to come its dramatic appearance in the south was to surprise Scott and Markham.

Nansen came to London in November 1892, outlined his plan and was treated with British naval scepticism. Nares warned against committing a ship to such hazard: 'The adopted Arctic axioms for successfully navigating an icy region are that it is absolutely necessary to keep close to a coast line and that the further we advance from civilization, the more desirable it is to ensure a reasonably safe line of retreat.' Others doubted that Nansen would ever be seen again, but the Norwegian listened politely to every objection and decided that his plan need not be altered. The *Journal* of the Society reported: 'The veterans advised him not to fly in the face of all Arctic practice and tradition, and begged him not to throw his life away on such a reckless adventure.' But was it not the case that all polar travel was still shrouded in doubt and ignorance? So little was known reliably that there could hardly be any proven tradition. Trial and error was the only safe method, and flexibility the surest approach.

The *Fram* set out in 1893 and, after many adventures, completed its journey and proved Nansen's point in 1896. The Society sent its President, Markham, to Norway to greet Nansen and later that year it gave him a gold medal. This was as generous a gesture as the earlier warning had been solicitous. But there is every indication that Markham and others were more challenged by the Norwegian success than able to learn from it. Indeed by the time of Scott's death in the Antarctic there was the beginning of an orthodoxy in polar travel, and it was largely based on Norwegian experience and example. The way in which British explorers proved unable to respond to Norwegian findings – it is not that they were unaware of them – runs through this story and is one substantial explanation for the eventual British tragedy.

Markham may have referred to the prestige Nansen had won for Norway when he approached the Admiralty late in 1896 for support for an expedition to the south. He saw the First Lord of the Admiralty and was fended off with caution and prevarication. The Admiralty was intent on the safety of seas nearer home, and if they said they approved of the idea, it is possible that Markham had so reserved the expedition for the Society and himself that the Navy could see no more role for itself than providing money and equipment. Had he been honest, Markham must have concurred with that view. The running of an expedition, he would have argued, was in the cause of 'geography' and surely a country would rally to the aid of individuals so eager to bring honour to that country? The Navy pondered and said they would rather not. The best Markham could get from them, beyond enthusiastic support, was a donation to match funds raised first by the Society, and the promise of some men and officers.

The funds came very slowly from the public, as if Markham never thought realistically about how they could be raised. He may have believed that Britain would automatically release its money to his deserving venture, leaving no need to go out and procure that money. Was there something of the same helpless caprice in finding a man to command the expedition?

Markham was never shy of dramatizing the way he had chosen Scott as commander. In his own account it reads like an episode from an adventure story for boys. Events may have transpired exactly as Markham describes them; in old age he could easily have believed that; more important, the impressionable Scott's sense of destiny must have been moulded by the older man's romantic patronage. Whatever the case, we depend upon Markham's account for knowing why Scott was inspired to lead two expeditions to the Antarctic. That account says more about the reckless company kept by duty and impulse in Markham's mind, than about the thorough assessment of character, skills and flexibility required by a commander on so testing a journey.

Years later Markham claimed that it was as early as 1887 when, in his own mind, he selected a commander for the Antarctic. His travels then had taken him to St Kitts in the British West Indies, where he was guest of his cousin,

Commodore Albert Markham, in command of the West Indies Training Squadron. Markham enjoyed the company of the young midshipmen. No doubt he had rich stories of his travels to tell them, while they must have reminded him of his own youth. With the first British expedition still fourteen years away, it is doubtful whether Markham had either the patience or foresight to determine then and there on an eighteen-year-old who would one day lead. But that is the tale Markham told in *The Lands of Silence*, a history of Arctic and Antarctic exploration written shortly before his death. Three midshipmen especially struck him in the Training Squadron: Tommy Smyth of the *Active*, his cousin's ship; Hyde Parker from the *Volage*; and, on the *Rover*, Robert Falcon Scott.

Did much really depend on a race between the cutters of these ships? The cutters started at anchor, with a crew under the command of a midshipman. At the firing of a gun, they furled awnings, weighed anchor, stepped masts and made sail. The cutters hurtled back and forth between buoys, then pulled down masts and rowed the last stretch. The race was close, but the *Rover*'s cutter won under its young officer – Scott of the *Rover*!

A few days later Scott was at a dinner party on the *Active* and Markham 'was struck by his intelligence, information and the charm of his manner'. They met twice more before the momentous decision. In 1897, when Scott was a lieutenant on the *Empress of India*, Markham was cruising round Spain on the *Royal Sovereign*. At Vigo or Gibraltar he encountered Scott and 'was more than ever impressed by his evident vocation for command'. Then, two years later in June 1899, Scott came out of Victoria Station and happened to see Markham passing by in the Buckingham Palace Road. He introduced himself and heard then, for the first time, of plans for an Antarctic expedition, plans still dawdling and firmly in Markham's control. Two days later

Scott submitted a written application for the post of commander.

No doubt Markham was impressed by the midshipman and by the lieutenant. But it is just as certain that he met many young naval officers in his travels, and was confident that the British Navy was led at all levels by sound men. He knew too little of Scott to base plans on such a fragmentary acquaintance. Yet he was a man stirred by any hint of providence or destiny. Stopped in the street, he may have quickly reminded himself of this officer, later been impressed by coincidence and within a day carried to decision by the turbulent blend of chance and prescience.

Markham took some precautions. He claims to have consulted Captain Egerton, who put Scott's name at the head of a list of contenders. Yet Scott was not an automatic choice. It would be a year before he was confirmed as commander. Markham had scant evidence to justify a choice that fitted in too well with a scheme of adventure to be contested. Whatever design or forethought there may have been, Markham described the decision in dramatic terms – to others of course and no doubt to Scott himself, who must have been moved by the old man's favour. Remember that, in the space of two days, his life was transformed, his prospects altered from those of a serving lieutenant to the leader of a great expedition. Scott himself, so often an unresolved, tentative personality, may have been the man most stirred by Markham's fancy: 'My final conclusion was that Scott was the destined man to command the Antarctic expedition. He was then 18. . . . The fatal mistake, in selecting commanders for former polar expeditions, has been to seek for experience instead of youth. Both cannot be united, and youth is absolutely essential. Old men should supply information and the results of experience, and should stay at home, making room for the younger and therefore more efficient leaders. . . . Elderly men are not accessible to new ideas and have not the energy and capacity necessary to meet emergencies. How can novel forms of effort be expected from still old organisms hampered by experience!'

2
Scott's Early
Life

Aged thirty-six, in London in the summer of 1904, Robert Falcon Scott was back from his first expedition to the Antarctic, during which he had passed two winters, personally sledged farther south than man had been before, and on that same journey made one abiding friend and set off a bitter rivalry. He was famous, promoted and invited out; yet he lived with his mother and two sisters in London while he sat down to write the narrative of the expedition. He confessed that the writing was a struggle and acknowledged the help of both Dr Leonard Huxley and Sir Clements Markham, to whom the two-volume *Voyage of the 'Discovery'* was eventually dedicated as 'the father of the expedition and its most constant friend'. In the first chapter of that book Scott entered into a routine but obligatory account of the history of Antarctic exploration. He then turned to the circumstances leading up to his own expedition and confessed that, before the commanding hand of Markham fell upon his shoulder, 'I had no predilection for Polar exploration'. The candour reveals a man still young, unresolved and a little more vacant than the conventional picture of a leader of firm resolution. In the same breath he admitted that his own story 'is exceedingly tame'. That is an exaggeration. But Scott's youth and early manhood were not especially productive of purpose or determination. Such doldrums may have irked the young man, and never fully deserted him. It needs to be recalled even now, to be set beside the reputation of national hero and the enormous granite statue of commander in Polar clothes that his widow sculpted and which stands in Waterloo Place, London, sheltered by foliage in summer and exposed in winter.

The child's face was round, soft and dreamy, even when the boy wore the uniform of a cadet on the *Britannia*. It is a kindly face, attentive but shy, the face of one of E. Nesbit's Bastable children, formed in a comfortable Devon home and in games in the garden with sisters and a younger brother. The face is steady and calm; it promises a steadfast man, if one of no special speed, wit or insight.

The explorer was a family man, as were many of the men who went with him. He wrote faithfully from the south to his relatives and took pains to provide for them before he went. If any part of him travelled to evade their fond attentions, or to free himself from responsibility, it was not a part of which Scott himself was conscious.

The family was Devonian, but with stories of Scottish and French backgrounds. The first Robert Scott in Devon had been born in Leith in 1745, the son of a man caught up in the Jacobite uprising. Robert Falcon Scott must have heard and expanded on legends of family heroism and of a great-great-grandfather taken away to France while very young to avoid the reprisals of the Duke of Cumberland. This exile did not return to England until he was in his thirties and he settled then in Holbeton, a small town in the South Hams, a beautiful and secluded part of Devon between Plymouth and Torquay with Dartmoor to the north. It is hilly country, wooded and threaded with narrow lanes that run down to a rough coast of many tiny coves. Smugglers' country, and an intricate shore for children to explore.

No wonder that the family turned to the Navy. Robert

Scott had four sons who went to sea and served in the Napoleonic wars. Two died as midshipmen, but two flourished in the provident trade of ships' pursers. They retired from the Navy in the 1820s and on the proceeds of their service bought a brewery in Hoegate Street, Plymouth. One of the brothers, another Robert, also bought a house, Outlands, in the village of Stoke Damerel, only a few miles from Devonport, the naval quarter of Plymouth.

The brewer Robert had five sons. One became a surgeon in the Navy, three served in the Indian Army, one – Edward Lustington – rising to the rank of General, and the youngest, John, who was born in 1830, was schooled for the beer business. In a family of travellers and fighting men he was made to be pacific and home-loving. If that sometimes rankled, it may explain how he became partial to the beer he made. The comforts and prosperity of his family seem to have led to indolence and complacency that fluctuated with irritable petulance at having to accommodate his wife's parents and his own elderly aunt, Charlotte. He married in 1862 Hannah Cuming, the daughter of a Lloyd's surveyor, and they had four girls and two boys to fill Outlands. The third of these children, and the elder son, was Robert Falcon, born in Devonport on 6 June 1868. It was a large household, crammed with people in the way that Victorian interiors were filled with soft, padded furniture and enough ornaments for servants to spend the morning dusting and polishing. It was a docile time to be born, and a beguiling, if sometimes nearly becalmed, setting.

The children had a nurse, and no sharp wants. But the family seldom ventured out of Devon and the child explorer made his first adventures in the garden and in the near-by country. His younger sister, Grace, has left stories of the boy trudging home after a wilful pony had tossed him and attempting to sail a tub on a stream that ran through the garden.

Nothing except a naval career seems to have awaited Robert Falcon Scott. It was not only the Scott family who had allegiance to the Navy; his mother's brother was Admiral Harry Cuming, and this may have been the strongest influence on his own inclinations, since he was devoted to his mother and impressed by her thorough pleasure in planning. He had a governess at home with the other children and at the age of eight went to a private school in Stoke Damerel. Then, at thirteen, he was briefly at Stubbington House school, in Fareham – his first significant period away from home – the recognized place for coaching towards a naval cadetship. From there, on 15 July 1881, he went to the *Britannia*, a boy dressed up in a uniform and subject to just that elision of adolescence that Markham had suffered.

It was a brief academic education, and not a distinguished one. Yet in later life Scott mixed with trained scientists and men of letters. He impressed the former with his aptitude for learning new subjects and his respect for scientific method. Scott may have had an undue determination to stress the 'scientific' side of his expeditions, as if guilty of brazen adventure, but few scientists who knew him ever doubted his appreciation of scientific work. Among writers, politicians and presidents of societies Scott held his own. It may have been at the cost of some nervous strain; he may have been overawed at dinner parties, though he met his future wife at one and seemed to her the most attractive man there. And if he wrote at first with labour and some awkwardness, the one thing that unquestionably grew in depth and compulsion in his second fatal journey was his power of description. It is, finally, Scott's words that are remembered, and he was better read than most naval officers, especially in poetry and modern novels. Something of this must have begun in his short preparatory education. It is appropriate that one who read of adventure and travel should have left as his finest memorial a travel journal that is still eloquent. At the end of his tether, Scott found the words to give a lasting imaginative life to his ordeal and to make us see a relationship between suffering and duty. There is even the impression in the last journal of a man discovering himself.

When we wonder what would have become of Scott had he returned from the Pole alive, the readiest answer is that he would have risen quickly in the Navy. But that would not have satisfied all his character. In the south he discovered an interest in the patronage of science that sometimes makes him sound like the director of a research establishment. In his crisis he became a writer of gripping directness. If he was himself confused by the strains of naval commander, scientific patron and writer, and if that very turbulence had so much to do with the character of his second expedition, then it is a mistake to suppose that he would ever have settled his own contradictions. Part of the fascination of Scott lies in the churning of unusual, unfledged interests. He was a quiet, withdrawn man capable of bouts of anger and enthusiasm, the signs of a struggle within.

Yet he took the Navy seriously and made his way as dutifully as any boy drafted into the service before he had acquired the mind and independence to be critical. Whatever doubts he had could be treated with the several codes that the Navy employed to make life simple. For instance Scott was never an easy mixer, certainly not as fluent as Shackleton. That came from shyness, uncertainty and even a fear of the strength of his own feelings. The Navy regularized the dealings between men on the basis of rank, duty and ship's law, and thus we find Scott in later life confessing that he could not lead an expedition unless comprised of Navy men and adhering to Navy law.

In 1883, aged fifteen, he passed out of the *Britannia*,

seventh in a class of twenty-six, with first-class certificates in mathematics and seamanship. His first posting, in August of that year, was on the *Boadicea* as a midshipman.

Not much can be said about Scott as a young officer, because in an age of repetitive training and the slow, waiting process of seniority only the record survives. He served also on the *Lion*, the *Monarch* and the *Rover*, where he was first seen by Markham. He had aptitude beyond the ability to win a cutter's race. His captain on the *Rover* had a good opinion of him and was prepared for Midshipman Scott to keep a full officer's watch, as long as it was in daylight.

Soon after the encounter with Markham in the Caribbean, Scott was made sub-lieutenant and posted to the *Amphion*, at Esquimalt, the Pacific station base on Vancouver Island. Still not twenty, he was a self-possessed traveller. On the last stage of his journey to the *Amphion*, he went from San Francisco to Esquimalt on a steamer taking miners and their families to Alaska. This vessel ran into bad weather and the saloons were a picture of misery and alarm before Scott took charge, quelled the panic and organized a cleaning-up operation. The Navy prided itself on training young men for emergencies, even if it had a restricted sense of the nature of emergency. The sub-lieutenant must have been encouraged to see that he could brace, bully or rouse people out of their sea-sickness. It may have consoled his own recurring vulnerability to queasiness.

He was on the Pacific station for nearly four years and came back an adult. His sisters noticed how much he had grown, hardened and matured. Furthermore he returned with a scheme for his career that was practical and far-seeing. Convinced that he now needed some special expertise, he looked to the mechanical novelty of the torpedo. It is the first sign of his interest in machines and of his sense of the future awaiting the Navy. In 1891 he began a two-year training period on the *Vernon*, the Naval Torpedo School in Portsmouth. He had already passed his lieutenant's exam, coming top of his class at the Royal Naval College, Greenwich. For so promising an officer it was a calculated attempt upon the future to forsake a life at sea, further travel and overseas posting for a long confinement in Portsmouth, exercising in the Solent and Spithead and spending hours over drawing-boards and models.

He was able to take his leaves at Outlands and see more of his family. This enabled him and brother Archie, now in the army, to sail their boat in Plymouth harbour, to ride and play golf and to join in the social activities of smart young people in Plymouth. Scott's mother sometimes sailed with the children, though his father stayed at home, more and more burdened by his dilatory handling of financial matters.

From the *Vernon*, in the autumn of 1894, Scott was posted to the *Vulcan*, the torpedo-school ship in the Mediterranean. He was now regarded as a specialist and sometimes fearful of being imprisoned by it. Too considerate to admit the full extent of his debts, Scott's father wondered whether Robert would not be better off in general service. Scott responded with a faith in the newest form of naval warfare and his own chances as part of it: 'my reasons for remaining in the ship are firstly that I look upon her as a latent success, as a splendid but undeveloped and misused experiment dependent on her present handling to establish her utility, a utility which in war time would be apparent and patent to all. For this reason I take a very great interest in her welfare and do as much as lays in my power to forward it. Secondly, and in consequence of my first reason, I have hopes of establishing a reputation for myself.'

He had become ambitious, even if as a child he struck people as a day-dreamer. Of course day-dreamers are usually planning the future, and the logic of the Navy was to plan. It is remarkable that Scott saw a war coming in which the torpedo might be crucial. He told his father that he was not losing too much of the other side of naval experience. In the Mediterranean fleet he went on several exercises, took part in regattas and sports and drew the eye of the admiral on inspection. But he had his doubts. Fellows on the *Vernon* had thought the posting to *Vulcan* 'not good' and Scott already had a temper that led to quarrels, especially with superior officers set in old ways. He had to guard against abruptness; just as often he needed to drag himself out of lethargy. There were these contradictory impulses, and all the while Scott watched himself and nurtured an indistinct feeling of destiny. There sometimes appeared, in his bearing or his letters, a glimpse of how seriously, even passionately, he regarded himself: 'I am conscious that by self-advertisement I might make myself heard now, but the position is a delicate one, and I should be sorry to advocate anything in which I did not believe. Meanwhile things constantly annoy and irritate one – but as you see, I work for a larger than ordinary stake.'

We can hear there the reserved perfectionist, a man vexed by small disorders and misunderstandings but sometimes too introspective to voice his frustration without revealing its disproportion. And, although the Navy offered uniform, travel, ceremony and respect, it was a service marooned by years of peace. In a long naval career there is no note of Scott being on a ship that fired a shot in anger. That 'larger than ordinary stake' might have sounded arrogant, especially from an officer of more modest means than many of his colleagues. It suggested a commitment of hope to the future that would not easily tolerate failure or thwarting. Years later, near the South Pole, Scott knew that he had been forestalled, and perhaps in that instant recognized how vulnerable he had made himself to failure and disappointment.

The Navy of the 1890s already put pressure on Scott

financially. The pay barely met the needs of an aspiring officer, and it was assumed that he had means of his own. Now the Scott family had to face a drastic reduction in its circumstances. The education of the children, Robert's progress in the Navy and his younger brother Archie's in the Army had been paid for from the proceeds of the sale of the Plymouth brewery. John Scott was being pressed by creditors and compelled to make up for his years of semi-retirement. Over sixty, he had to let Outlands, the house that all the family loved, and move to a smaller place near Shepton Mallet in Somerset. In 1896 he was driven to apply for the managership of a small brewery in Bath. As such, the Scotts were the victims of middle-class complacency in the face of more competitive times. There was a real loss of comforts and leisure, and for Robert Scott a sudden obstacle in the way of his career. He had never been extravagant, never drank and rarely went on the spree with fellow-officers. Now his uniform became shabby for want of a replacement and he secured a transfer to the backwater of *Defiance*, a depot-ship at Devonport, so that he could assist the family.

Then, as he approached the age of thirty, the hopeful young officer was severely hit by fate and, within a year, made the chief support of his mother and sisters. The rigours of moving and of renewed work, especially work for another master, proved too great a strain on John Scott. He died in October 1897 of dropsy and heart disease. At this the family gave up their new home. One sister married, to William Ellison-Macartney, while two others went to London and opened a business as dressmakers in Beauchamp Place. Mrs Scott accompanied them, and Robert and Archie agreed to finance the venture. Archie had been in the Royal Artillery, an expensive regiment, and to make ends meet he secured a transfer to a cheaper West African regiment.

It speaks for enterprise that there was no recrimination and so much readiness to make a new life. Scott's mother was the most hurt by the change and Robert had to reassure her that it was no humiliation for the girls to work. He thought that London had made them more interesting and intelligent and 'I honestly think we shall some day be grateful to fortune for lifting us out of the "sleepy hollow" of the old Plymouth life'.

Scott himself went back to sea and, after short periods on the *Empress of India* and *Jupiter*, he took up a post on *Majestic*, the flagship of the Channel Fleet. Archie, always more animated and sociable than his older brother, was made an aide-de-camp to the Governor of the Gold Coast. But in 1898 he came home on leave. The brothers had a happy time together when Archie was allowed a cruise on the *Majestic*. But a month later he was dead of typhoid. Their mother was distraught and blamed herself for the collapse of the family fortunes. Scott comforted her and insisted: 'If ever children had cause to worship their mother, we feel we have, dear, and it hurts to hear you blaming yourself: you can never be a burden, but only the bond that keeps us all closer together, – the fine example that will guide us all our lives.'

In private, the death of the beloved, lively brother seems to have preyed upon Scott's morbid capacity. There were moods in which this withdrawn romantic thought himself victimized by fate. So many bad luck stories throughout Scott's life may only mean that he told them about himself. Sudden inexplicable loss wounded him. There seems to have been no deep religious conviction to sooth the loss, only the puzzled anguish of one whose plans for a grand future could so easily be overturned. Scott leaned on the future, putting great store by it; and as a naval officer in times of peace he may have had too little exposure to situations in which things went wrong. A lack of adaptability in his approach could mean that adversity or difficulty were interpreted as his own bad luck or a malign destiny.

Scott was caught in the position of having to care for his family. One is reminded of his last words – 'For Gods sake look after our people' – an ambiguous cry, a mixture of pathos, nobility, frustration and anger. But the call to God, it seems to me, was more a roar of desperation than a convinced spirit. It was the last hope of a man who felt burdened, who persistently sought out responsibility but who was wearied by its weight. Scott himself may have been guiltily aware of the need to care for people he had neglected or put at risk.

There is a note of guilt in a letter of Scott's to one of his sisters soon after the death of Archie. That letter also gives glimpses of Scott's sense of fineness in man and perplexing obscurity in God:

It is good to hear there was no pain and it is easy to understand that he died like a man. All his life, wherever he went, people felt the better for his coming. I don't think he ever did an unkind thing and no form of meanness was in him. It is a strange chance that has taken him who perhaps of all of us found the keenest pleasure in life, who was always content and never grumbled. Of course, now we know he never ought to have gone to West Africa. After watching him carefully, I saw that despite his health he was not strong and I meant to have a long talk with you on the subject. Too late – doesn't it always seem the ending of our wretched little mortal plans? Good God, it is past all understanding. He and you and I were very close together, weren't we? I know what your loss is, knowing my own.

The rather faintly drawn idol that Archie was to the family has a fellow in Scott's life, his most supportive friend, a man who died beside him, Edward Wilson.

It was less than a year after Archie's death that Scott saw Sir Clements Markham in the street, crossed over to talk to him and triggered the older man's capricious notion of destiny. But he did step over, because he was himself a man who believed in such turning points, even if his timidity may have made him hesitate at the kerb. He would have approached Markham taut with hope, and the patron of discovery may have sensed that bristling readiness: the two men were made for each other. The one required upstanding naval virtues and enough deference to absorb advice; the other believed that the life he had led was still tame and fettered.

When Scott went south for the first time he entrusted his mother to his brother-in-law, which was sensible. But for every effort he took to look after her, he was also turning away, risking his life and the loss of her sole remaining male relative. Scott's men seldom reflected on what their journeys allowed them to escape. Yet some of them were loitering in their occupations, several of them had cramping domestic circumstances and virtually all of them rejoiced in the expansiveness of the great white south. By their own estimate, Polar exploration did involve the regrettable contingency of leaving loved ones; most of them would have rebuked suggestions that they were released from some home restrictions. At this distance, however, it is impossible to ignore that aspect. So many of the men were made healthier, happier and fulfilled in the south, not least Scott.

He was aspiring and lofty in his plans, but moody and temperamental that they so seldom came to fruition. Often enough he stared into space, forgetful of company or of what he was doing. Since his childhood, the family had laughed proudly at his untidiness, or at the way he would play golf and, between the hitting of a shot and walking after it, forget entirely where it had gone. More seriously, Scott worried over his health and the way in which lassitude and the feeling of being trapped sometimes sapped his strength. There is no hint of real illness or weakness.

Instead, he was what is called a 'delicate' child, and sometimes 'run down' as a young man. He had the ailments of a nervous temperament, but he was anxious with his own failings and fretted over them. When he came back from sledge journeys as strong as or stronger than any man, there was the reassurance that he was sound, that he had found a great effort to dissolve his doubts.

But, at this stage, sea air and exercise could not prevent a succession of disorders. In his early twenties he tried to keep journals for himself, surely more personal and searching than was common among sub-lieutenants. We may see how quickly his sense of weakness could be developed into a philosophy of the unconvinced speculator:

It is only given to us cold, slowly-wrought natures to feel this dreary deadly tightening at the heart, this slow sickness which holds one for weeks. How can I bear it? I write of the future, of the hopes of being more worthy, but shall I ever be? Can I alone, poor weak wretch that I am, bear up against it all? The daily round, the petty annoyance, the ill-health, the sickness of heart . . . How? how can one fight against it all? No one will ever see these words, therefore I may freely write 'What does it all mean?'

That unspecific, creeping debility is not too far from the tone of some of Edgar Allan Poe's stories, and it shows how impressionable, romantic and pessimistic a man Scott could be. This is very far from the stereotype of the British Navy, and it is not often attributed to the brave commander who struggled through the blizzard until weakness overcame him. But Scott was not a stereotype, and might not have struggled so much if his character had been more clear-cut and consistent.

Detached, uneasy and introspective, his solemn handsomeness did not go with easy chatter. Some people believed that he was inexperienced with women. But he seems to have been deeply interested in them. As his sister

said: 'The sailor's life and his romantic nature caused him
to idealize women.' In his late teens, he had been infatuated
with a married woman; during his period at Vancouver he
was friendly with Kathleen O'Reilly, the daughter of a
judge who lived in the town of Victoria. Few things
measure the depths in Scott so well as the nature of his wife,
and it is likely that in youth no woman properly engrossed
him just as no job or adventure consumed all his nervous
energy.

He may have dreamed of a woman and noted that real
women were not a match for the flawless passion and
mystery of creatures in fiction and poetry. Scott was well
read in romantic literature and the address book he kept as
a young man includes, in pencil, Browning's *A Woman's
Last Word*. It may have been the idealized version of
romantic failure, the ennoblement of some rejection in
Scott's life or a further mark of the way he was moved by
disappointment:

> Let's contend no more love,
> Sigh nor weep
> All be as before love
> Only sleep.
>
> What so weak as words are
> I and thou
> In debate like birds are
> Hawk on bough
>
> Hush and silence
> Cheek on cheek.
>
> What so false as truth is
> False is thee
> Where the serpent tooth is
> Shun the tree.
>
> Where the apple reddens
> A sure pry

Let us lose our Edens
Eve and I

Be a god and hold me
With a charm
Be a man and fold me
With thine arm.

Teach me only teach love
As I ought
I will speak thy speech love
Think thy thought.

Next if thou require it
Both demands
Laying flesh and spirit
In thy hands

This must be tomorrow
Not tonight
I must bury sorrow
Out of sight

I must a little weep love
(Foolish me)
And so fall asleep love
Loved by thee.

3
Preparing for
Discovery

Amid the long-drawn-out preparations for what was to be the *Discovery* expedition, there occurred the first significant penetration of the Antarctic. This was something more than earlier attempts to make a circumnavigation of the Antarctic land mass or the periodic ventures by whalers as far as the coastline. It received little credit in Britain and hardly impressed Sir Clements Markham or the Royal Geographical Society. After the *Discovery* expedition Markham spoke rhetorically of the continent having been known only to birds before Scott. But two years before Scott crossed the Buckingham Palace Road men spent thirteen months gripped by the frozen sea of Antarctica – not on the land – the half-fascinated, half-fearful pioneers who endured the first dreaded Antarctic winter. It is a sign of the general ignorance of Antarctica before 1900 that the winter was regarded with such awe, whereas other more searching vistas and dangers were simply not comprehended. One man in that first wintering party, and one of the most enterprising in the hitherto unexperienced darkness, was the Norwegian Roald Amundsen. We should bear in mind that Amundsen had gone beyond the Antarctic circle and encountered some of the problems of the area before Scott even contemplated such a journey. Too many Britons, and Markham especially, forgot or were unaware of this when they later reproached Amundsen for intruding on Scott's preserve. Claims of priority litter this story, and they are invariably the specious attempt to dress up national or personal prejudice.

The expedition in question was refreshingly free from national monopoly, and in the accounts that survive it seems to have been muddled and aimless, but undeniably human. While so many Antarctic explorers emerge from their diaries as resolute, single-minded and possessed of the attitudes and horizons of a dutiful school prefect, the records of the *Belgica* convey real men. Whereas Scott's men lectured one another on a variety of topics, the *Belgica* party held a beauty contest based on magazine photographs of girls dreamed over in the 'Ladyless South'.* In inspiration and organization the expedition was Belgian and under the command of Lieutenant Adrien de Gerlache de Gomery. It sailed from Ostend in August 1897 in a Norwegian ship and with a party of eight Belgians, five Norwegians, two Russians, a Rumanian and an American. Amundsen was the first mate.

He was then twenty-five, having been born to the south of Oslo in 1872. It was an uneventful childhood, but one that introduced him to snowy landscapes, the use of ski and long-distance trekking. His life intensified in his early teens when he set himself deliberately on a professional career of adventure, blatant and ruthless enough eventually to offend and throw doubt on self-righteous British thoughts of patriotic and scientific purpose. Amundsen's father died when he was fourteen, leaving the heritage of a brusque, piratical merchant adventurer and a mother who – like Scott's – was alarmed at every prospect of her son's going far afield. A year later Amundsen happened to read the

* The competition awarded marks to the ladies in the 'excellence of special parts': the most beautiful face; luxuriant hair; flashing eyes; mouth (Cupid's bow); shapely hands (tapering fingers); arms; sloping, alabaster shoulders; supple waist; *les jambes* and feet.

works of Sir John Franklin and narratives of his mysterious disappearance. One wonders whether anyone dared tell Markham that Amundsen's inspiration was the very incident that had been such a personal adventure for the president of the Royal Geographical Society.

That news might have provoked Markham's gout or the thin, spidery hand that left such venomous comments in his journals and letters. There was a gulf between a Markham and an Amundsen that no shared interest could bridge: it was a gulf that had to do with character, upbringing and the way in which contemporaries can live in different times. In assessing that gulf, the mistake is to take sides: the two men were as zealous and limited as one another.

Years later, in a quick sketch of the surface of a life that may have had little more than a surface, Amundsen described how reading Franklin appealed to him:

A strange ambition burned within me to endure these same sufferings. Perhaps the idealism of youth, which often takes a turn towards martyrdom, found its crusade in me in the form of Arctic exploration . . . Secretly – because I would never have dared to mention the idea to my mother, who I knew would be unsympathetic – I irretrievably decided to be an Arctic explorer.

I have suggested that, as an old man, Markham allowed sentiment to melt his recollection of earlier events. In fairness it should be allowed that, by 1927, Amundsen too emphasized youthful decision. Yet he was a blunt man only rarely diffident about admitting his aims, and so intent on doing anything not yet done by men that his career restricts our sense of what an exploring, inquiring man might be. From the age of fifteen he prepared himself with the narrow diligence of an athlete. Without any taste for it he played football, a game that haunts the unused energies of Polar travellers. More important, he grasped the usefulness of long-distance skiing, in Norway an activity that lies close to national ideals of hardiness and self-sufficiency. 'At every opportunity of freedom from school, from November to April, I went out in the open, exploring the hills and mountains which rise in every direction around Oslo, increasing my skill in traversing ice and snow and hardening my muscles for the great adventure.' There speaks the spirit 'in training'. It was a sense of anticipation that in some ways overwhelmed Scott's confused motives, and imposed a 'race' upon Antarctica in 1911–12.

No one with a close knowledge of Scott and Amundsen could have hesitated over who would win the race. With reason and feeling, Scott protested at the tension of competition Amundsen had introduced; but he could not shrug it off. To be first and to be famous did matter to Scott. He could not be candid about their importance, but that was because of his complexity as a character. His youth had nurtured incompatible strains of ambition and relaxation, whereas Amundsen slept in winter with the windows open as part of 'my conscientious hardening process'. In being less hard, Scott became the more interesting and vulnerable man.

Amundsen went to university, reading medicine, but withdrew when his mother died and did obligatory national service. At that time he made a lone, winter journey on ski of over seventy miles across a dangerous, exposed plateau. In every physical way he was suited to and experienced in the arduous business of Polar travel. All his life Amundsen was a lean, gaunt man, wiry and as strong as he had intended. He marched on ski as naturally as Scott might stroll about the deck of a ship.

At the age of twenty-two the Norwegian went to sea as an ordinary seaman on a sailing ship, and worked his way up to the rank of mate. To bodily vigour he now added a familiarity with lower ranks and service in the Merchant

Navy. His successful expedition to the Pole contrasts with Scott's in many ways, not least in the sociability of the small company and its flexible handling of the obstacles to success.

The *Belgica* sailed south with a directness that shows how little was then known of Antarctica. For in 1897 there was only a haphazard, untested map of the Antarctic continent; nothing was known of the hinterland. The features that had impressed most observers were the enormous size of the pack ice that surrounded the land, the difficulty of penetrating it and the danger of being crushed by its pressure. De Gerlache went down the length of South America and blundered into the most confused and misleading part of Antarctica: the crooked Graham Land peninsula with its scattering of islands. The *Belgica* made its way in and out of this muddle, establishing straits previously unknown and making many brief landings on the mainland to collect specimens. 'Specimens of what?' we might ask, of them and subsequent explorers. Specimens of whatever they found, is the only answer.

De Gerlache then took the ship farther south and went into the Bellingshausen Sea, and increasing ice. Nothing reveals the uncertain purpose of the *Belgica* so much as the way de Gerlache hankered after wintering in the ice while his officers and scientists persistently advised against it. Although there was no sharp dissent, it was a situation not unlike that facing Columbus. Neither the bold nor the cautious knew what risks they were calculating. In the last resort it was the commander's decision. As Frederick Cook, the American doctor on the *Belgica*, wrote: 'Everybody is opposed to it, but if it must be, they are inclined to submit gracefully to the unquestionable fate.'

The *Belgica* was soon caught in the ice. For some while still it drifted with the pack, the ship squeaking and groaning at the contrary movements. Then ship and pack stuck fast. In not much short of a year's imprisonment, there appear to have been no recriminations, even if few behaved gracefully. It was an immense ordeal, partly because nervous apprehension had prepared the party for it, but also because the dark, the cold, the damp, an unsuitable diet, confined company and too little to do undermined physical and mental health. No one learned those lessons as well as Amundsen; he and Cook seem to have been more determined than the others to remain alert, observant and ready to experiment. A bond formed between them, and the active function of leadership often passed into their hands.

So trapped, amid such a spectacular desert, the party succumbed to inertia as the baleful night set in. Cook, the volatile guardian of the men's well-being, noted: 'The curtain of blackness which has fallen over the outer world of icy desolation has also descended upon the inner world of our souls. Around the tables, in the laboratory, lost in dreams of melancholy from which, now and then, one arouses with an empty attempt at enthusiasm.' There were scientists in the party, and observatory huts built on the ice; but very few could engage in or understand the rather cursory study of weather and magnetism. The men whose task it was to work the ship lived in the forecastle, apart from the officers and scientists and denied any regular activity. The divisions between men and officers, so taken for granted at the end of the nineteenth century, could become confused on Polar expeditions. To readers today it may seem incongruous that a ship isolated and turned in upon itself, so far from European civilization, should insist on such proprieties. But few Polar explorers saw any alternative. If a gentleman had built a country house on the ice, he would never have dreamed of mixing freely with the servants he hired and transported south. Yet some commanders, officers and scientists had enough unease over these curious circumstances to assert, time and again, the good fellowship that united a party.

Cook's account of the *Belgica* voyage is unusually honest about the friction of close company and about the days on which men grew appalled by the sight of one another. This irritation, the depression of living in the dark and the onset of anaemia and constipation were intensified by the problems of diet. No fresh food could be carried on such voyages; no tropical ports could be resorted to for fruit and vegetables. The menu on the *Belgica* was neither monotonous nor plain, but it lacked essential vitamins. There was an excess of cereals, corn meal, biscuits and macaroni. As for meat, they lived on pemmican and tinned delicacies. The latter were rich, smooth and not always well preserved. The canning process inevitably entailed the stifling of freshness and the loss of several nutritive elements. Pemmican, almost synonymous with Polar travel, was a concoction of dried meat and various meals that could be made into a stew with the addition of water, or simply gnawed at like some tough biscuit. The *Belgica* had two Norwegian variants of pemmican – kydbolla and fiskabolla, the one a meat base, the other fish, largely despised by the party, but examples of the special Norwegian familiarity with dried and concentrated foods.

Only Gerlache and Amundsen would eat fiskabolla, which some men alleged was the sweepings from a fish market. The rest of the party kept to the expensive and familiar pastes and patés, sausages and hashes, thus aggravating their tendency to scurvy. Cook observed the symptoms:

Physically we are steadily losing strength, though our weight remains nearly the same, with a slight increase in some. All seem puffy about the eyes and ankles, the muscles, which were hard earlier, are now soft, though not reduced in size. We are pale, and the skin is unusually oily. The hair grows rapidly and the skin about the nails has a tendency to creep over them, seemingly to protect them from the cold. The heart action is failing in force and is decidedly irregular.

Deterioration was general. One of the officers, Danco, who had a weak heart, became seriously ill, and very few were free from scurvy. Just as alarming were the signs of mental breakdown: some of the sailors were said to have become 'insane'. It has been suggested that Cook himself was so neurotic that he added to the moodiness of men already prepared for the worst.* Certainly, compared with later expeditions, the *Belgica* made only modest physical demands on its party. But pioneers suffer most in the imagination, and there was a blend of lethargy and illness on the ship that threatened their survival. Indeed Lieutenant Danco died in the middle of the winter, and Amundsen himself fell ill.

There was a remedy at hand, and Cook and Amundsen were its advocates. The one source of fresh meat was seals and penguins. The two men had slaughtered as many of both as they could before the darkness and made a deep-freeze of the carcasses on the ice. The difficulty lay in persuading Europeans to reject a tinned goose liver paté for a fresh seal steak or penguin stew. Some explorers never overcame their aversion to alien foods and flavours that mingled meat, fish, sea water and a sickening oiliness. De Gerlache loathed the taste and at first forbade the men to eat seal or penguin. But, when the commander was too weak to protest, Amundsen went to the stove personally

---

* Cook (1865–1940) was to become the centre of a great Polar controversy that raised new doubts about his own stability. In the years 1907–9, he led an expedition to the North Pole, in competition with Peary. Cook claimed to have reached the Pole on 21 April 1908. But Peary challenged this and an assembly of scientists in Copenhagen dismissed Cook's claim. Was he really there, a liar or an imaginative man lost in the wilderness? Despite being discredited, in 1909 he duly published a book, *My Attainment of the Pole*.

and began a campaign of conversion until all the party could stomach seal and penguin, with undeniable benefits to their health.

Not only in this treatment was Amundsen prominent. He was actively interested in getting out onto the ice and going on journeys. Cook thought him 'the biggest, the strongest, the bravest, and generally the best dressed man for sudden emergencies'. In matters of clothing, skis and sledges Amundsen advanced by trial and error. On the few real sledging journeys made by the *Belgica* he was notably involved. No one doubted his prowess on ski or his readiness to go out of sight and sound of the ship. On one occasion Cook and Amundsen together scaled the top of an iceberg seven miles from the ship. These excursions required that the men pull their sledges themselves, and, since the means of sledge power was to become one of the key issues in Polar travel, it is important to see that Amundsen had tried man-handling and disliked it.

The *Belgica* was held in the ice for an unusually long period, and there were fears of a second winter's imprisonment. Again Amundsen and Cook suggested ways of freeing the ship. At first they tried to blast an escape with high explosives and, when that failed, they instigated the laborious process of cutting a channel in the ice. At last the ship was freed, and there was a welcome rush of water under the keel. They were back within the reach of newspapers in March 1899, able to read of the Spanish–American war and the Dreyfus case and eager to tell the world of their experiences.

Frederick Cook's account of the *Belgica* expedition, *Through the First Antarctic Night*, was published in London in 1900, at just the time Scott was appointed leader of the British expedition and embarked upon its detailed preparation. At this distance it is difficult to discover whether he read Cook's book, much less ascertain that its lessons influenced him. But one criticism of the *Discovery* expedition, made by some of its members, was that it had a limited library of Polar books.

Another Antarctic expedition had taken place, only shortly after the *Belgica* venture, and it too left no evident impact on Scott's plans other than leading him to one quarter of the continent. Carsten Borchgrevink* went south in the *Southern Cross*, sponsored by Sir George Newnes the newspaper owner, surveyed the coast of Victoria Land and spent the winter of 1899 in a hut at Cape Adare. Borchgrevink was a scientist, but the intervening hand of a tycoon in popular education may have been enough to earn Markham's disapproval. It was not in Markham's nature to expect lessons from foreigners, and Scott may have been too busy to digest the implications of the *Belgica*.

It was a persistent pattern of Scott's expeditions that he was burdened with the details of administration. In part that is because of his own discomfort at an office desk, as a fund-raiser and as a public speaker. But it is also a consequence of the scale of the British expeditions and the uncertain way in which they were mounted.

Markham's long enthusiasm for the Antarctic appears to have been so personal that it obstructed his capacity to collaborate, to delegate or to enter practically into the indignity of raising money. From the time that he took up the presidency of the Royal Geographical Society in 1893 to the end of 1898 Markham had raised only £14,000. The bulk of it had come from very few sources. Despite sweeping claims about what the expedition might do for British interests and prestige, Markham never embraced public appeal. Instead he sought money privately, wherever

* Borchgrevink (1864–1934) was a Norwegian naturalist who had participated in the first landfall on Antarctica in 1895 when he was on board a whaler that put men ashore.

he had influence himself. He would not have calculated this, but such methods kept the expedition under his guidance and away from public scrutiny. In other words, Markham pursued his own idea of what was good for Britain, and pursued it without great success.

At times he spent as much as he raised. At a Franklin commemoration, he presided over a steamer excursion carrying nearly 300 people from Westminster to Greenwich, lunching on the way on board and returning in the evening to dinner at the Geographical Club with the Duke of York and the American ambassador. 'It was a very successful gathering,' said Markham's cousin, 'and it assisted very materially in propagating interest in Polar research.' This homily cannot conceal the way several years' campaigning had produced only £5,000 from the Geographical Society, voted unanimously on Markham's proposal, another £5,000 from Sir Alfred Harmsworth, £1,000 from the Royal Society, £1,500 from two sister spinsters, the Misses Dawson Lambton, and not much else. The total was woefully inadequate for the sort of enterprise Markham planned. It was only in early 1899 that a member of the Geographical Society, Mr Llewellyn Longstaff, was moved to contribute £25,000 – nearly trebling the total overnight. Longstaff was sixty, formerly a lieutenant-colonel and a leading commercial figure in Hull. He is one of the most instrumental and least-remembered benefactors of British exploration. Although the expedition was developing as a very private venture, Longstaff appears to have asked for no direct say in the planning. He was to make only one plea, yet it was the means of much distress in Scott's sensitive mind.

Longstaff's generosity prompted the government to guarantee £45,000, so long as an equivalent sum could be raised by the expedition. Longstaff's gift brought the total to nearly £40,000 and the residue was raised, but not reliably until the actual departure of the *Discovery*.

The organization of the expedition had been complicated by the way in which, with its modest contribution, the Royal Society became co-sponsor of the project. Markham hoped that the two societies in concert would prove irresistible to the government. But in the event the partnership was uneasy and added to the bureaucratic detail surrounding Scott.

The body that confirmed Scott as leader was a Joint Committee of sixteen, formed from the two societies and including eminent scientists as well as explorers. What might have been a sensible joining of forces only proved the disharmony of two motives for Polar research. The year that elapsed between the Buckingham Palace Road and Scott's confirmation as commander was a time of argument among the two factions: some wanted a naval officer in command, while others – chiefly the Royal Society – saw more benefit in a trained scientist. Markham was nettled by this 'grinding of their own particular axes', and ground his own the harder. But the controversy clouded the expedition and may account for Scott's dogged attempt to make himself conversant with the sciences.

The strain of balancing exploration and research affected both of Scott's journeys south. It was an issue he never settled, and one that compelled an insecure, aloof man to put his own vulnerability in jeopardy. Amundsen had returned from the Antarctic convinced of the virtue of a single commander and uncompromising purpose. He made a short contribution to Cook's book that stressed how far a dual command produced tension: 'Inevitably this resulted in a division of responsibility between the commander and the skipper, incessant friction, divided counsels, and a lowered morale for the subordinate members of the expedition. . . . I was resolved, therefore, that I should never lead an expedition until I was prepared to remedy this defect.'

Some sections of the Royal Society actively opposed Scott's appointment, and it is notable that Professor J. W. Gregory was selected as chief scientist before Scott was confirmed. One cannot underestimate the ordeal of a naval lieutenant just promoted to commander having to deal with the Joint Committee. Markham was on his side in every argument, but Scott may soon have recognized the handicaps of Markham's full-blooded support. It is to his credit that he proved decisive in such unfamiliar business; yet the pressure accounted for some of the mistakes of the expedition.

In June 1900 Scott's task was awesome. He came up to London to live there for the first time, with his mother and sisters in rooms above a shop in Royal Hospital Road, Chelsea. From there he would walk and run to work – the latter as part of a personal training plan – through Green Park to the expedition's offices in Savile Row. There he was supposed to coordinate an expedition that had the Prince of Wales as its patron, the Duke of York as vice-patron and a Joint Committee of which Lord Lister was chairman and Markham vice-president. Furthermore the Joint Committee, aware of so many areas and disciplines contained within the expedition, had already appointed nine sub-committees, with an intermediary executive committee to report back to the Joint Committee.

Scott saw how nearly the venture was being throttled by its own elaborate procedure. He wrote boldly to the Royal Society, saying that if there were still doubts over his interpretation of his role then he would resign. Next he cut through the web of committees and replaced them with a finance committee consisting of the treasurers of the two societies, a representative from the Treasury and Cyril Longhurst, the secretary to the expedition.

There remained too much work for the commander. Markham was nominally in charge of supplies and personnel, but Scott had both to honour the older man's whim and to do the detailed work he neglected. Without any prior experience, he had to arrange the ordering of pemmican from America and Denmark. In the autumn of 1900, with Markham, he travelled to Norway to discuss sledging techniques, the use of dogs and ski, and to meet Nansen. The two men were impressed with one another. Scott wrote to his mother: 'He is quite a great man, absolutely straightforward and wholly practical, so our business flies along apace. I wish to goodness it would go as well in England.' Nansen noted in Scott 'his light, wiry figure, his intelligent, handsome face, that earnest, fixed look, and those expressive lips so seriously determined and yet ready to smile'. Nansen was generous with advice and Scott acknowledged that Oslo was the centre of the sledging industry. Yet the most valuable word that Nansen had to give was not properly heeded. Like any other Norwegian, Nansen believed in dogs for pulling sledges. The *Discovery* did take dogs, but little faith in them and no special training in handling them. The explanation for this is clear: Markham distrusted dog power, and Scott flinched from the necessary severity in handling them. The error marked Scott's expeditions and led inexorably to his death. But the reasons for the error are complex and have to do with the nature of the English gentleman Scott aspired to be.

On their way back from Norway Scott and Markham visited Count Erich von Drygalski in Germany who was well advanced with plans to winter in the Antarctic. Scott's disposition to pessimism was daunted by the German's thoroughness, and the entire trip may have overwhelmed him with a sense of how much detail there was in Antarctic travel, and how much expertise he lacked himself. But he arrived back in London the more convinced of the need to wind up slowness. It was better perhaps that he make some mistakes, and have plans advance, than see decision delayed by caution and the need to satisfy so many opinions. He took more authority for himself and moved the expedition's office to Burlington House, only down the road but a gesture of independence.

Far more serious was the dispute he had with Gregory. As if inwardly conscious of Amundsen's advice, Scott had given orders for acquiring some scientific equipment. The details are now obscure: Scott may have acted rashly or even provocatively; equally, departure could have been put back a year if the chronic balancing of committees had gone on. Scott knew how long this expedition had been preparing, and how intransigent the schemes of experts could be. But Gregory had not been consulted and he chose to resign, taking with him two members of the Joint Committee. This hostility was to recur during and after the expedition. The incident may have established in Scott's mind that the scientists had to be under his control; but it left an insecure man aware of his own shortcomings in discussions with scientists. George Murray was made temporary director of the scientific staff in Gregory's place.

Of more interest to Scott was the appointment of men and officers for the party. In this respect he shared Markham's preference for the Navy. Between them, and in the unusual circumstances of an expedition sponsored by two learned societies, the two men managed to achieve their own version of the Navy. Instructions were given to a Dundee shipyard for the building of the *Discovery*, to the design of the Chief Constructor of the Admiralty. When it was launched, it was technically a merchant ship running as nearly as possible under Navy law, but with Markham as its registered manager.

Scott himself was apprehensive of having to deal with other than Navy men; merchant seamen would have grown up outside the Naval Discipline Act. Furthermore there was a palpable sense of superiority enjoyed by the

Navy when it looked at the Merchant Navy. Apart from the natural rivalry of two forms of sea-going, the Navy was more prestigious, more elitist and the preserve of officers with private means. Scott had had to make sacrifices to stay in the Navy. The encouragement for them was the mixture of altruism, prejudice and calculation that thought it more honourable and more practical to be ready for a war at sea than to carry passengers and cargo round the world.

Markham had quit the Navy as a young man because his independence resented strict discipline and because he hated the use of corporal punishment. But his faith in a naval party was unflawed, or so it seemed. He endorsed the heavy bias towards service personnel and petitioned the Admiralty to release more officers and men than they had at first allowed. This zeal may have been an attempt to make up for an initiative of Markham's made before his re-acquaintance with Scott in the summer of 1899. That initiative is the most searching doubt to be thrown upon Markham's own adoption of the Scott legend, of youthful promise sublimely brought to fruition.

At some time in 1897 or 1898 Markham had approached Albert Armitage with a view to the latter's leading the Antarctic expedition. Armitage was a Scot, born in 1864 – thus four years older than Scott – who had trained on the *Worcester* as a sea cadet and in 1880 joined the P. & O. Company as a junior officer. By 1892 he was a sub-lieutenant in the Merchant Navy. Markham's invitation was not arbitrary or unreasonable, for in the years 1894–7 Armitage served as second-in-command on the Jackson-Harmsworth expedition to Franz Josef Land. He was therefore one of the few young officers in either branch of the British Navy with Polar experience. According to Armitage, Markham wrote to him while he was still in the north 'asking me to return home in order to go on an Antarctic Expedition, and on my return to England he requested me to keep in touch with him: prepared to take command of one'.

We have only Armitage's word for this; and he did not speak openly of it until the 1920s. Yet several things support the claim: Armitage had rare attributes; Markham was searching for a leader, all the more strenuously if one allows that he may have needed to be reminded of Scott. At the same time Armitage could have inflated the first offer, just as Markham might have thought better of it on meeting the man. In Armitage's eyes his own chances slumped as soon as government support became likely. Then a naval commander was inevitable. A younger man, with 'no experience of ice-work whatever' got the position and Armitage was asked to be second-in-command. At first he refused, and only eventually accepted upon certain guarantees. More than twenty years later, in 1922, Armitage wrote to H. R. Mill to say: 'Those word-of-honour promises were all broken by Scott as I was warned they would be by two of his brother Naval Officers and by some of the Committee of the Expedition.'

This is an uncertain, rancorous story, and some have chosen to dismiss the elderly Armitage as eaten up by bitterness. No doubt he was the victim of his own feelings, but most men suffer in that way. His version of Scott is not implausible. Others felt the temper of the commander; glimpses of ambition often show through; and nagging uncertainty may drive a man to occasional ruthlessness with himself and with others. Many men who served under Scott admired him. But one rank in particular had an uncomfortable time with him: his second-in-command.

The Admiralty loaned Scott three lieutenants: Charles Royds, Michael Barne and Reginald Skelton, the latter an engineering expert who had served with Scott on the *Majestic*. 'No more lieutenants could be obtained from the Admiralty,' wrote Markham, 'so Captain Scott had to turn elsewhere and accepted Ernest Shackleton as the junior executive.' That offhand account of making do with second best only appeared in 1921, in *The Lands of Silence*, Markham's posthumously published history of Polar exploration. As so often with Markham, the dismissal concealed a more interesting story and attempted to patronize Scott's most serious rival. There are still adherents of Scott or Shackleton in Polar circles. This stems from the arguments as to how and why the two men quarrelled, but fundamentally it is because of the clash of character and the different conceptions of duty and adventure embodied in their careers. They annoyed and needed one another like fellow-neurotics. If there had been only Scott or only Shackleton, who knows if there would have been the rising tide in British Polar activity in these years.

Shackleton's family was from Yorkshire, but they were living in Kilkea, Co. Kildare, when he was born in 1874. He spent his first ten years in Ireland, the last period in Dublin, and ever afterwards was liable to be teased by critics for his Irish impulsiveness, his Blarney enthusiasm and, in Markham's phrase, 'the rough life he had led'. Shackleton derived his greatest energy from resentment, rivalry and a feeling of possible slight, so that when he bridled at jokes about Ireland or naval taunts at the merchant service he was actually fuelling his ambitions.

His family moved to England in 1884 and, as his father took up a doctor's practice in Croydon, so Shackleton attended Dulwich College. He was an odd mixture, loving boxing, gymnastics and poetry, not academic but talkative and amusing. In later life he experimented with the story that he had run away to sea, but in fact his secure, professional father had him apprenticed at the age of seventeen to the North-Western Shipping Company. Shackleton spent the next ten years rising to be first mate and then third officer, and working finally for the Union Castle line. In

1900 Shackleton was on board the liner *Gaika* on a voyage to Cape Town. One of the passengers was Cedric Longstaff, the son of the Hull businessman who stood second only to the government among the expedition's patrons. The two men were both in their twenties and no doubt talked together. Soon afterwards the Longstaffs approached Markham and made their only known request for the expedition – that Shackleton should go with it. Markham was in no position to be obstructive. He spoke to Scott who asked Armitage to look at Shackleton's record, perhaps on the principle that one merchant officer should deal with another. Armitage met Shackleton's superiors and reported back: 'His brother officers considered him to be a very good fellow, always quoting poetry and full of erratic ideas.' Shackleton was in, and Markham took steps to have him given a proper commission in the Royal Navy Reserve.

In summary, it is worth noting that Markham had reasons for guilt about the inclusion of Armitage and Shackleton. In both cases rumours were to spring up over the circumstances of the appointments, spiked by animosity. They were the only two Merchant Navy officers in the party and they were to feel victimized on that account. But if Shackleton was accepted late in the day, in a lowly position, and with a helping hand, he still became a leading figure in the expedition, a spirited member of the party, a prominent organizer and one of the three men who went on the sledge journey south: Scott, Shackleton and Edward Wilson.

Wilson was universally admired among his companions, and the fact that he was so close to Scott serves to reveal aspects of the leader that few other men coaxed into the open. Wilson brought out the best in him, as he did in so many others. There is a reticent saintliness in Wilson. He is the one unmistakably religious spirit in the group, in whom the great sacrifice looks natural and dignified and not strained, extravagant or tragic. He is a difficult man to convey because he was modest, resigned and self-effacing. He did not obtrude himself in his two expeditions, and yet nearly every man he travelled with confirmed that he was a moral centre for the party, both an example and a discreet, helpful councillor. He still seems an admirable man, and yet he does not quite escape the incongruity of a decent padre in the trenches in the Great War. For Wilson's virtues leave one question unanswered – why were they so meekly devoted to so remote and confused a venture? The strength of character seen in Wilson by so many was not enough to correct the headstrong misguidedness of the party.

Like Shackleton, Wilson was a doctor's son, born in Cheltenham in 1872. The family mingled Quaker and military traditions, and they may both be seen in the bearing of Wilson himself. From an early age he was fascinated by nature and by drawing. He was a friendly child, a fair athlete, but inclined to fall into solemn Victorian piety. He said of his own years at preparatory school: 'I failed to get a scholarship but learned a first-class morality. From the year 1884 when I went to Wilkinson's school at Clifton I have had an increasing disgust for impure talk, impurity in every shape, – a thing for which I shall always be grateful to that wonderfully high-toned school. I never heard a dirty word or a doubtful joke or jest there, and when I came into the thick of it afterwards I never had any share in it.'

He went on to Cheltenham as a day-boy, won prizes for drawing and developed as a rambler, a collector of birds' eggs and a rapt observer of wild life. The walker was a figure celebrated in Victorian poetry, and Wilson seems to have been an ideal example of the solitary walker in pursuit of bodily fitness, spiritual calm and the attempt to be absorbed by nature. He went on long expeditions as a boy, around his mother's farm estate, Crippetts, and as far afield as Snowdonia, sleeping in the open and learning every plant, rock and creature as he went. The way in which the Victorian love of nature changes gradually into the formal study of botany, geology and zoology is exemplified by Edward Wilson. In that sense the journey to the Pole was only the last walk amid scenery of savage beauty always reduced to a milky, tasteful pantheism in Wilson's watercolours.

In the autumn of 1891 he went up to Caius College, Cambridge, to read Natural Sciences, to row himself into delicious exhaustion and to hold on to his faith. At Cambridge, for the first time, there appears the Wilson who was a good mixer, a sympathetic listener, a source of advice, but a man always a little withdrawn from the hurly-burly. A fellow student described him in exactly the terms that Polar explorers were to use:

He was essentially a very just, tolerant, and extraordinarily strong man. He was utterly fearless and would condemn a man's action which was not pure and sound in the strongest possible way. He had a tremendous belief in his own powers; there was nothing that he would not attempt to do, and yet he was the most beautifully modest man in the world. He was completely unselfish, and had no idea of self-advertisement nor of advancing himself except in his work. He was absolutely without any personal ambition, but was just intensely keen on doing the work he had in hand to the very best of his ability. His faith was the essence of his life; his religious views were simple but very strongly held.

So many shining accounts can reduce Wilson to a featureless statue. He was more interesting than that and, as with so many explorers, his going south was an attempt to test a flawed constitution and settle turbulent thoughts. In 1894 Wilson's exam results were excellent: he took his B.A., first-class honours in the natural science tripos (Pt 1) and the first part of his M.B. As his prize, Wilson chose a volume of Ruskin, a man close to his own ideals – as draughtsman, observer of nature and as social humanist – but a man by then demented, a philosopher stranded by the Victorian age's advance on modern times.

Wilson may have felt that tension. A part of him was anxious to get into hospital work, but he yielded to pressure that he stay on at Cambridge for the second part of both his M.B. and tripos. In the event, he failed both and moved to London, to work at St George's Hospital and lodgings in Westbourne Grove and Paddington. He was very sensitive to the duty of a doctor and agonized over the dilemma of a man torn between his career and the cause of healing. 'I am quite convinced that everyone should follow his own conscience,' he wrote to his mother, 'so long as it does not interfere with any responsibility previously undertaken. If we find it does, we have made an error and we must just take the consequences.'

He sometimes seemed solitary and when he moved to live in a mission house in Battersea he thought it 'a good healthy change for me, as I hate Society, and here I shall have to learn to put up with a certain amount every day'. He was overworked, he smoked heavily and loathed himself for the habit. Sometimes he veered from moods of suicidal misery to 'feelings of extraordinary freedom and happiness'. It was part of his discipline never to waste a moment. When he was not at the hospital, he rowed, played rugby and walked to the zoo, the Natural History Museum and the National Gallery, where he was in awe of the great Turner pictures.

On Sundays he conducted children's services at Battersea. This was not easy for him and he was often unbearably irritated by the restless audience eating sweets and sniffing and scratching:

All the while I am telling them how nice it is to be like Christ and how soon they will get to the 'Jungle Book' if they'll only

be a little quieter, and the hokey-pokey man has settled his
barrow close outside the shop window and someone is scrambl-
ing up to the boarding outside to see how we are getting on inside, and a Band of Church Army or perhaps the Green Foresters
or the Oddfellows with a local drum and fife band come down
the street, and then I thank God for a respite and wonder why
I haven't filled the room with dead little Battersea boys.

He found solace in the company of a young lady,
Oriana Souper, but at first he was unsure whether he was
suited to marriage. In 1897 he passed his exams and abided
by parental opposition to his plan to go to Africa with the
South London Missions. Wilson was anxious to do his best
for his fellow-men, but he was neither comfortable nor
fulfilled in any of the ways that presented themselves. This
strain affected his health, and in early 1898, as he read a life
of St Francis, he suffered a recurring fever that was diagnosed
as tuberculosis.

As part of his cure he went to Norway and then to Davos
in Switzerland. On these trips he was largely alone, walking
and sketching scenery, and becoming convinced of the
withering effect of urban doldrums. When told to rest, he
fretted. Therein may lie one motive behind those immense
walks in the snow. He doubted that any cure lay in idleness:
'The killing part about it is the lack of occupation, nothing
but idle loafing, terribly depressing and demoralizing.'
Some sort of unease in the late Victorian era detected
unsoundness in 'loafing' and had a bursting energy to put
the world right. But it was a blind energy too often, unclear
about the social and political causes of the world's tension.
I do not mean to be disparaging if I suggest that Wilson
walked off that tension in the snow; rather it is meant as an
insight into frustrated nobility.

Convalescence and the mountains did begin to heal
Wilson. In the autumn of 1899 he went back to work,
became engaged to Miss Souper and passed his final M.B.

Then in June 1900 Dr Philip Sclater, president of the Zoology Society, urged Wilson to apply for the position of junior surgeon and zoologist on the Antarctic expedition. Wilson was hesitant and doubted that he had either the qualities or the necessary interest in Polar travel. Two years earlier he had attended a lecture by Nansen in London. The man had impressed him more than the matter and, significantly, Wilson had been upset by a photograph of a man leading one of the dogs, guessing that he was on the point of slaughtering the animal.

Wilson's uncle, Major-General Sir Charles Wilson, approached Markham, and Sclater was on the appointments committee, so that Wilson easily won an interview with Scott. However, he went up for it with his arm in a sling, having contracted blood-poisoning at a hospital post-mortem. Scott liked him and offered him the post if his health continued to improve. In 1901 Wilson had two medical examinations, and it seems likely that in the last resort Scott personally overruled objections to a tubercular surgeon. Wilson was accepted and a month before departure he married Oriana Souper.

Including Scott, there were six officers on the *Discovery*. As well as Wilson, he took with him Reginald Koettlitz as first surgeon and botanist, Thomas Hodgson as biologist, Hartley Ferrar the geologist and Louis Bernacchi as physicist – a scientific staff of five, considered adequate to cover every foreseeable discovery. Bernacchi had served with Borchgrevink and had been in the shore party that wintered at Cape Adare, while Koettlitz was a German doctor who had abandoned his Dover practice to go with the Jackson-Harmsworth expedition. The presence of two men who had been to Polar regions may have inhibited Scott. Koettlitz especially was a cantankerous, stolid man, not easily amenable, while Bernacchi seems to have had to keep his experience in rein for fear of offending his commander.

There were in addition twenty-seven men, twenty of whom were serving in the Navy. These men were picked up here and there. Some flourished, some were dismissed. Markham had been involved in the selection, and he was not averse to disqualifying one because his nose was too long or picking another by the sound of his name. But some of those twenty-seven are worth naming for the large parts they were to play: Frank Wild, Thomas Crean, William Lashly and Edgar Evans, a strong Welshman who had served with Scott on the *Majestic* and who became something of a talisman to the commander so that, when he faltered, on the way back from the Pole, it was enough to diminish Scott's spirit and to remind him of bad luck.

4
The Discovery
Expedition

The story of the *Discovery* expedition should begin with the muted clash of hope and certainty that sets out in a ship already called *Discovery*. For when we speak of explorers venturing into 'the unknown' in the name of 'human knowledge', we may not notice that such men are sometimes confident of what they will find and unaware of many other possibilities in the unknown. In exploration, that which is 'discovered' is usually affected by the means and resources employed, by the questions adopted at the outset and by the intellectual temperament of the explorers. The strenuous marching through jungle, desert and wasteland may discover trivialities compared with the revelations that come to men and women in their own minds in their own gardens. To call a ship *Discovery* can restrict the meaning of that word and the depth of human curiosity. That is why the purposeful naming of Scott's first Antarctic vessel is so characteristic of abundant narrowness and confidence at the close of the age of geographical exploration.

Thus, on the one hand, the *Discovery* lays down a method by which men might live, work and relax in Antarctica, rather than just clench themselves against cold, dark and brooding. Scott's first expedition mapped out a coastline on which men could land, established the general geographical nature of the continent and demonstrated a way of travelling and existing on it. Compared with the cautious forays made by the *Belgica* party, Scott acted with a wonderful purpose and firmness. His several plans were effectively carried out; he returned with every semblance of success.

Yet, in another light, the *Discovery* expedition was amateurish, almost innocent in its recklessness and the origin of several misleading conclusions. Regarded from the stance of Scott's second expedition, it appears as primitive and fumbling as the *Belgica* adventure might have looked to Scott in 1904. There is a lesson to be drawn from this: that nothing is ever discovered in the sense that it is settled. Man's imaginative horizons recede from his grasp the more surely that grasp is informed. The yearning to know will never overcome the neurosis that has to doubt. That is why the experience of discovery is as much intellectual and emotional as it is physical. Scott himself was second to the Pole – a ridiculous distinction that shrinks beside his own discovery of the nature of failure, and the way in which his response to it moved other people.

The *Discovery* left London at the end of July 1901. But British expeditions seldom went south as directly as Amundsen would nine years later. Instead Scott made his way by the landmarks of the British Empire, showing the flag, entertaining dignitaries and keeping the coffers open. On the first expedition, Scott stopped at Cowes – then enjoying its annual yachting regatta – and entertained the new king, Edward VII, on board. As the two men met, the king allowed the naval commander's mother to pin on her son's coat the Victorian order, one of many decorations and institutions founded in that year to honour the long reign of Queen Victoria. The queen had been dead for only six months and court mourning made the visit an informal one, largely instigated by Markham and Scott's admiral, George Egerton.

The death of Victoria is an obvious transition in British history, as unavoidable as the turning of the century. Even at the time people recognized its significance, not because they believed that an old lady could or should live much longer, but because it seemed to relieve Britain of the weight of so many archaic things and to promise a future even more threatening without the care of the great maternal figure. Now, perhaps, events could move on freely. A few may have looked forward to that release, but the majority of Englishmen felt the loss as something that could set loose an unspecific turbulence in the world. In South Africa a young lieutenant engaged in the Boer War wrote to his mother on learning the news: 'We heard about the Queen's death while on the march and were all very much cut up. It is awfully sad and the worst thing that could happen to England.' That officer's name was Oates.

When the *Discovery* reached Cape Town in October, it stopped there for eleven days – despite being nine days behind schedule – and several of the party went on a trip to a prisoner-of-war camp for Boers. Very few of them would have disapproved of such camps or questioned the justice of the war being fought in South Africa. In this, as in other matters, Edward Wilson may have had to decide whether to voice or suppress the beginnings of an argument. His severe moral sense prompted this prediction: 'A nation should be judged on exactly the same ground as an individual. As a nation we have the vilest of sins which everyone extols as the glories of Imperialism. *One day* all this part of our history will be looked upon in its proper light.'

Such an admission, in a family letter, made Wilson an exception, in Britain as a whole, let alone in the company of the young men on the *Discovery*. Yet his instinctive pacifism was tempered by conservatism, and it would be a mistake to portray Wilson as a radical. He was a troubled member of his age, but too much a part of it to throw off the practical rationalizations of imperialism. A man as good as Wilson might go south to escape this disgust in himself: 'Now that I know what the duties of a soldier are in war I would sooner shoot myself than anyone else by a long, long way. I simply could not do it. The very thought of it now is a ghastly nightmare to me, chiefly the result of a very realistic account of our sinful – though as things are, necessary – cruelty over the bombardment of Kronje in the Modder. It made me cry like a baby and I threw away the paper in perfect disgust.' Wilson was a devout man. Yet in being able to reconcile sin and necessity he illustrates the compromise of the English Christian gentleman.

Like most new ships, the *Discovery* leaked and had come to Cape Town more slowly than had been planned. On the way, there were brief stops at Madeira and South Trinidad, and time for the routine to settle. For the men it may have come as a disappointment to find that the system was naval. 'Routine about the same as yesterday,' wrote Able Seaman Thomas Williamson in his diary. 'They must seem to think that we are some automobile or traction engine which only wants oiling to keep it on the go, instead of human beings.'

Those first months were not always harmonious. George Murray, the temporary director of the scientific staff, departed at Cape Town, leaving Scott in unchallenged command. Scott kept a captain's remoteness, and Wilson's first impression was that he was serving under a 'quick-tempered and very impatient' man. Wilson's closest companion was Shackleton, whose lively humour amused most people. The junior officer soon emerged as a leading character in charge of ward-room catering and putting together entertainments. To some, Shackleton himself was a show; but the more strictly naval members were critical of his brashness. One evening in the ward room Shackleton was nominally fined by the president when, for the fifth time, he sought to settle a discussion with a wager.

It was not long before Scott, and most of the others, were proclaiming the special unity of the group. But Polar expeditions jammed men, officers and scientists together in cramped quarters. The occasional spurt of resentment that Wilson had felt at Battersea Sunday School overtook him on board the *Discovery*: 'I am more thankful than I can say for having been brought to this life because it is such an education. But God knows it is just about as much as I can stand at times, and there is absolutely no escape. I have never had my temper so tried as it is every day now, but I don't intend to give way.'

On many nights Wilson would stay talking with Shackleton on the deck of the *Discovery*. He was impressed by Shackleton's broad enthusiasm for poetry and his readiness to quote from memory. The early bond between these two is significant, but it did not last. In time Wilson was to give his allegiance to Scott, as if he saw sounder depths in a man who may have read poetry to himself in his own cabin. Scott was sometimes so caught up in his thoughts that he was absent-minded: at one meal he poured milk onto his plate of curry and was jolted out of reverie by the respectful laughter of other officers. His steward, Charles Hare, thought he was 'over-sensitive and allowed himself to get worked up if things did not go as planned'. There is the melancholy perfectionist brought up in a service where the commander is constitutionally infallible. Scientists, more accustomed to open argument, could unwittingly trespass on Scott's insecurity. Bernacchi once helpfully proposed a scheme for the ship's boats and 'was told, in no uncertain terms, to attend to my own speciality'.

This illustrates the effort Scott was to make in taking scientists into his confidence, and encourages caution in dealing with the assertions of democratic discussion. There are discrepancies in different accounts of Scott, and there is no need to iron them out. A more plausible answer is that Scott himself was made volatile by the strain of his position. He had never commanded before, let alone so novel an expedition, or so unusual a company. He was utterly conscientious and must have agonized over every hint of temper or remoteness that he yielded to. At the same time he would have been anxious never to step outside the emphatic role of commander for fear of relaxing discipline. To take too much advice from Bernacchi might only reveal that the commander was less experienced than a subordinate. Add to that the problem of taking on vital supplies and seeing to their safe storage and it is easy to sympathize with Scott's occasional pettiness. Even in the Atlantic, leakage had caused serious damage to the stores: 'the greater part of the provisions are in a dilapidated state, and those at the bottom are utterly destroyed, a bad look out on someone's part I think'. At one Sunday service Scott concluded with a lecture on waste and said that he had spied little bits of biscuit floating astern that they would all be sorry to have lost. Indeed there were to be times when men scavenged for crumbs broken off in munching a precious biscuit.

Wilson was already warming to Scott, and this description from a letter written on the voyage is worth quoting as a sign of growing sympathy, despite several details that could be challenged by other testimony:

He is thoughtful for each individual and does little kindnesses which show it. He is ready to listen to everybody too, and joins heartily in all the humbug that goes on. I have a great admiration for him, and he is in no Service rut but is always anxious to see both sides of every question, and I have never known him to be unfair. One of the best points about him too is that he is very definite about everything; nothing is left vague or indeterminate. In every argument he goes straight for the main point, and always knows exactly what he is driving at. There will be no fear of our wandering about aimlessly in the Southern regions.

The *Discovery* sailed east across the Southern Indian Ocean by way of Macquarie Island to Lyttelton in New Zealand. She remained there another three weeks, the crew showing many visitors over the ship and being entertained ashore. 'I think the people are very nice in every thing and every way,' wrote Stoker William Lashly. 'They really seem to think we want a little enjoyment before we leave here.'

Lashly was a teetotaller, but many well-wishers must have wanted to give sailors a binge before they went to the austere Antarctic. No doubt New Zealand girls could be touched by the sacrifice that the men were making. Yet there is even less to report of the private lives of the sailors than of the scientists and officers. And, when the *Discovery* returned, Scott's report to the Admiralty resounded with this unequivocal satisfaction: 'Both in New Zealand and at home they have been feted, and made much of, and fully exposed to all the temptations which so frequently demoralize men of their class. It must be considered no small addition to their credit that they have come through such an ordeal unscathed and have preserved their good name to the end.'

Today an unwitting humour has grown up between those lines. Scott's tone seems tensely innocent. Not all of his men can have come through unscathed. Williamson's private despair over naval discipline may have been shared and may have extended to other desperate orthodoxies. The real poignancy of Scott's comment lies in his certainty that one class of men is more susceptible to demoralization than another, and in the Galahad lordliness that can sound priggish or virginal.

The *Discovery* left Lyttelton a few days before Christmas 1901. Cheering crowds lined the quay, but the celebrations had a tragic repercussion, an instance of Scott's bad luck. In order to wave back to the crowds, Seaman Charles Bonner had climbed the mainmast. As the ship met open sea, it pitched in the swell and Bonner was thrown to the deck, clutching the weathervane. He was killed outright and when the ship put in at Port Chalmers, to take on coal, Bonner was buried. He was replaced by Thomas Crean, a large Irish seaman from the *Ringarooma*. So an accident introduced one of the greatest lower-deck personalities to Antarctica. Crean was from Annascaul in Co. Kerry and he had left a crowded home for the Navy at the age of fifteen. At first it had seemed to him spartan and cruel, and he tried to desert. Antarctic exploration made Crean a hero, and gave him a career and great crises to prove his fortitude. Yet we need not sentimentalize the seamen who went south. Their officers sometimes spoke of them as if they were endlessly patient, loyal and supple oak trees. But it is doubtful how much they knew or wanted to know of the men's home lives or private thoughts. Crean had left an impoverished household for a hard service from which chance rescued him. The seamen in the story are men without wills of their own, carried along like driftwood, proof of how often the services were a refuge for the helpless poor.

Not that these men were stupid or unaware. On the contrary, some of them kept journals in the Antarctic that are filled with shrewd observation. Time and again the seamen met the physical and mental challenge of Polar travel. But the Navy could only countenance a subordinate and obedient role for them. No one would have dreamed of asking for Seaman Williamson's critical opinions. Of all the small ways in which Shackleton offended the naval officers, none was as unconventional or generous as his friendship with Seaman Frank Wild. Wild became the devoted second-in-command to Shackleton, and a proof that ratings could manage the unimaginable promotion to command. He owed his chance to Shackleton and to the way the young merchant officer talked to him on the *Discovery* and began to help him with his navigation studies.

From New Zealand Scott took the *Discovery* south to the area of the Ross Sea. By tradition this was the British sphere of influence in Antarctica, while Borchgrevink's expedition promised easiest access to the hinterland. The instructions given to Scott were sweeping but superficial: to discover the 'nature, condition and extent' of land in that area and to make a magnetic survey with the reservation that 'Neither of those objects is to be sacrificed to the other'. The most significant South Polar expedition was still that of Sir James Ross, in 1839–43. He had broken through the pack ice and mapped out some 500 miles of coast. In the process he had discovered the existence of the Ice Barrier in Ross Bay and a volcano at the western end of it which he had named after his ship, Mount Erebus. It remained uncertain as to what lay beyond the ice barrier. Did it extend to the Pole? Was there land beyond it, on which the Pole was located? Or was the Pole even amid some farther frozen sea?

Scott's specific task was:

to explore the ice barrier of Sir James Ross to its Eastern extremity; to discover the land which was believed by Ross to flank the barrier to the eastward, or to ascertain that it does not exist, and generally to endeavour to solve the very important physical and geographical questions connected with this remarkable ice formation.

If you should decide to winter in the ice your efforts as regards geographical exploration should be directed to three objects, namely – an advance into the Western mountains, an advance to the South, and an exploration of the volcanic regions.

Early in January 1902 the *Discovery* sighted Cape
Adare where Borchgrevink's party had wintered in 1899.
Bernacchi, the veteran of that expedition, led a party
ashore and in the hut that had been used three years before
they left flags and a message in a tin. That ritual captures
the bare initiative of men on the threshold of the unknown.
Still today we collect the emblems and oddities of our
culture and deposit them on the Moon or in the foundations
of new buildings. It is easy to challenge anyone's choice of
which artefacts represent our culture, but surely there is a
hint of surrealist farce in going so far into the frozen
wilderness, making a first landfall and leaving there a
flag and a message not much more informative than
'Kilroy was here'? Their other duty at Cape Adare was
more sombre: to visit the grave of Hanson who had died
during Borchgrevink's stay.

Back in the ship they worked their way south to within
sight of Mount Erebus on Ross Island. Scott was now
looking for an eventual anchorage. Between Ross Island
and South Victoria Land there is a strait – McMurdo
Sound – accessible in summer, frozen in winter, which
seemed to offer some security. But, while reasonable
weather lasted, Scott sailed eastwards along the shore of
Ross Island and made another landing at its eastern tip,
Cape Crozier, the site of a penguin rookery. More messages
were left there before the *Discovery* embarked on its major
eastward journey. By the end of January they saw land
previously undiscovered, stretching away to the north-
east. They named it King Edward VII Land. To this day
the map of Antarctica is decorated with the names of
European rulers, the beloved ones left at home by explorers
and the explorers themselves. The grandiose obscurity
reads oddly, and there is no nationalist pride to change a
Leopoldville into Kinshasa. Scott invariably used such
stately names, and called both his son and an Antarctic

mountain after Clements Markham. But some explorers felt the incongruity of pompous labelling. During the *Belgica* expedition, Frederick Cook wrote:

We were discussing the matter of raising flags and the formality of taking possession of newly discovered lands. The conclusion at which we arrived was, that the first chart of a new country was quite good enough a deed to the title of land, as the empty formality of pinning a bit of bunting to a temporary post and drinking to the health of the Royal Ruler, as is the custom of British explorers.

That duty done, the *Discovery* turned back westwards and manoeuvred its way into McMurdo Sound under the lee of what was thereafter known as Hut Point, the south-western corner of Ross Island. There the ship would be frozen in the ice and a winter hut built on the land. This is a distinctive part of Scott's method: the adjacent ship and hut. On his second expedition, the ship – the *Terra Nova* – was sent back to New Zealand for the Polar winter. This was a more sensible policy, for if the *Discovery* had been crushed in the ice – a real fear – no relief vessel would have known where to find the land party. Even so, the *Discovery*'s land establishments were used sparingly – for some scientific work, for storage and as a theatre. In retrospect the progress from men reluctant to leave their ship to men content to live in a large bungalow while their ship sailed north for fresh provisions seems halting. Nothing accounts for it better than the genuine trepidation and the great psychological significance of a ship to sailors.

Work began immediately in such a variety of forms that there was a good deal of confusion. Gradually, however, the ignorance and prejudice of British methods asserted themselves. Nothing so illustrates Scott's inexperience as the several wrong directions taken in those first months. The kind Wilson came to the sad conclusion that very few of the scientists were well equipped in their own areas. 'With the single exception of Hodgson,' he wrote, 'we are all intensely ignorant of anything but the elementary knowledge of our several jobs.'

On the voyage south Scott had experimented with signal kites and lost every one of them. Now they were ashore he meant to employ the two balloons provided by the War Office. A group of the men had even had a short course at Aldershot in how to work the balloons. Ideally they might provide an ingenious means of making geographical observations. Scott went up himself, and Shackleton and Skelton later got a view of over twenty miles. But the Polar winds made the ascents very risky, and in the low temperatures more gas was required than had been anticipated. In fact the equipment was unpredictable and the men had only a sketchy knowledge of how to use it. Wilson watched with alarm: 'If some of these experts don't come to grief over it out here, it will only be because God has pity on the foolish. Had any one used the valve in the morning it would not have closed properly and nothing could have prevented the whole show from dropping to earth like a stone.'

The balloons were not used again. Like the kites, they were a sign of Scott's impetuous technological enterprise. Wilson noted that he was 'always trying new and knacky things on his own'. Short of hard science but a proven innovator at the torpedo school, Scott's temperament was often that of an inventor. In that mood he seems volatile and inquiring, even harebrained at times. But in other ways he too easily fell into misguided orthodoxies. Seaman Williamson wrote in his journal, 'it seems as though they cannot forget that Navy idea or commandment of, thou shalt not miss scrubbing decks no matter under what circumstances'. When the water froze on the decks Williamson complained that the labour was 'something terrible'.

Of far more significance was the start of Polar sledging by the British. Although a journey south began with the great test of a sea voyage culminating in the tricky passage through the ice, and although wintering in the Antarctic was still a substantial ordeal, Scott's priority was to travel on the ice and land. That entailed British sailors and scientists walking regularly, with or without ski, and somehow pulling sledges with them, in thick snow, in blizzards and in temperatures well below freezing point. This was simply outside British experience, whereas it was something that Norwegians, and many Americans, had known from childhood.

Very few of the party had skied before, or done any real training in Britain. Once ashore the skis were allocated and the explorers had to learn as best they could. Many of them could not go many yards without falling over. Charles Ford, a steward, went out by himself and had a fall in which he broke his leg in two places. Scott himself badly injured a knee towards the end of February so that he was prevented from going on a sledging journey.

While Scott was crocked, the first large sledging expedition set out, with disastrous results. Several men got frost-bite. Able Seaman Hare was lost when he went back for forgotten ski boots. In searching for Hare, more men fell or lost contact with the main party. Five men were caught on a slope and Seaman Vince, in boots that did not grip, slid helplessly into the sea. His body was never found. There was something close to panic before the desperate men straggled back to the ship. Hare was out in the open for nearly two days and had a miraculous escape.

No one would have been more appalled than Scott, a commander excluded from a journey that incurred the expedition's second fatality. Every possible thing was wrong: the men were clumsy on ski; they were uncertain about what boots to wear; they too carelessly went off alone; the sledges were badly packed; the tents took too long to erect; even the primus stoves were faulty – the loss of Vince could be traced directly to the breaking of one camp when the men were unable to make hot food. Scott admitted: 'Not a single article of the outfit had been tested, and amid the general ignorance that prevailed the lack of system was painfully apparent in everything.'

Later in his own journal Scott remarked on the way in which the whole party learned from these mistakes. He claimed that the success of subsequent sledging journeys would not have been achieved otherwise. Many errors must have been corrected, yet in 1911 Scott was still rebuking the uneven loading of sledges. Even on this first expedition the more knowing Bernacchi regretted that men were allowed to play football on the ice or daydream when they would have been better employed in practising tent routine or in competitive dog and sledge races.

In their first month ashore the two men with Polar experience – Armitage and Bernacchi – had split the twenty dogs into two teams. Bernacchi treated his kindly, in the way the British assured one another they always regarded dogs. If this team faltered, men pulled on the traces to encourage and help the dogs. This was expressly against the advice Nansen had offered Scott. The Norwegian insisted that draught animals, and the sledge dogs in particular, should be shown no affection. They worked as hard as they were made to; their hardiness responded best to stern domination. Armitage's team was handled in this manner, and duly lost the race. But this test of dog-handling had been an entertainment, with non-participants taking sides and cheering. Bernacchi's dogs responded cheerfully to assistance; it was a little while before they took it for granted.

Perhaps that test was decisive. But, even if Armitage's team had won, the result might have been ignored. After all, Scott had sought out Nansen and then rejected his experience. The British difficulty with dogs in the Antarctic was inbred, and was part of their sentimental fondness for animals. Markham's memory went back to a British tradition that had preferred man-hauling, and this bias coincided with a particular aversion in Scott to the cruel treatment of animals.

There is no reason to believe that the British have ever been more tender to dogs than have other nations. But the keeping of household pets was a Victorian habit, especially in those comfortable homes that produced Scott and the other officers. It was against the law in Britain to make dogs work. Certainly in the south the British were betrayed by their willingness to talk to the animals. Not only did men join in the pulling work. When some dogs were idle or lazy, men carried them. Unfortunately this had the effect of making the dogs fight amongst themselves, as if jealous of human attention. There is a note of perplexity in Scott's account of quarrelsome, malingering dogs, and there were many moments of bitter comedy, hopelessly tangled tracery, barking dogs and frustrated men.

The party had no dog trainer, and neither the will nor the knowledge to bully the dogs. In addition it is possible that the initial selection had been ill advised and haphazard, while much of the dog food had been contaminated by the ship's leak. This was only discovered when the dogs began to suffer from the rotten stores.

The British might have been more honest to do without dogs altogether, so strong was their resistance to the necessary harshness. Years later, after the conclusive proof of Amundsen's journey, Markham could still write 'If dogs are treated with humanity, they are in the writer's opinion not so good as men in a long journey'. Gradually, on the first expedition, dog-handling was abandoned and men alone pulled the sledges. The effort of this was devastating, and it directly contributed to the hunger that caused Scott's death. But, beneath every controversy over the handling of dogs there lay a fatal British romanticizing of the unassisted effort of the explorer. Scott may have been its most ardent adherent, and here is the voice of impractical self-sufficiency, of men who relished the blunt test of man against the elements, whatever geographical or scientific pretexts they might claim. It involves a sublime self-destructiveness that had its finest hour when Oates walked out of the tent and away into the blizzard, infinite space and undying glory:

In my mind no journey ever made with dogs can approach the height of that fine conception which is realized when a party of men go forth to face hardships, dangers, and difficulties with their own unaided efforts, and by days and weeks of hard physical labour succeed in solving some problems of the great unknown. Surely in this case the conquest is more nobly and splendidly won.

It is not far from the joy that comes with exhausted strength.

Scott took pride in standing up to the work and it served to reinforce his moral confidence and his passionate feeling for honourable performance. It also excused him from a squeamishness that was unusual in any man and unexpected in a commander. The Norwegian use of dogs involved the eventual slaughter of some animals to feed the others; in the last resort it approved of working the dogs to death and of the men eating the dogs. Yet the sight of blood, let alone the scarlet stains on snow, always upset Scott. This is rather more than the sea captain's vulnerability to sea-sickness, something that makes eminence human; it was a distaste he could not overcome and which seriously hindered his judgement.

On the voyage south Wilson had detected this sensitivity

in Scott. After dinner one night there was a heated argument on blood sports in which Wilson the zoologist opposed several sportsmen officers: 'I was practically unsupported in arguing that it was a relic of barbarity which was certainly fated to die out in time in any civilized nation, an end to be devoutly hoped for. As I expected I found myself in a hornet's nest. The young naval officer hasn't thought much about such things. Only the Captain had ever realized that the question of sport had another side to it.'

Scott forced himself to watch Wilson skinning specimen birds on the *Discovery*, but was sickened by the sight. The dangers of this became apparent when Scott shrank from the slaughter of seals and penguins that would provide a store of fresh meat. Scurvy was rife on this first expedition, partly because of dietary deficiencies, but also because of Scott's temperamental reluctance to give orders for slaughter. Even *in extremis*, when he, Wilson and Shackleton were on their sledge journey south and compelled to destroy dogs, Scott's feelings disabled him and added to his shame. This passage is full of anguish and of the way in which Scott tortured himself with his own failings. Not many men who went south with him were as introspective:

I must confess that I personally have taken no part in the slaughter; it is a moral cowardice of which I am heartily ashamed, and I know perfectly well that my companions hate the whole thing as much as I do. At the first this horrid duty was performed by Wilson, because it was tacitly agreed that he would be by far the most expert, and later, when I was perfectly capable of taking a share, I suppose I must have shrunk from it so obviously that he, with his usual self-sacrifice, volunteered to do the whole thing throughout. And so it has been arranged, and I occupy the somewhat unenviable position of allowing someone else to do my share of the dirty work.

For the first time an expedition to Antarctica had a secure base on the continent. Therefore, no matter how many useful explorations east and west, no matter how regularly the scientists recorded the weather and searched for specimens, the attention of the party always leaned to the south. Scott's plan was to sledge south in the summer season of 1901–2. He cannot have hoped for the Pole itself; this was an attempt to discover what sort of terrain lay to the south.

His first instinct was to take only one man with him and in choosing Wilson Scott admitted his own need for companionship, not to mention the power of inclination in dictating his choice. The two men had grown closer, and Wilson had begun to occupy the position of intermediary and peacemaker that he was to fill on the second expedition. 'The Captain and I understand one another better than anyone else on the ship, I think,' wrote Wilson, who found that Scott listened to his suggestions and acted on them. Wilson sensed his privileged position and it is likely that others saw the best way to Scott lying through this moderate, quietly spoken man. Even Scott may have appreciated the means others had of speaking to him, and enjoyed the society of one man with whom he did not always have to be commander. They differed on the question of religious faith, and left the matter alone.

Yet Wilson's best friend was still the impulsive Shackleton. They spent a lot of time together and jointly produced the *South Polar Times*, a newspaper to be circulated among the party. Shackleton edited the text and Wilson illustrated it in an office made out of packing cases. As they worked, Shackleton chattered and regaled Wilson with jokes, games and a fund of stories. Understandably Shackleton most enjoyed the company of an educated civilian who knew London as well as he did: but it shows Wilson's versatility, his capacity to lend himself to various men, that he was the nearest companion of men as different as Scott and Shackleton.

Scott asked Wilson to go south with him in the winter of 1901: a notoriously delicate child inviting a man only recently recovered from tuberculosis on a gruelling journey. Wilson apparently suggested that they take a third with them in case of sickness. Scott interpreted this as a request that Shackleton go too, since Wilson's high regard for him was well known. Scott had been impressed with Shackleton, but it indicates his wish to please Wilson that he invited the Merchant Navy man. What is strange is the fact that Wilson already doubted Shackleton's stamina, but did not volunteer that medical opinion for fear of spoiling his friend's chances. Here we have to allow for a reticence between colleagues that seems contradictory but which is more plausible among late Victorians separated by the barrier of the Navy and by the shyness of one and the near quietism of the other. It is a vital trait for the understanding of the expedition. Without it there might not have been all the mistakes there were, there might have been some overt homosexual relations; but without it too there might have been no need for implacably private Englishmen to be gathered together in Antarctica.

No activity conveyed the simultaneous companionship and isolation better than sledging. Often the wind was too loud for them to hear each other speak; all too soon each man was so tired that he became enclosed in his own ordeal of labour. Many explorers report the long silences of such journeys. The introspective would then have time for thought, but the pessimistic could become more than usually brooding and irritable and the cheerful might lapse into melancholy. It is a simplification to cast Wilson, Scott and Shackleton in those three roles. But the sketch does emphasize the extent to which the great walks in the snow changed men, confirmed their character or sometimes led them towards breakdown. Although harness joined the men, they could be cut off in their own worlds. Scott gave this account of the trio:

Shackleton in front, with harness slung over his shoulder, was bent forward with his whole weight on the trace; in spite of his breathless work, now and again he would raise and half-turn his head in an effort to cheer on the team . . . Behind these, again, came myself with the whip, giving forth one long string of threats and occasionally bringing the last down with a crack on the snow . . . On the opposite side of the leading sledge was Wilson, pulling away in grim silence.

As the dogs wilted or shirked, so the men reduced themselves to the state of the dogs. It was more than they could endure. Already, in winter quarters and in earlier sledge parties, there had been complaints of scurvy. Basic diet on the *Discovery* was plain, small and suspect, and the men soon lost confidence and interest in their food. They complained of the tasteless pemmican and were suspicious of the tinned meat. There were instances of food poisoning, and many stores had been spoiled by damp on the voyage. Crucially the party lacked fruit and vegetables and was disinclined to take fresh seal and penguin as substitutes. Scurvy had the added horror of being an illness without explanation. No one fully grasped its causes or understood a remedy. The gloominess of attitude that often accompanies the physical symptoms – swollen limbs, bad teeth, tiredness – was thought to be a possible cause. Thus men dreaded both scurvy and the depression that could precede it.

It must be added that economy and mistake had made Scott work to a daily sledging ration of only $7\frac{1}{2}$ oz. of pemmican, whereas earlier parties had eaten twice that amount. Granted that the diet made the men vulnerable to scurvy, as soon as heavy man-hauling began, their condition rapidly deteriorated. This is the abiding failure of

Scott's two expeditions, and it is the more poignant in that the men hardly knew what was happening to them. Only the reduced daily mileage confronted their exhaustion and instilled in them a sense of failure.

Their actual menu – bacon and biscuit for breakfast; biscuit, Bovril, chocolate and sugar at midday; and at night a pemmican soup with pea meal, bacon powder and powdered cheese, washed down with cocoa – stimulated feverish food dreams of roast duck; fresh bread and golden syrup; steaks in thick gravy with onions; huge fruit salads and bowls of lettuce, cucumber and tomatoes; sirloin of beef with crisp brown fat; jam tarts and a bowl of cream; the remains in a porridge saucepan. It is easy to smile at these dormitory fantasies, but they were the cry of the spirit protesting undernourishment: the chief reason for the eventual loss of Scott and his four companions, if never realized by them.

Shackleton soon developed a bad cough, and Wilson the symptoms of scurvy. With the dogs letting them down, the men were forced into the soul-destroying business of relaying: dividing a load, taking half on a stretch and then going back for the rest. Next Scott developed scurvy and Wilson contracted snow-blindness so that he had to be led by the others. Further isolated, Wilson imagined himself walking through English beechwoods 'and the swish-swish of the ski was as though brushing through dead leaves'.

Their farthest south was 82°16′, still on the Ice Barrier but in sight of the mountains that were the beginning of the land plateau. Compared with the later expedition, it was a short distance to have come. But they had seen a way to the Pole and, feebly and painfully, worked out a sledging system for getting there. No matter that they were not much more than 300 miles from their base, once they turned back they faced the fearful equation of time and strength that years later was to undermine Scott.

Within days they were compelled to slaughter the last dogs, if only because their sledges were weighed down with food for the dogs who were now trotting along beside men pulling sledges. Still, the killing was difficult and disheartening for all three, none of whom was anywhere near sound. Scott may have been despondent at the limited achievement and Shackleton went into a rapid decline. Wilson's private estimate, that he 'hasn't the legs that the job wants', may simply have been a lucky guess that coincided with a cough and the worst case of scurvy.

What happened as Shackleton deteriorated is still a matter for argument, less over his physical condition than the way in which the three men responded to it. Shackleton was a flamboyant boaster, but intensely ambitious of success and physical vindication. That winter he had entertained the company by play-acting the successful traveller to the Pole being received by the crowned heads of Europe. He yearned to make a mark, to prove himself to Scott and the Navy, to impress his fiancée, Emily Dorman, and to reassure himself. Scott was less open about the wish to be famous, but no less tied to it. Failure always depressed him and sometimes aggravated his brooding. It is also possible that he nursed some blame for the dogs towards Shackleton who had been nominally in charge of them. It is more likely that he became suddenly alarmed at the prospect of losing another man and of risking loss of the entire party.

Wilson became not just an intermediary, but a greater personality through the work he did in keeping the unhappy trio together. There were undoubtedly arguments, rows, even quarrels, but none has been directly reported by one of the participants. Armitage was the source of the most striking anecdote which, he claimed, came in the first instance from Wilson, with later confirmation from Shackleton:

Wilson and Shackleton were packing the sledges after break-fast one morning. Suddenly they heard Scott shout to them 'Come here you B.Fs.' They went to him, and Wilson quietly said 'Were you speaking to me'. 'No Billy' said Scott. 'Then it must have been me' said Shackleton. He received no answer. He then said 'Right, you are the worst B.F. of the lot, and every time that you dare to speak to me like that you will get it back.'

This is a petty exchange of words, understandable in wretchedly tired and anxious men. Yet the outburst gives a clue to how often in Antarctica Englishmen suppressed their natural feelings. Subsequent events suggest that it merely voiced an antagonism between Scott and Shackleton made raw by the situation in which the one was a burden on the other. As they struggled to get back, Shackleton was made first to walk beside the sledge. Then he was spared all work in making camp or cooking. Such kindnesses may have been a special aggravation to Shackleton, for Scott and Wilson both had to insist that he rest and that he stop claiming greater strength than he actually possessed.

How ill was Shackleton? Wilson thought he might not survive and on one occasion the invalid heard his fate being discussed. Shackleton may have resented Scott's supervision of him as much as he regretted his own break-down. At the same time he seems to have been a difficult man to treat; the reluctance to own up to his weakness must have made the others' task more onerous, no matter that they admired his courage. The most telling indication of what happened on that return is that Wilson became Scott's man. One day Wilson 'had it out with Scott' and may have compelled the commander to recognize the difficulties others had with him. If so, it was tactfully and persuasively done. Wilson must have been impressed by Scott's candour and idealism, and the commander discovered a true confidant. In the last resort, Scott and Wilson put Shackleton on the sledge and dragged him back to base. That was a mercy that Shackleton's pride was not able to tolerate.

There may have been no other 'incident'. In the aftermath the three men perhaps struggled to recall the actuality of what had been a mood nearly hysterical with illness and fatigue. It was a decisive journey: Shackleton was ever afterwards labouring to prove himself sound; Scott found a real target, the Pole; and Wilson discovered something like a quest for himself. He had not been entirely happy to go on the southern journey, since it interrupted his ornithology – 'I am afraid this long southern journey is taking me right away from my proper sphere of work to monotonous hard pulling over an icy desert where we shall see neither beast nor bird, nor life of any kind, nor land, and nothing whatever to sketch.' It is not easy to define Wilson's quest, which was almost mystical. It shines out of his paintings, which are so suggestive of a demure Turner who has felt something holy in blizzard, aurora and reflection of light. 'Surely God means us to find out all we can of his works,' Wilson had written about the reason for exploring the wilderness. As he recovered from the trip, reading Ruskin, rather than Darwin's *Origin of Species* which he had taken sledging, he considered how far his God existed in the beautiful prospects of Antarctica: 'I feel inclined to kneel before anything that goes to my heart as being very beautiful, and the more humble and lowly and unasserting it is the more I feel inclined to kneel before it as representing to me the presence of something very near to God and very holy. It is this feeling which has in the old days again and again led me to kneel and kiss a flower in the woods.'

When we read Wilson, it is like the voice of the last great rambler of the Romantic movement.

The southern party reached Hut Point ten days after the arrival of the relief ship, the *Morning*. It had been part of the original plan that a ship would seek out the *Discovery* after one year: to replenish its supplies, bring back news and invalids, or even to rescue the entire party. Among the patrons of the expedition there were differing opinions as to what message it would give Scott. Some wished for an immediate recall and, between them, Markham and Scott turned a blind eye to that wish. As the *Morning* set out, Markham could easily have argued that its orders must not be definite since no one could predict what it would find. However, there was an unmistakable need for economies and Scott took the opportunity to call for volunteers who would return with the *Morning*.

He thought eight should go and wrote, a little ingenuously: 'The result is curiously satisfactory . . . there are eight names on the list, and not only that, but these names are precisely those which I should have placed there had I undertaken the selection myself.' It does not ring true that so forceful a commander wishing to be rid of some men should not have ordered them home, or persuaded them. To call for volunteers and be pleased that fate realized his wishes suggests that there may have been a group of men on the *Discovery* who were, in Markham's word, 'idlers', or some who had been unhappy. What adds to the effect of policy is that nearly all the Merchant Navy men were included in those returning. This had the appearance of a purge. Shackleton was sent back – 'He ought not to risk further hardships in his present state of health' – and protested the decision. There is a controversy over the medical verdicts on Shackleton: Armitage claimed that Koettlitz believed Shackleton was as able to continue as Scott. Furthermore Armitage alleged that pressure was put upon him to return, but that he insisted on staying since his appointment was independent of Scott. Armitage also said that Scott responded to his defence of Shackleton, 'If he does not go back sick he will go in disgrace'.

Armitage's criticism of Scott is difficult to appraise. It was made years later, in confidence, and has been called the fruit of bitterness. No one else has described the Scott–Armitage scene, but details of the story are corroborated elsewhere. It serves to stress the width of the gulf between Navy and Merchant Navy and Armitage's belief that Scott was jealous of the glory, looked upon the Antarctic as his domain and treated the expedition as his. This helps explain the sense of injury Scott had when others intruded on the expanse of Antarctica, and it may be the reaction of the relatively sheltered life of a naval commander.

The second year of the *Discovery* expedition was full of incident and adventure, if hardly a justification for staying on. Scott had no thought of another journey due south, but he seems to have been anxious for more hard sledging. Of several journeys undertaken, the most notable was the western journey. This gave Scott great personal satisfaction and reinforced his notions on sledge travel. Without dogs very creditable distances were managed – an average of over fifteen miles a day – and the spirit of robust man-hauling was confirmed. Scott also initiated the method of taking a large party and dropping off numbers along the way. Essentially, this allowed many to carry and deposit supplies for a few.

The western journey ended with Scott sledging with two seamen and concluding 'There is no class of men so eminently adapted by training to cope with the troubles and tricks of sledging life as sailors'. The men with him were Lashly and Edgar Evans, two fine physical specimens. The three men shared every danger and slept in one large sleeping bag. Scott admitted that he had never learned as much about lower-deck life in so short a time. It was not a gesture towards equality, yet it does seem a modest extension of Scott's horizons.

After the fraught journey of the year before, Scott must have enjoyed the greater unanimity. Vaguely the point may have dawned on him that the sailor could be stronger than officer or scientist. This is impossible to prove, but on the occasions when sailors were fully tested in sledging their record was good. At the end Edgar Evans failed, and thereby disheartened men who had come to look on him as a droll Samson. But by Scott's own standards it is a sign of enlightenment that Evans was even included in the last five. With Evans and Lashly in 1903 Scott had perhaps his most satisfying sledge journey: long, hard, dangerous but successful. There were shattering adventures, such as the moment when Scott and Evans dangled in a crevasse with Lashly braced against their weight.

Scott's account of this adventure contains an interesting picture of the naive, almost lugubrious awe in the Welshman Evans. It is worth quoting, to convey the atmosphere of their camp and the stoicism of Evans:

> Evans' astonishment at the events of the day seemed to grow ever deeper, and was exhibited in the most amusing manner. With his sock half on he would pause and think out our adventures in some new light and would say suddenly, 'Well, Sir, but what about that snow bridge?' or, if so and so hadn't happened, 'where should we be now', and then the soliloquy would end with 'my word, but it was a close call!'

The *Discovery* was compelled to return. When Markham came to send a second relief ship, the funds of the expedition had run out. He turned to the government for aid but met with objections. If some felt that the expedition had already been prolonged by collusion between Markham and Scott, there was now a concerted and vocal opposition. All the old rifts between the Geographical and the Royal Societies opened up and scepticism was expressed about the scientific work that had been done. Some of the press criticized the financial affairs of the expedition and complained that 'funds have to be begged for in an emergency when there should have been ample for all purposes. More than this, as far as knowledge of what has been done is concerned, the public has really had nothing whatever for its money.' Markham was indignant, but the attacks were reasonable and only illuminated the private nature of the expedition. Even when they returned, the scientific work remained in question just as to this very day the claims of science in explorers' prospectuses can sound remote pretexts. There was of necessity little news of the expedition, and Markham had to go cap in hand.

Altogether the situation was made to sound like an emergency when the party was as safe as it had ever been. The government agreed to assist on the condition that it took over the *Morning* and had charge of the 'rescue'. They also bought another ship, the *Terra Nova*, to accompany the *Morning*. The two ships reached McMurdo Sound in January 1904 with orders for Scott to return and with a deadline, by which time *Discovery* men resented the urgency and reacted in the way of Shackleton when packed off home. They were also very unwilling to relinquish what had been their home. Dynamite was used to blast a way through the ice and by 5 March the *Discovery* sailed north with its two relief ships.

For the first time there had been a significant, if minor, incursion on Antarctica by man. Scott came back aware of some errors, blind to others, a stronger man, a man with friend and enemy, and a man with a claim on the south – as he felt – no matter that inhuman emptiness might be its most appropriate and abiding state:

For countless ages the great sombre mountains about us have

loomed through the gloomy polar night with never an eye to mark their grandeur, and for countless ages the wind-swept snow has drifted over these great deserts with never a footprint to break its white surface; for one brief moment the eternal solitude is broken by a hive of human insects; for one brief moment they settle, eat, sleep, trample, and gaze, and then they must be gone, and all must be surrendered again to the desolation of the ages.

Scott seldom indulged social philosophy in his journal, but taken in isolation that passage is as mournful and poignant as the explorer of new lands who finds only an overwhelming desert. The picture of man is petty and insignificant and reminds one of some of the complaints of civilized life that Scott's men hoped to evade in the south. Scott was depressive and anxious, but far from a critic of his times. Even so, the intuition that life is but a brief moment in which we settle, eat, sleep, trample and gaze is near to the uneasy bitterness of twentieth-century pessimism. It is the mood of the wasteland discovered amid the most extreme and perfect terrestrial desolation. One appeal of the south to Scott's rather austerely neglected subconscious may have been that the rippled white expanses quietly confirmed his own disquiet. The south was a desert that made the riddle of inquiry tragic. Amundsen never dreamed of that pattern; Scott searched it out and put his flags on it.

5
Fame and
Marriage

Scott found himself famous, welcome and regarded as
someone who had made his mark; but he remained steadfast in doubt. Success only multiplied the ordeals of encounter for a shy man and made a sceptic suspicious of the
grounds for acclaim. He would never fully credit the prevailing standards of fame and success, and did not move
with the zealous aptitude of a climber. In the years between
his two expeditions he was not evidently preoccupied with
the challenge of Antarctica. In comparison Shackleton went
hither and thither for money, position and popularity, and
for a second chance at the south. Shackleton was more
energetic, more committed to himself and far less searching
of Edwardian values. A more conspicuous figure than
Scott, he managed to appropriate much of the name and
attention that his former commander could have exploited.
As so often, Scott hesitated and reflected. In these interim
years he was more in search of himself than contriving
another opportunity in the south.

In the way that Scott courted responsibilities but was
burdened by them, his return in 1904 entailed a series of
lectures and the anticipated difficulty of writing the official
account of the *Discovery* expedition. He never reconciled
himself to public speaking and was distressed by the
pressure to assert or display himself for a large audience of
strangers. In such circumstances he was neither beguiling

nor fluent; even in the easier surroundings of small groups of like-minded men he could retreat into the guarded isolation of the naval commander. Justified or not, he believed that he offered little as an individual, that his personality was hemmed in. Of all the Polar explorers of this era, Scott neglected the appeal of the subject to the ordinary man; and yet he found himself labouring to describe Antarctica for the public and then to persuade the armchair traveller into funding his expedition. Some criticized the way Scott treated his expeditions as private properties or limited companies. But it may be nearer the truth that he looked on the enormous ventures as expressive of an inner self. It was a manifestation of his day-dreams, even if he adopted the justifications of patriotism and science.

The writing took longer than he planned: his leave of absence had to be extended by the Admiralty from six to nine months. *The Voyage of the 'Discovery'*, published by Smith, Elder in 1905, was a popular success, but it is a plain book, at best conscientious, methodical and aware of the splendour of the ice continent. Scott acknowledged literary help and advice, and was weighed down by a sense of duty to the two societies and to all the men who took part. Very often the voice of the book is that of an observer, rather than the leader. As a writer Scott is reluctant to speak up for himself: he omits all the difficulty with Shackleton – which is understandable in view of the discretion that then ruled. But he barely reveals the rapture of desolation, as if he did not yet feel it. Again Scott emerged as a writer only when failure was unmistakable and tragedy crowding in with the cold. In the last stages of the second expedition no one looked over Scott's draft; but by then he had no need of editing. He was free as soon as he saw Amundsen's black flag in the distance ahead.

The writing brought him the friendship of his publisher,

Reginald Smith, and renewed collaboration with Wilson. The three men put the text and Wilson's illustrations together in the publisher's London office, and had relaxing week-ends at his house in Kirriemuir. One fruit of fame was that Scott now moved in London literary and social circles, a pleasure he took with absent-minded alarm. The abstracted hero, the forgetful adventurer, was a character of just the fey appeal to attract another of Scott's new friends, J. M. Barrie, the dramatist. Not that Scott calculated the impression he made. That would have appalled him, and the risk of acting may have made him all the more repressed on platforms or at the dinner table. But when his attention wandered, he was suddenly likely to be the celebrity of the year arriving at a dinner with no dinner jacket under his overcoat. The friendship with Barrie is unexpected: not many naval officers would have achieved such rapt harmony with the author of *Peter Pan* and *Mary Rose*. But it was deep, honest and lasted to the end when Scott wrote a dying letter to Barrie that contains this almost anguished confession: 'I never met a man in my life whom I admired and loved more than you, but I could never show you how much your friendship meant to me, for you had much to give and I nothing.'

It is the dubiousness of Barrie as an intimate companion that tells us something about Scott. Barrie's charm – great at that time – now seems wistful, immature and sickly. As a man he was soulfully consumed in remorse for his lost mother, and turned towards a dainty reverence of whimsy as an escape from reality. His professional success does not hide the fact that few notable writers were as cut off from his time, as intent on presenting fairyland in a fashion that adults could accept. I am hard on Barrie to illuminate how the downcast abstraction in Scott could turn into maudlin self-pity. Scott was not cheerful, and lacked that dry merriment which makes Shaw so much more satisfactory a pessimist. The ability to see Polar enterprise in personal terms could sound petulant and foolish when disappointed. Barrie did not write those last passages of Scott's journal, but their friendship, their similar dismay at pain and problem, their solemn fallacy that heroism could dispel difficulty, surely help to clarify Scott's character. There was in him the commander that Peter Pan might have become. Imagine Peter thrust into the trench setting of *Journey's End* and the doleful appreciation of disaster is more understandable.

Lecturing occupied as much time as Scott was prepared to give it. In November 1904 he spoke to a crowd of 7,000 in the Albert Hall, so tense that he hurried and forgot to thank every deserving member of the expedition, so anxious that he was bewildered by the great applause as he ended. Such an occasion is worth recalling in view of the unhappy lecture tour Scott was to undertake five years later in search of funds. Had he stretched out his hand at the Albert Hall and required that the British send him south again, he might have had money in a month. That he did not ask is suggestive that he did not yet mean to go back, and that he was temperamentally reluctant about asking. When the need came, he showed himself a cold, diffident beseecher and a tight-lipped advocate of prospects. No lecturing was undertaken without Admiralty approval, and Scott had assured the First Sea Lord, Lord Walter Kerr: 'I have no wish whatever to advertise myself. I should be very sorry to do anything that the Admiralty or the service at large thought unbecoming a naval officer. Except in this matter I have mentioned [the Albert Hall lecture], I am trying to keep as quiet as possible. Of course it is a little difficult at present.'

Nor did Scott avoid all difficulty. Not every naval officer led exploratory expeditions; not even Scott could fail to see how much it might assist his career. It was his character not to wish to be thought pushing; that does not mean that he was anything but an intensely if timidly ambitious man. But on his return he was promoted to Captain and made a Companion of the Victorian Order. As well as awards from continental geographical societies, in August 1905 he received an invitation to Balmoral for a short stay with the king during which he would give a lecture to the royal household. The visit left him a little overpowered, but he dined with the king, shot with the Prince of Wales and felt so relaxed that his lecture ran longer than planned. 'All sort of nice things said afterwards,' he wrote to his mother, drollest of all the remark of the prime minister, Mr Balfour, that he regarded himself as the father of the expedition. The complacent acquiring of unmerited prestige by politicians baffled Scott in much the same way that their leaders' deviousness was loyally ignored by military men during the First World War.

Scott now addressed himself to the duties he had had to neglect in going south. He moved his mother into a house, 56 Oakley Street, and lived with her and his sisters. Towards the end of 1905, as it became necessary for him to return to active service, he was awarded a gold medal by the American Ambassador in London. In the speech he made, he said that 'in all probability' his professional duties would prevent him from going south again. Coming at a time when Scott was fêted as never before, and had had time to assess and describe his expedition, that shows the incomplete hold Antarctica had upon him. It also suggests that only the pressure of others would send him south a second time, just as it had the first.

In January 1906 he took up a position as assistant director of Naval Intelligence at the Admiralty. This may have been a graceful gesture by the Navy to prolong and capitalize on Scott's celebrity in London. But Scott himself was tiring of entertainment, even though he had met several young ladies, often actress friends of his sister Effie, and been the uniformed stalwart on whose arm leaned the frail Mabel Beardsley (sister of Aubrey) and the more robust Pauline Chase, best known for her portrayal of Peter Pan. Young women sought him and hostesses plied him with invitations. No doubt his stories of adventure and the fact of his presence were sufficient. But it is hard to imagine Scott thriving on the tortuous and articulate gatherings Henry James described in *The Awkward Age*. Society then was formal to the point of stuffiness when it chose, but beneath the surface rules were wavering. Attitudes, manners and convention found themselves in the abyss where men and women could expect no comfort or safety from God, family, country or civilization. On the edge of artistic circles Scott must have felt the seething disillusion of Europe, and scorned it along with the many brave heresies that were flourishing. Scott's wish not to offend the Navy code and his desire to honour his country came after the startling, shit-boasting debut in Paris of Alfred Jarry's Père Ubu, a craven, unscrupulous beast king, as far from old ideas of kingship as Edward VII was from the placid squire of Balmoral. Scott had met his own king and was surely unaware of Ubu, but the several levels of Edward's life marked a new diversity in human behaviour that Scott himself would have resisted desperately. The hint of a monster in man was a warning pressure that strengthened Scott's insistent manners.

By August 1906 Scott was ready for a sea posting: as flag captain to Admiral Egerton in *Victorious*. That summer, cruising round Majorca, *Victorious* had Clements Markham as a passenger. Once again the old man talked to Scott long into the night and stressed those things not yet done which needed to be done. Markham's urging was not enough on its own, but within the year Scott had the added incentives of a rival and a demanding woman to impress. It is the case that Markham recalled his thoughts to the south and had an immediate effect. Days later Scott wrote to Barrie, admitting that he might return to the Antarctic. But this was on the long finger and accounts for Scott's illogical feeling that no one else should trespass upon his portion for as long as he contemplated the idea of going back. He may have persuaded himself that, as of the summer of 1906, he was preparing a return; but his actions were sluggish, haphazard and unfocused. He left himself open to usurpation, and to being driven to act less by positive resolve than in response to Shackleton's initiative.

This is still the period in which Scott devoted himself to the Navy. Nothing he said supports the point, but it is possible that this doggedly honourable man felt that the service deserved so many years of him before he was free to think of another expedition. Therein lies the man who saw a certain self-indulgence in going to the South Pole. The Navy might have argued against his loyalty, for Scott's reputation as an explorer was his greatest service to the Admiralty. As an officer at sea Scott did his job, was diligent and ingenious, but he never convinced himself that he and the Navy were thoroughly suited.

In 1907 there occurred an incident that seemed to reinforce the legend of Scott's misfortune, and which may have been a cloud on his record. On 1 January he was made captain of the *Albemarle*, a battleship in the Atlantic fleet. In the second week of February the new captain took his ship on secret night manoeuvres some 150 miles west of Lisbon 'and came within an ace of an appalling catastrophe'. What happened is still as unclear as the actual encounters at, say, the battle of Jutland some years later. The accident in 1907, and the confusion at Jutland, both speak for the way in which large fleets of heavy ships had put an impossible strain on 'line of battle' tactics. The *Albemarle* was one of eight ships advancing in a staggered line with only 220 yards between the ships. It was eight in the evening when the line accelerated. Scott was on deck and only went below after the *Albemarle* had put on speed. He then carried some cipher signals to Admiral Egerton's cabin and 'felt the engines had stopped suddenly and the next moment they were going astern'. He dashed up to the deck and saw the outline of the next ship, the *Commonwealth*, on their bow. The impact came – 'a sickening sensation . . . one felt only a jarring drag as though a colossal brake had been put on'. There were two collisions, with the *Commonwealth* suffering worst. The *Albemarle* did what it could to help and Scott described the sight in a way that catches his own horror:

It was pitchy black but her lights were close to us outlining the huge hull, and as she rose and fell with the sea and one saw the twinkling lights and the illuminated figures on her decks, she represented a picture of helplessness and a possibility of catastrophe which is not easily forgotten. It was perhaps some half hour before she reported that there was no danger of sinking.

It is in such moments that we feel closest to Scott, as if he was then fulfilled. Gloomy premonitions are confirmed by mishap, since doubt at least has vanished.

The cause of the accident was so obvious that it may explain why the court of inquiry was not made public. Ahead in the line one ship had swung to starboard. The one behind had had to follow suit to avoid collision; the one behind that was the *Albemarle*, which took the same evasive action and thus ran into the side of the *Commonwealth*. The *Commonwealth* was holed below the waterline and then struck again as the two ships swung out of control. Eventually they both reached Gibraltar, where the *Commonwealth* was found to have taken in over 100 tons of water. The *Albemarle* was at sea again in a day, but the *Commonwealth* needed three months of repairs.

Scott wrote to his mother asking her not to be alarmed by newspaper reports. But the threat of an inquiry was real and Scott conceded that he should not have left the bridge so soon after a change of speed. He was never a man to spare himself, but the Admiralty's verdict – that no one was to blame – seems fairer; it might have encouraged the realization that large battle fleets in close order were a danger to themselves. Scott's years of captaincy go over and over the same scheme of manoeuvres, formations and exercises, battle practice and gun-laying, signalling and navigation. Yet, in Scott's mind, 'it is only since the accident that the full dangers of the formation and the circumstances under which we were placed in it, have become evident to me'. If the foreshadowing of Jutland needs underlining, when Scott left the *Albemarle*, he was replaced by Jellicoe, British commander at that battle.

After seven months on the *Albemarle* Scott was allowed back to London on half-pay. Was this in any way a rebuke in connection with the *Commonwealth* collision? Or were the Admiralty nudging Scott into enlarging his own plans for Polar travel, especially as Shackleton began to capture attention and support? Whatever the answer, these were worrying times for Scott as he approached forty, an age for which he had long seemed qualified. His flux was stirred and agitated by the rapid development of the most important relationship in his life.

The ladies of explorers are invariably demure, devoted and silent creatures, hopelessly stay-at-home during their husbands' excursions, the tender figures seen on receding quays, at repose in photographs adorning the walls of whatever hut, igloo or den their men inhabit, and even wreathed in mourning, elegant faded flowers, at splendid funerals. We know them as the people who must have been the first to read letters and diaries written at the ends of the earth; and we wonder if they ever noticed, with sadness or pride, that those personal letters may have been written by men conscious of writing themselves into posterity. The travelling men talk to themselves in these letters about the way they have stranded their wives, and about how they would never have done such a thing except to please the ladies. We rarely hear protest from the women, and their repressed personalities lead us into asking what sort of love and marriage it is that drives men south.

Scott's wife was not of this retiring, humble flock. She was a strong, declaratory character who could overawe her men. Kathleen Scott was not concerned with Polar travel, except in so far as it was her husband's bane and destiny. Yet his second journey owes so much to her sense of stirring dedication that we have to see her as prompter of it. Leadership in Scott was a duty that he accepted from the inspiration of others. That said, their short affair was exhausting, passionate and always tinged with the melancholy offstage threat of failure. It is a reasonable use of words to speak of their 'affair' since they both treasured moods and commitments that were wild, personal and beyond the conventional limits of marriage. For both of them, the value of a relationship was and had to be a gesture towards what life ought to be. There are categorizations easily fallen into: that she was an artist and bohemian, while he was a Navy man and an explorer. Perhaps neither role fits; perhaps they were two vulnerably innocent romantics, she a little of the bully and he a willing victim. They were alike in earnestness and lack of irony; they shared an unquestioning conception of integrity; but their determined advance on purpose is now the impulse that makes them seem marooned. The strength of their affair grew out of their magnificent blindness to the shaky grounds for their own confidence. Otherwise it is only in legend and poetry that love is enacted in huge, vain and fatal journeys.

But one thing emerges from this interpretation: while some explorers went away to be free of homely burdens and loving ties, for the Scotts it was a separation that concentrated the deep, imaginative nature of their love. Lovers may part because being together seems drab beside the purity of the idea of love.

Kathleen Bruce was thirteen years younger than Scott: an older man offered her caring and security; a younger woman might illuminate him with vitality and freshness. She was the daughter of a Nottinghamshire clergyman who was also a canon at York Minster where her uncle had been archbishop. That family pattern was not hers. Passionately attached to the thrill of art, she attended the Slade School and, at the turn of the century, studied and lived in Paris on her own, meeting Rodin and becoming the acolyte of Isadora Duncan. Some biographers of Scott have seized on her as a fully fledged member of the *avant-garde*, tribute to Scott's wide-ranging mind. But the Paris she visited was the city of Jarry, of Méliès, Rousseau, Satie and Apollinaire, as well as of the sensual romanticism of Rodin and the florid, arty confusion of health and art that filled Isadora Duncan. The pungent anarchy of that Paris, the eery calm that portended surrealism, the pioneering daring that art might be meaningless to keep pace with life – these trends passed her by.

The artist and the captain first met in the spring of 1907, possibly at the time when Scott was in London for the *Commonwealth* inquiry. She was lately back from Greece, where, in her phrase, she had been 'vagabonding' – roaming the country and sleeping in the open, turning nut-brown and exhilarated by the nearness of Isadora's fulsome ideals. This was far from conventional, but it never slipped below the ladylike. The true English lady could go on solitary rambles through wild parts of the Earth and return not just intact, but reinforced. Burnished skin gilded the height, dark hair and very pronounced features: as a young woman Kathleen moved with the rapturous concentration of someone convinced of natural movement as a means to fulfilment.

The occasion of their meeting was a luncheon party given by Mabel Beardsley in Chelsea. Kathleen sat between Barrie and Max Beerbohm and thought how 'difficult' English men were. 'Far down the other side of the table was a naval officer, Captain Scott. He was not very young, perhaps forty, nor very good looking; but he looked very healthy and alert, and I glowed rather foolishly and suddenly when I clearly saw him ask his neighbour who I was.'

They were introduced after lunch and he remarked on her sunburn and the startling blue of her eyes. Amid the pale faces of salon gentlefolk, this made a striking resemblance, for Scott was invariably brown and had deep violet eyes. He listened to her account of vagabonding – there may have been a lyrical fervour in it – and was entranced. The first appeal grew out of a shared delight in that heady walking for the spirit's sake.

Then the meeting took an amusing but characteristic turn. She had to leave to catch a train; he followed her – he had had great meetings in the streets near Victoria before. But she was carrying her own large suitcase, and Scott deliberately loitered, held at bay by the thought that 'English gentlemen don't carry large objects in the streets'. It is an eery reserve, and incongruous prelude to the wilful hauling of more than his own weight across flawless prairies of snow. Abandon and inhibition are close partners in Scott.

They did not meet again for nearly a year. Did Scott ever regret the caution that left her with her case? They were at the same tea party, once more arranged by Mabel Beardsley, who was not indifferent to Scott herself. When Kathleen arrived, she saw Scott caught on a sofa with an elderly lady. She veered away, shy and tremulous, and talked to Ernest Thesiger, the actor, and Henry James – a group that one longs to overhear.

But as the tea party revolved, Scott and Kathleen came face to face. This time there was no hesitation. She was overwhelmed by his 'almost purple' eyes and hardly minded the dull hair beginning to thin. He offered to take her home and, on the spur of the moment, she abandoned a dinner rendezvous in Soho and agreed to go with him. She was not yet fully recovered from having her appendix out and took it for granted that he would call a hansom. But this love was based on walking, and he 'started striding forth westward at a good rate. Anxious but excited I fell in, and side by side we walked, laughing, talking, jostling each other, as we lunged along the river-side in hilarious high spirits.'

Thereafter they met or corresponded regularly. Something like a formal proposal was made by Scott in January 1908. But between then and the marriage, in September, there was time for fretful questioning on Scott's part and real doubts on hers. He was at sea for most of the time, on *Essex* and *Bulwark*, and the courtship was marked by a sort of delirious agonizing over separation and obstacles.

Kathleen treasured her freedom and knew that Scott would want her to abandon several old friendships. In his absence she sat for the portrait painter Charles Shannon who was himself in love with her. 'As I sat there in the quiet, temple-like studio, I made my decision.' She told Shannon and may have added that this 'rock-like naval officer was just exactly what I had been setting up in my mind as a contrast to my artist friends'. Shannon, stunned, walked out into the street and had a comic accident with a bus. Kathleen remained a sculptress all her life, but she had turned her back on bohemianism.

If she had looked to Scott for a 'rock-like' base, disappointment over that may have given her most doubts. There is no question about the strength of Scott's love; yet he spent nine months fearful of shadowy difficulties that they faced. 'I want to marry you very badly,' he wrote to her in January, 'but it is absurd to pretend I can do so without facing a great difficulty and risking a great deal for others as well as myself.' His first concern was that he could not leave his mother unprovided for. Yet she specifically told him to live more for himself: 'You have carried the burden of the family since 1894, it is time now for you to think of yourself and your future.'

A Navy captain was not in the worst position for marriage; able seamen managed it and had large families. But poverty was a looming worry in Scott's letters, and it was sharpened by something like paranoia when he discovered that the *Essex* posting involved a salary of only £720 a year, £110 less than he had thought he would earn. Coming after six months of half-pay, this is another hint of Admiralty coolness. Even so, in 1908 £720 was a comfortable sum of money, especially for a man who had the chance of extra income from writing and lecturing. But the worry persisted. Scott became obsessed that Kathleen should have the clothes she wanted, and, more important, that she should not appear to be the victim of poverty: 'Now does your sweetness see? Kathleen, am I dreadfully sensitive to appearances? – but you will understand, won't you?' When ashore at Swanage he was depressed by the circumstances of service officers: 'I have been looking at poverty here as represented by those who live on pay alone. I don't find it attractive to them. I don't believe it would be attractive to you or me – lodgings – ceaseless gossip of appointments – what will this or that person do next?'

The disproportionate preoccupation with poverty must have exasperated Kathleen sometimes. It helps to reveal

Scott's insecurity, and the irrational pitch it could reach. Such worries bespeak an inescapable grounding in the safety of middle-class comfort and in the unconscious snobbery of avoiding extravagance. So long a history of family making-do had numbed Scott permanently, and the rift of self-doubt in his character has every debilitating trace of fallen gentry. Is there another lure in the south here? That it was a world free of cost of living?

Doubts over his own means were also a way of uncovering his own sense that he and Kathleen were too unalike. Here the anxiety is more complex. Kathleen clearly jostled Scott out of many set attitudes and feelings; he liked that change but felt endangered by it. Very soon he spoke to Kathleen as someone who had lessons for him that he might not be able to absorb. He interpreted the 'horrible difference' she detected as a criticism of his caution, and that only made him the more circumspect:

it seems that I have already sorely troubled the serenity of your life, and banished some of its sweetness. Don't let me be a trouble to you.

Yet oh my dear, there is another side of me, born of hereditary instinct of caution, and fostered by the circumstances which have made the struggle for existence an especially hard one for me. Can you understand? I review a past – a real fight – from an almost desperate position to the bare right to live as my fellows.

The spectator must find it hard to believe that Scott ever knew a truly 'desperate position' – until the very end, that is. But that was a desperation that cleansed and absolved all the confusions of ordinary life that had preyed upon him. In the summer of 1908 he took his ships on exercises, felt increasingly a square peg in a round hole in the Navy and arranged for the purchase of a house for himself and Kathleen – in Buckingham Palace Road. One part of him warmed to her love of the open air – 'You are the spirit of all this to me, though we have loved each other in crowded places. I want you to be with me when the sun shines free of fog.' Another begged her to change him, knock shackles off him, before it was too late: 'Oh dear me what a task you have before you.'

Even as late as the end of July Scott could not face his future with equanimity or unalloyed pleasure. 'I am afraid of what I shall be to you. Shall I be always trusted? Will it come natural to you to tell me things, intimate things, or will you grow to think me only fitted for the outer court-yard of your heart?'

She had sent him a photograph of Isadora Duncan, replete with her love of headstrong liberty. The pose seems to have disturbed Scott, given him a glimpse of a taste for abandon that unnerved him. 'I see the beauty of it, yet it is for you, not for me. Will many things be for one and not for the other?' He admired her independence of the ways of the masses, her strident advocacy of beauty, and her unrepressed capacity for dreaming. His own dreamy days, he claimed, were over – 'The dreaming part of me was and is a failure' – and he was inclined to hide behind the portrait of discipline-tied naval officer. Yet Kathleen's dreams may have been slight beside Scott's unwitting resort to the day dream of a sluggish older man whipped into shape by a brilliant younger woman. These letters were edged with self-pity but more tellingly by a form of self-dramatizing morbid rhetoric:

'Do you see in all this the shadow of a train of thought, and the shadow of sadness which it has brought to me? I want you to be near my soul, and I pause to wonder if I have a soul that such a free-thinking creature as you could ever find companionable.'

They were married on 2 September 1908, with Kathleen whispering to him at the altar that she would as soon take the handsome best man. A son was born a year later, and named Peter Markham. All along it had been Kathleen's dominating urge to mother a son; it was likely that at times she wondered if a husband was merely a means to that end. But, with the son delivered, she 'fell for the first time gloriously, passionately, wildly in love with my husband. I did not know I had not been so before, but I knew now. He became my god; the father of my son and my god . . . Now my determined, my masterful, virginity, sustained through such strong vicissitudes, seemed not, as I had sometimes feared, mere selfish prudery, but the purposeful and inevitable highway to this culminating joy and peace.'

They lived together less than two years.

6
Shackleton's Intrusion

Scott's men are those who died with him, those who went to Antarctica with him, more or less sharing his goals, more or less admiring followers. At a distance they are those who lived in England and were moved to pity and wonder by the report of his fate. But the category extends to men who were rivals of Scott's, men who are visible now partly in the way his light fell on them. Thus Amundsen is a winner made to look mean or simple-minded by Scott's grand failure. That hardly troubled Amundsen. His blunt, practical nature may not have detected the undertones of Scott's coming second. But Shackleton seethed with frustration at Scott's implacable intrusion on his own life. He needs to be seen as one of Scott's men, if only because he felt that so much of what he did was a response to Scott. The stringently glorious end that Scott achieved was something that a Shackleton had to live with in helpless, competitive envy. Scott had wandered into a posterity that may have been the compelling requirement of Shackleton's life. That Scott had accomplished it without design can only have ground harder on Shackleton's spirit.

History still regards Shackleton as an opposite of or alternative to Scott. While the sea captain is gentlemanly, solemn, self-sacrificing and a representative of the establishment, Shackleton is painted as an impetuous, ambitious outsider. It was a crude polarity that was dishonest to both of them. They revealed the worst in one another, and as self-deceiving competitors they made a tortuous dance out of the polite postures that could disguise personal ambition. The closer one looks at the antagonism between the two men, the harder it is to accept the claims of science and patriotism with which they overlaid their journeys. Nothing would have driven them south except a lust for recognition and importance which is as vain and noble as the urge that drives the politician, the artist or the inventor: the wish to be known; the chance that he will die with the fatuous hope of not being forgotten.

Shackleton once told his sister – another Kathleen – that she could not conceive the exhilaration there was 'to walk over places where no one has been before'. That wish for uniqueness is so strong, so basic, that it is a part of all creative urges. Shackleton or Scott would as readily have walked into the virgin obscurity of hot coals as of snow. To go where no one else has gone is akin to the wish to fly, to identify the laws of relativity, to invent the cinema, to interpret dreams or write such music as Charles Ives composed at the time Scott and Shackleton went south. This was a period of such rabid invention that the extent of experience and the purpose of life were being more drastically altered, and more quickly, than ever before. As social and political creatures, Scott and Shackleton were staid and unenterprising. Their taste in the arts would not have run to Ives or Picasso's *Les Demoiselles d'Avignon*. Freud would have flustered them. Yet going south was their version of human uniqueness, and of the loneliness that surrounds it, that characterizes the artistic *avant-garde* before the First World War. Going south is as wild, extremist and fearful as Picasso's African women in Avignon, as Ives's musical inquiry into discord, as Jarry's Père Ubu predicting monstrousness in men.

The twentieth-century imagination reveals its special juxtaposition of contrary forms and moods when one notes that the lyrical naivety of Georges Méliès's film, *Conquête du Pole*, is contemporary with Herbert Ponting's sombre documentary film of Scott in the south. For Méliès, the explorer was the dashing envoy of Europe in frock coat and topee, as blithe and as inventive as Phileas Fogg, a man ineffably careless of real geography who regards far places as the backdrop for his daft daring. In Ponting's film the explorer is a figure in furs in a wilderness. His beard is bristling with frost, and his eyes wince at the brightness. He looks out at interminable spaciousness and is awed by the threatening alternative to our imagination and culture of so much emptiness. Méliès offers a whimsical dream for the armchair explorer; Ponting hints at the numbed movements of man-embryo. And as these two films coincide, the two sorts of explorer overlap in Ernest Shackleton.

Shackleton was brought back from his first sight of the Antarctica on the relief ship, *Morning*. That voyage may have been necessary to restore his exhausted body, but it can only have aggravated the torment of a proud man who believed he had failed and who resented the propriety of his commander sending him home. How easily Shackleton must have reasoned to himself that he had been made a scapegoat, a boisterous intrusion on the settled company of Navy men finally removed. The man who thinks himself victimized is often someone with the instinct that he is exceptional. To cast out that sort of man only reinforces his tremendous belief that he has capacities, hopes and integrity uncommon among men. Whatever the gap or animosity between Shackleton and Scott, Shackleton may have learned to reason that they were alike in seeking glory in the south but that Shackleton went about it honestly, while

Scott hid behind the uniform of duty and what the Royal Navy expected of a commander. If, out in the waste and in fear of dying, Scott had briefly freed himself of that barricade, and cursed Shackleton for slowness, then that might only have proved to Shackleton how often Scott was a humbug. It was part of Shackleton's zeal that he told himself he was an uncomplicated, cheerful adventurer. Yet the rivalry with Scott was to wind so intricately that it forced Shackleton into the appearance of dishonesty and trickery. I doubt that Shackleton betrayed Scott, since betrayal was anathema to his spirit. But there was an insecurity about Scott that could make the acts of other men look devious. Thus the followers of Scott or Shackleton are not just taking sides in a petty quarrel, but standing up for notions of how men should live. And in that respect Scott compares well with Shackleton. Shackleton was enough of the Victorian boy to love adventure for its own sake. He was brave, intuitive and even lucky. The men who followed him adored him, happy to have their worries lifted from them. Scott spread worry around him, but in competition with Shackleton he takes on vestiges of the image of a robust explorer.

Shackleton wept as the *Morning* sailed north, aware that he could hardly do other than report to England the success and durability of Scott and that he would be regarded as an invalid sent home early. Vigour for Shackleton was a sign of virtue. He regarded death as a logical conclusion to the total exhaustion of human energy. Before setting out on the southern journey he had written to his fiancée, Emily Dorman, in the way of a man who might prefer to perish in the wilderness than come back with a stain on his reputation and a suspicion as to his vitality:

Beloved I hope you may never have to read this, but darling loved one if it comes to you you will know that your lover left this world with all his heart yours my last thoughts will be of you

my own dear Heart. . . . Beloved do not grieve for me for it has
been a man's work and I have helped my little mite towards the
increase of knowledge: Child there are millions in this world who
have not had this chance. I cannot say more my heart is so full of
love and longing for you and words will not avail, they are so
poor in such a case. Child we may meet again in another world,
and I believe in God, that is all I can say, but it covers all things:
I have tried to do my best as a man the rest I leave to him.

So much of the breathless muddle of Shackleton's
character is in that letter. He is youthful and rhetorical
enough to foresee that he is writing a letter that may be
read only when he is dead, and to be the more stirred by
that pathos. The more inhibited Scott only identified
his own tragedy when he was already lost. He did not
anticipate as Shackleton did: Scott's fatal misjudgement
led him to exactly the heroic ending that something in
Shackleton yearned for. The letter to Emily Dorman is
flooded with the narrow simplicity of the Edwardian
adventurer: the protestation that he will have added a
'little mite' towards the sum of knowledge – as if the head-
hunter in Borneo or the shopkeeper in Brixton did not have
the same claim upon culture and posterity. He seeks in a
wife the meek qualities of true woman and little girl, and he
is prepared to spend much of his marriage so far from his
wife that she has a succession of similar letters to console
her. And there is the matter-of-fact, almost dismissive
belief in God to tidy up all outstanding queries. Shackleton's
god is as vague and uncomplicated a figure as the captain of
a school, never questioned or examined. It is a faith as
convenient as that of generals in 1914 who called on God to
protect their attacks, the spiritual gesture of a pragmatic
people clinging to the last link with the notion of God. 'I
have tried to do my best as a man the rest I leave to Him' is
tinged with self-exculpation, and it might be the sigh of
Europe on the eve of cataclysm. Shackleton was hellbent

on being a hero in an age too confused and warped for heroes.

In Britain he had the inescapable task of acting as postman for the expedition, reporting to its sponsors and giving some public lectures on progress to date. He was suited to this latter task, even if it may have irked him. Shackleton was amusing, talkative and demonstrative: he got on with men and could enthrall large audiences. 'Irishness' in English eyes often meant a glibness, the sort of verbal dexterity that laid Wilde and Shaw open to charges of being unsound. Those lectures did not last long but they may have persuaded Shackleton that he had at least one ability Scott lacked: to convey enthusiasm and raise funds. The next few years are a tribute to Shackleton's deftness as a leader of independent expeditions. While Scott delayed over going south again, and was depressed by the chores of fund-raising, Shackleton simply mounted another southern venture without any of the institutional support that Scott had had. Scott needed to feel national and official pressure urging him south; Shackleton was personally drawn there, and was much less shy of returning because of so unequivocal an urge.

In Europe Shackleton led an unsettled, nervy life that only convinced his critics that he was a fluctuating man. No one career held him, other than the wish to be an explorer, a traveller who acted out the virtues of danger, hardship and discovering the limits of one's powers. Unconsciously Shackleton was one of the first of those twentieth-century moralists who demonstrate the mystical power of being outward bound to a comfortable, constipated race of metropolitans.

It is easy to present Shackleton's restlessness as a shallow, unscrupulous opportunism. Scott, and Scott's faithful supporters, took that view, but only because they were more complex and less candid than Shackleton. They could not respond to the way Shackleton relished the journey, danger and the glory of return for their own sake. Granted that in this period no explorer was as certain of the need for exploration as he claimed in his own prospectus, still Shackleton's lack of inhibition was extreme and likely to alarm the more cautious and compromised travellers. There were many critics of Polar travel who argued that it was self-indulgent, without purpose, a compound of needless risk and schoolboy excitement. Scott tried to suppress such opposition, in its public forms and in the occasional bursts of light it had in his own soul. Shackleton was the more shocking for being ready to accept that hostile portrait of the blithe traveller. But Shackleton is redeemed by history for adhering to the irrational and the obsessive. He now survives in a glow of purity that seems far-sighted, lucid and poetic. He is the Polar traveller who helps us to feel the disarray of the civilized society that he persistently deserted.

Early in 1904 Shackleton resigned his Merchant Navy commission, not because he accepted the lowly status it had in Navy eyes but because he needed to be unattached. For the next few years he was frankly in search of money and fame, the bases of a second trip south. He was willing to search high and low for them, and the flexibility of the man makes a striking contrast with Scott's commitment to the senior service.

His work on the *South Polar Times* had given him a flavour of journalism, and he took a position as sub-editor on the *Royal Magazine*. He was ignorant about the job, but a quick learner, a natural story-teller and 'brimming over with original, unconventional, racy ideas, which, whether practical or not, were always stimulating and suggestive'. Those are the words of Shackleton's editor, a man who guided the novice's innocence, listened with fascination to his stories and detected an adaptable energy in the young

man that would have flourished in any trade. The editor
noted Shackleton s readiness to work, his skill with people
and was convinced 'that if he had gone to a stock-broker, a
butcher, or a carpenter, or a theatrical manager and asked
for a job, he would have got it. There was something about
him that compelled confidence. And none of these good
folk would have regretted taking him on.'

He left journalism and became secretary to the Royal
Scottish Geographical Society. He and Emily Dorman
were married by now, and they lived in Edinburgh on £200
a year in a curious, provincial version of the travellers'
establishment. No doubt Shackleton hoped to meet and
become familiar with the very class of people who had been
behind Scott's expedition. He was like a would-be novelist
going to work for a publisher. But the Scottish Geographical Society was not the most necessary of institutions, and it
had little enough work for Shackleton to take on a variety
of outside activities that soon overwhelmed the secretary-
ship.

In July 1905 he resigned and plunged into business
ventures and the brief hope of making a name in politics. In
the general election of January 1906 he stood without success
as a Liberal-Unionist at Dundee. All this while he darted
from one commercial scheme to another, like a gambler at
roulette arbitrarily fixing on numbers that will make his
fortune. Some of these plans sound like the germ of
Conrad novels. For a time he nursed one momentous
coup, writing to his wife in the rapt tones of a conspirator:
'Don't say anything darling to a soul: for it is dead secret.'
The plan may always have been moonshine, yet it is no
more fanciful than other free-enterprise schemes of the
period and shows how much more adventurous than
Scott Shackleton was. While Scott carried out night
manoeuvres, anxious not to collide with his companion
ships, early in 1906 Shackleton had a 'little steam boat

company' competing for the contract to bring 40,000 Russian troops back from the Far East and the calamitous war with Japan. He was in telegraphic communication with Russian princes, haggling over a price per head, dreaming of a personal profit of £10,000 and wondering where he might get his hands on enough big ships. The scheme fell through. It may never have stood a realistic chance. But Shackleton was not a man with a precise sense of where reality, chance and hope met. He gathered a romantic aura about him and admitted to his wife that it was 'awfully exciting'.

However, nothing could equal Shackleton's secretive passion over his plans to return to Antarctica. Throughout 1906 he used his business contacts to muster funds for an expedition. Like the outsider who only arouses distrust in the establishment, Shackleton did not publicize these plans. For a chronic privateer, no venture can have the satisfaction of one that is his alone. And Shackleton himself was suspicious of the good-will of the establishment: an easy mixer with men, he was temperamentally unsuited to institutions, and they in turn regarded him as shifty and self-seeking.

Shackleton would have no great patrons, and no committee structure to impede him. It was his expedition alone, and he would supervise everything. Yet he called it the British Antarctic Expedition and told his wife 'I am representing 400 million British subjects'. By February 1907, by dint of bargaining with business colleagues over the notional proceeds of a book and lecture series, Shackleton had some £20,000 guaranteed and the confidence to make a public announcement. It seemed a vindication of Shackleton's love of independence that an individual could suddenly spring into public gaze with such an enterprise all prepared. In fact, many aspects were still vague. But the wilful surprise of his action guaranteed the institutional disapproval that he anticipated, and provoked in Scott the very anxiety that he hoped for.

Secrecy had been adopted by Shackleton for several reasons: because the lone wolf depends on surprise; because fund-raising is as delicate a business as diplomacy; and because Shackleton thought it natural and reasonable to want to beat Scott to the start. Nothing from Scott indicated the will to compete. But the lone wolf expects everyone else to be as fierce and solitary as himself; and wolfishness gives even the sheep no option except to fight.

By the middle of February 1907 Shackleton was in the open and running. His finances were still shaky, and he was never chary of striking secret and contradictory deals with different supporters. But there was a sweeping, all-embracing candour reported in the *Geographical Journal* which is the furtive operator convincing himself of openness and, incidentally, owning up to the reason for the game that Scott hedged on: 'I do not intend to sacrifice the scientific utility of the expedition to a mere record-breaking journey, but say frankly, all the same, that one of my great efforts will be to reach the southern geographical pole.'

Scott was at sea when the first announcement was made, but it is possible that he had had early warning from Wilson or Mulock,* both of whom Shackleton had asked to accompany him. Mulock had replied to Shackleton that he was already committed to Scott. In the event Wilson too would decline Shackleton's pressing invitation, ostensibly on the grounds of other work that had to be finished. Yet Wilson was to become go-between for the mutual prickliness of Scott and Shackleton, and Scott's letters make it clear that he had asked Wilson to take on that role. Being

* G. F. A. Mulock, as a sub-lieutenant on the *Morning*, had taken Shackleton's place in the latter part of the *Discovery* expedition. Though sounded out by Scott for a second expedition, Mulock took no part in it.

cut off from Shackleton's plans must have agitated Scott. In addition he may have been very apprehensive of dealing with Shackleton personally. Furthermore Scott was a man who feared usurpation and would have felt harried into making his own decision by the headstrong Shackleton. Scott wrote to Shackleton saying that he had told the president and secretary of the Royal Geographical Society, in confidence, that he would be going again. But he had set no date, made very few plans and seemed less than convinced that he would ever go. It ought to have been so much easier for Scott to raise a second expedition, if only because of the extra reputation he enjoyed and a hypothetical priority to which he now laid claim.

What followed shows the actual vanity and pettiness of men who asked to be viewed as patriotic, public-spirited and scientifically inquisitive. Thousands of miles away from the ample wilderness of Antarctica Scott asserted that he had a right to the McMurdo Sound base. It is a lurid glimpse of the property instinct lurking within protestations of open-minded exploration. For Shackleton this claim carried the extra burden of a spurious honour and fairness. Scott did not say, 'Get off – that's mine!' but presented his case in such a light that Shackleton would feel a cheat by going to McMurdo. This was the Navy code of self-interest swelling into self-righteousness. It was also exactly the ploy to wound Shackleton, who thought of himself as so open a competitor that he loathed the suggestion of foul play.

Only that characteristic explains why Shackleton tolerated Scott's special plea. Yet Shackleton was horribly caught by the thrust. In raising funds, he had stressed the importance of a familiar base, and even as he agreed to Scott's veto on McMurdo he asked Scott to give him time to persuade his backers. But, before this agreement was made, there was a very awkward period of stand-off that only Wilson could settle. The tension of that sledge journey was now reproduced as the three men wrote to and through one another. At first Shackleton argued with Wilson's refusal of the invitation to go south. No doubt Shackleton longed to have Wilson's experience. But Wilson was a talisman for both Scott and Shackleton. Whichever way Wilson went would serve to define the quarrel and rivalry. And Shackleton must have grasped intuitively that Scott's territorial claim was so pompous as to depend upon the loyal support of Wilson. If Shackleton had wooed away Wilson, Scott must have conceded on McMurdo. But Wilson was definite about not going and told Shackleton to waste no more money on long, wheedling telegrams to him.

Shackleton recognized ultimate defeat in this, and so he accepted Scott's suggestion of seeking Wilson's advice on the matter of the base. Wilson wrote to Shackleton unambiguously, but in a vein that shows him as something other than the paragon his admirers describe. He absorbed Scott's position and exerted a moral pressure on Shackleton. It must be added that the finest English gentleman of legend who accepted Scott's special legalistic pleading on McMurdo Sound was also the celebrated naturalist unable to accompany Shackleton because he was conducting a survey into the disease of the grouse, commissioned not by any wild-life preservation society but by Lord Lovat, one of the leading killers of that game bird, a man vexed that disease should be cheating the shoot. Wilson told Shackleton: 'I think that if you go to McMurdo Sound and even reach the Pole – the gilt will be off the gingerbread because of the insinuation which will almost certainly appear in the minds of a good many, that you forestalled Scott who had a prior claim to the use of the base.'

Scott would be beaten to the Pole by Amundsen's brisk indifference to any suggestion of priority. And in 1907 he was ready to impede Shackleton, no matter that he could not himself be in Antarctica for at least another three years. When men fence off parts of the wilderness it only shows how far the location is a setting for their own fulfilment.

Shackleton yielded to the moral blackmail, possibly fearful that Scott would make a discreet public protest, but far more resolved in his own mind to avoid any hint of dishonour. Scott had overawed him, for the second time in his life. Sensing that, Scott asked for more time and hinted at larger proprietorial rights. Shackleton bridled at a suggestion from Wilson that Scott might claim all of King Edward VII Land: 'I have given way to him in the greatest thing of all, and my limit has been reached.'

Scott was bent on keeping Shackleton outside the line of 170°W, which would have effectively excluded Shackleton from the Ross Ice Shelf. 'I must tell you quite frankly,' wrote Shackleton, 'that my agreement to this proposition might perhaps make a position untenable to me on my Southward journey and that I do not see my way, at the present moment, to accede to this. I also consider that the unknown land or the disputed land of Wilkes is free to anybody who wishes to explore that part.'

In April 1907 Scott came ashore and sat down with Shackleton to divide the map of Antarctica between them. If anyone had been reminded of Renaissance princes sharing new worlds, he might have recalled how foolish such treaties looked in the light of history. Nevertheless in May Shackleton committed to paper a plan 'I shall rigidly adhere to': he gave up McMurdo Sound; he said he would keep his side of 170°W; he said that he would land at either Barrier Inlet or King Edward VII Land. Shackleton restricted his movements in advance in several other ways and concluded the letter by hoping that it met Scott's points: 'Should your ship not winter in the Antarctic, I will send you down a chart of whatever exploration I may have made.'

Of course Shackleton could have ignored Scott's claims and gone straight to McMurdo. But, as events transpired, he signed the treaty, went south and found himself compelled to break the agreement and use McMurdo. Some have endorsed Scott's view that this was calculated treachery. I think that misunderstands the character of the two men. Shackleton was not able to land where he wished. Anyone with more experience of Antarctica would have recognized the danger of making binding promises in advance. In those days, in the ships used, the way of the ice and weather could be decisive in providing a landing site. Shackleton was trapped by his own concession and by the maze of honour and dishonour Scott had created.

As it was, Scott made a fair copy of Shackleton's letter and sent it back with this grim comment: 'If as you say you will rigidly adhere to it, I do not think our plans will clash and I shall feel on sure ground in developing my own.' Scott's tone of injured premonition reveals a man who waited to be wronged. It is as if his dilatoriness and indecision now picked on Shackleton as a ritual betrayer. Was there a part of Scott that yearned for Shackleton to have done with the Pole, but to get there under a cloud so that many would recollect that cheating and his own fatal luck had deprived Scott of the prize? When Shackleton eventually landed at McMurdo Sound, Scott conceded that he was not surprised; it may be nearer the truth that he was confirmed. This irony remains: Shackleton admitted wanting the Pole, yet still went south long after it had been won; Scott was never as candid about that extreme pinpoint on the globe, but who can imagine him persistently returning to Antarctica, for the sake of knowing the nature of rocks and weather, for the sake of travel itself?

Shackleton had the support of not one officer or scientist

who had been with Scott. Yet his party of fourteen bristled with fervour, initiative and a range of men that their leader's instinct and caprice had drawn together. There was not a single naval officer in the party; only the meteorologist, Jameson Boyd Adams, was a lieutenant in the Merchant Navy. But Shackleton had the personal allegiance of two petty officers in the Navy who had been on Scott's expedition: Ernest Joyce and Frank Wild. The Navy made no concession to the wishes of these two to go south again, even though men and officers alike had been given official leave to go with Scott. It indicates Shackleton's greater sense of unprivileged quality, and his attractiveness as a leader, that both Joyce and Wild wanted to forsake their Navy pension and security. Shackleton apparently guaranteed that they would not lose by coming with him and, in 1907 and 1909, Joyce and Wild bought themselves out of the Navy. Wild, originally a Yorkshire seaman who claimed descent from Captain Cook, was a tiny, muscular, fiery man who had found Shackleton willing to help him prepare for exams. He was to become Shackleton's lifelong associate and closest supporter.

Otherwise Shackleton had an odd mixture of aristocrat, artisan and academic, some famous, some unknown. Sir Philip Brocklehurst, assistant geologist, was a stalwart of Eton, the Derbyshire Yeomanry and Cambridge University, where he had boxed. He also put £2,000 into the expedition funds. Edgeworth David was professor of geology at Sydney University. Douglas Mawson, the physicist, was a lecturer at Adelaide University. George Marston was an art teacher from the Regent Street Polytechnic and Bernard Day was a mechanic from Wellingborough Grammar School and the engineering works of the Black Country. Eric Marshall had rowed and played football at Cambridge before abandoning the Church for a surgeon's career. Bertram Armytage and Alistair Mackay had fought in the

South Africa War while Raymond Priestley was barely
twenty, a teacher at his former school, Tewkesbury, who
had been reading in a Cambridge library one day when his
brother asked, ' "How would you like to go to the Antarctic, Ray?" and I said "I'd go anywhere to get out of this
damned place." ' In a matter of days he was interviewed
and accepted: 'But I could never understand why Shackleton
took me, because I had no degree, and I know there were
twelve people with Honours degrees after the job.'
Arbitrarily or not, Shackleton had acquired a man who
was to become one of the most distinguished of Antarctic
travellers.

Shackleton's ship, the *Nimrod*, left London in July 1907
under the command of Captain England. There was the
obligatory halt at Cowes for the king and queen to come on
board with flags to be left in the south, and then on to New
Zealand where, in early December, Shackleton himself
arrived to take over the expedition. On 1 January 1908 the
Nimrod, sailed south from Lyttelton, towed by the *Koonya*.

Shackleton was looking for Balloon Inlet or King
Edward VII Land as a landing place. There is no doubt that
he persisted as long as he could in that search, that he put his
ship and party at risk and that he made Captain England
perplexed and irritated by the attempt to keep faith with
Scott. But his dilemma was that of a man in a small ship in a
vaguely charted part of the world where every year the form
and movement of the ice is different. By 23 January the
Nimrod was between the pack ice and the Barrier. In
hazardous conditions they searched for Balloon Inlet and
were forced to the conclusion that it had broken away.
Shackleton resolved to sail east, to find a landing place on
King Edward VII Land. But the ice pack was closing in
again, and England was stressing the weakened condition
of the ship and the dangerous shortage of coal so that safe
return to New Zealand was jeopardized by every extra delay.

Still Shackleton insisted on another forty-eight hours, during which time the *Nimrod* was nearly trapped on several occasions as it searched for a clearing to the north that might herald a way to the east.

The men hardly understood Shackleton's agony. They were a 'laughing careless crowd' enjoying the sight of seal and penguin. England knew the pressure on Shackleton but must have deplored his leader's willingness to burn any surplus woodwork – including the deckhouse and the mizzen mast – for a better chance of going east. Eventually the weather worsened and took the decision for them. Shackleton wrote a long letter to his wife as the *Nimrod* sailed west, over the fatal line of 170°, towards McMurdo Sound. In part the letter is an exhaustive description of the ordeal, of icebergs the size of the Royal Exchange threatening to crush the ship against the Barrier – 'or a piece the size of the NBR Hotel and Prince's Hotel, great pieces twice the height of the Dean Bridge above the Water Leith, other pieces as big and as square as all Belgrave Terrace and Buckingham Terrace coming down on to you.'

It also admits the moment Shackleton accepted the trap laid for him by Scott's intimidating bargain, the cold pact of honour and the risk of worse weather, and the final clenching hold of the pack ice. The ship and his coal were at their limits, his ponies were exhausted: 'I realized that to push further on then would be madness. We could not lie where we were on the chance of it clearing up for it might be days and our precious stock of coal would dwindle away: the ship will not sail and must depend on coal alone: so with a heavy heart I gave orders for turning back.'

The letter is haunted by guilt; indeed that guilt could have led to disaster for Shackleton's party – nothing else so thoroughly reveals Scott's daunting effect on Shackleton. 'I never knew what it was to make such a decision' said Shackleton in the tone of a man who honourably believed in and was accustomed to uncomplicated issues: 'I am feeling more now than I can say darling and wish I were close to you telling it all to you instead of locking it up in my heart as I have to do to a great extent: and all the anxiety that I have been feeling coupled with the desire to really do the right thing has made me older than I can ever say.' He told his wife that his conscience was clear, but his heart sore, and at one point he foresaw 'the whole world' crying out at him for compromise. Shackleton suggested that Emily show parts of the letter to friends, 'but not to outside people and to no enemies. Not that I think there will be really except the Scott faction.'

The reaction in Britain was as Shackleton anticipated. The promise had never been publicized. Why should the public comprehend such demarcation in an area where expanse was the chief appeal to the imagination? Yet for those aware of it, and already committed to one side or the other, the incident was a proof of character. Markham 'strongly advised' that the *Geographical Journal* ignore the matter: 'The reason is that an excuse would be implied; when the public are not aware that any excuse is needed. It is a pity that Ernest worded his promise so strongly, and the best thing is that nothing more should be heard of it.'

In view of Markham's hostility to Shackleton, that is a tacit admission that the agreement had been a foolishness on both sides. Yet Scott devoured the wrong that had been done him like a hungry man. He had copies made of the letter of agreement: 'The breach of faith is so emphatic that I propose to let certain persons see the letter.' At first he told Kathleen Bruce that he was surprised by the breach of 'a perfectly plain distinct statement absolutely binding him in an honourable sense'. But it was not long before Scott's deeper feelings emerged. He sent Kathleen a copy of the agreement with the comment: 'You will see that by wintering in McMurdo Sound he has just gone bang through it, with unanswerable breach of faith. I had a suspicion he might, and find others had the same, also bit by bit I get evidence of similar actions in his history during the past few years. He seems to have almost deliberately adopted the part of plausible rogue and to have thrown scruples to the winds.'

That needs to be read in the context of the uncertainty Scott felt towards Kathleen Bruce, just as much as that of his rivalry with Shackleton. The hints of rumour and the allegation of chronic unscrupulousness in Shackleton still have no firmer evidence than the youthful adventurousness of the man.* The suggestions tell us more about Scott's anxieties with regard to a vital, dominating woman that he yearned to impress. But the most remarkable aspect of the light in which Scott chose to see Shackleton comes in his dismay over 'the terrible vulgarizing which Shackleton

---

* Anyone in search of reasons for disapproving of Shackleton would have found more in the career of his younger brother, Francis. A man of great charm and business enterprise, Francis Shackleton was rumoured as one of the men involved in the theft of the Irish Crown Jewels, a great scandal of 1907 that bubbled away for several years. The jewels were found to be missing in July 1907, the month in which the *Nimrod* left England. They had been in the care of Sir Arthur Vicars, Ulster King of Arms, in whose office at Dublin Castle Francis Shackleton held an honorary position. The matter is still confused by mystery, gossip, melodrama and farce, and Shackleton flourished in all these forms. It seems likely that he was at the centre of homosexual blackmail that prompted the theft, and it was his association with the Duke of Argyll that alarmed Edward VII into doing everything he could to draw wraps over the case. Francis Shackleton went on to large-scale bankruptcy, prison and a later life passed under the ashamed obscurity of a pseudonym. He nearly rose very high – as a businessman and a socialite – but he was scapegrace, precarious and, in the eyes of the establishment, flawed. The Shackleton brothers were not close, but not dissimilar, and Francis Shackleton's career is one that could only have shocked Scott. For more of this story, the reader should go to Francis Bamford and Viola Bankes, *Vicious Circle* (London, 1965).

had introduced into the Southern field of enterprise, hitherto so clean and wholesome'. The reader must judge whether that charge is deserved or specious, and assess how much it shows us of Scott's mind. It does indicate the deep, sub-conscious appeal of the Polar wasteland that Scott should treasure its clean wholesomeness. It is not too much to speak of the Pole possessing a virginity in his mind that served as an alternative to the spoiled, messy way of the real world. That phrase is eloquent with the despair of a man who feels unsuited to turbulent experience and who had convinced himself of some austere purity else-where. But, in terms of the rivalry with Shackleton, Scott horribly confuses his own ideal and his difficulty with people. This is the intractable solitary flinching from and crying out at his privacy being penetrated. It is a remark that discloses the passion of Polar travel and the way in which such enormous journeys by foot were attempting to cover spiritual distance.

Scott's disparagement of Shackleton must have been boosted by the news that he had quarrelled with Captain England. The popular press exaggerated the affair and implied a physical struggle. The truth may be more blurred and less dramatic, but it indicates the tension of the *Nimrod* expedition and shows how vulnerable Shackleton felt towards anything less than total loyalty. He was a great, inspiring leader to those happy to be led and inspired. Admiration brought out the best in him; argument could make him belligerent or spiteful. In the same way, Scott's implacable but lofty distaste was always likely to produce the very reactions it anticipated. And Shackleton's perilous wish to do his duty to Scott had surely provoked suspicion in Captain England.

The *Nimrod* duly landed at McMurdo Sound and began the business of putting men, equipment and supplies ashore. By now England's mind was torn between serving the shore party and ensuring that the ship returned safely to New Zealand. On any expedition the decision when to go north was critical, hazardous and fraught. The search for Balloon Inlet had added to that pressure: time had been squandered and the perpetual shortage of coal made more extreme. More important, England may have decided that Shackleton was too prone to confusing emotion and practicality. If the leader had risked all for the sake of a misguided promise, might he not endanger the ship to get more supplies ashore? The day came, in mid-February, when Shackleton urged England to put the *Nimrod* nearer to the land, and the captain refused. Both men were at the bridge at the time, and apparently Shackleton went so far as to handle the signal telegraph himself. Anger took both men below to England's cabin and the matter was dealt with there.

Calmer men would have agreed to overlook a brief conflict of will and judgement. They were both under strain, and it was a situation that probed the awkward relationship of expedition commander and ship's captain. At the same time it was too rash of Shackleton to take matters into his own hands, and more severe than was necessary to treat England as he did. For Shackleton decided that, once the *Nimrod* was back in New Zealand, England must be replaced. Shackleton put instructions to this effect on paper that were only given to England at Lyttelton. In view of his natural distress, England behaved very well. He did as he was told and resigned in favour of his own lieutenant, Dunlop. He still reported conscientiously on repairs that were necessary in the *Nimrod*, and made himself available at all times. The only part of Shackleton's orders he would not swallow was the explanation that his resignation was because of illness. He tolerated such public comment, but privately he told Kinsey, the New Zealand agent: 'I beg to inform you that I am perfectly sound both in body and mind, and that my resignation has been forced upon me.'

England's failing was very small, and one that a wiser commander might have treated as prudence. The fierce reaction shows how quickly Shackleton's vivacity could retract, and how brittle his confidence could be. What he took as the threat of disloyalty may have seemed the more real because he was still uneasy about what Scott would think of him. Ironically it was action that could not be improved as evidence for Scott's view of a vulgar, noisy pirate. Although England would not discuss the incident or its aftermath, newspaper reporters took sailors out on the town and gathered enough for sensational stories. The dispute with England must have convinced the shore party that their leader was both decisive and devoted to their cause. No two things could have heartened them more, and the atmosphere of Shackleton's expedition was consistently united and cheerful. He was known as the Boss, yet it was his practice to discuss problems openly before coming to decisions. Those who worked for him were unusually fervent in praising his sympathy for all sorts of men; they trusted his judgement and responded to his humorous treatment of danger and difficulty. There grew up about Shackleton the notion that he was most shrewd and quick in a crisis. For an 'adventurer', his journeys are notably free from disaster; time after time he brought men unscathed through spectacular perils. Some credit for this should go to the way he solicited and listened to others' opinions. But Shackleton also charmed his men, and made them feel so privileged that, in the words of Jameson Adams, they all recognized in their leader an 'almost supernatural intuition for selecting men who believed in him implicitly and who were proud to have the honour of participating in his great adventure'. That attitude can sometimes look through defects and mistakes if they are made without prejudice or secrecy. When men acknowledge great leadership in their leader, they are conspiring in a rapturous companionship in which self-congratulation has glossed authority. Because Shackleton went for the sake of adventure, he tolerated very few of the myths and barriers that Scott observed: rank, duty, science, patriotism and orders. Shackleton says in effect to his men 'we are here because we want to be, and we will not get through unless we live and work together'. This stance smacks of equality, yet it depends on the glowing conviction of its casual boss. Shackleton led by encouragement and jokes, by being the most boyish of the boys. Scott was far more detached, a middle-aged man in charge of boys. But the difference in style does not mean that Shackleton was any less autocratic. Only a dazzling tyrant could have made men perform as he did: men strove to carry out Scott's orders, but they wanted to please Shackleton. And, as Scott took pleasure in orderliness, so Shackleton needed the admiration of men. Tidiness convinced Scott of his own propriety; admiration reassured Shackleton that he was a success.

But despite differences of style, the British method of Polar travel embraced Shackleton as fully as it did Scott. Temperamentally Shackleton would not have been averse to any innovation in method and equipment that Scott had lacked. Yet in all major respects Shackleton meekly adopted policies that Scott had followed, no matter that they had had a dubious success. Granted the lack of resources, in terms of men and money, Shackleton's achievement was a tribute to courage, determination and the concentrated aim of reaching the Pole. Where Scott had simply explored south, Shackleton discarded inhibition and went for the Pole. In which case it is the more creditable that, getting so near – so very much nearer than Scott had managed – Shackleton resisted the urge to push on regardless, to die at the Pole. Instead he managed to calculate his rations, judging the moment to turn back exactly when the Pole was so near that the frustration must have been desperate. The stereotype of Shackleton, as the braggart, vainglorious hero, should recognize that he saved his men and declined the temptation of ultimate success. Such circumspection does not fit the stereotype, even if it explains why men trusted him. Equally it should be said that Scott did not act upon (if he foresaw) the harrowing equation of food, energy and distance that would overcome his own return. He went on because it was the plan, and it was Amundsen's black flag that signalled the full extent of failure to him, not the sort of calculations that Shackleton must have studied in his tent at night.

Shackleton's journey was prodigious: arguably no one at either Pole has done as well as he did. But he handicapped himself in every possible way. He took no skis on the Polar journey. Twelve pairs purchased in Norway 'were not used on the sledging journeys at all, but were useful around the winter quarters'. In those years Norwegian ski manufacturers must have smiled at the visits from English explorers who purchased their wares but steadfastly neglected to employ them properly. Again Shackleton endorsed the British orthodoxy that dogs had failed under Scott and that ponies were the surest means of transport. He took fifteen ponies from Manchuria in the belief that they were 'hardy, sure-footed and plucky'. Yet the voyage south found them frail, sea-sick and depressed: one pony had to be shot on landing because his sides had been rubbed raw on the ship. Four more were dead in a month, from eating sand and the shavings used to pack chemicals. Part of the trouble here was the lack of anyone skilled in the care of horses. Yet the Polar party still took four ponies with it. The ponies went lame, fed badly on tainted maize and were always likely to kick. On 21 and 28 November and again on 1 December ponies had to be shot. The last survivor fell into a crevasse on 1 December, leaving a weight of 1,000 lb. for the four men to haul, still on the lower slopes of the Beardmore Glacier. They had the cold comfort of hard pony maize to chew on and the lesson that Manchuria is not Antarctica.

The unwieldy British prejudice over animal traction meant that while Shackleton was disappointed by his ponies, 'I had not expected my dogs to do as well as they actually did'. He accepted without demur or scrutiny the unsatisfactory performance of Scott's dogs, and was then surprised at the way in which they regularly exceeded his expectations. Originally he took only a duty number of dogs, but the adaptable animals bred, so that he had twenty-two before he was finished. It was always the theoretical capacity of a pony for hauling a much greater weight that misled the British; the same principle had made Shackleton experiment with a motor vehicle. But the ponies were temperamental. The sea voyage struck at their constitution, and Polar cold demoralized them. In variable footings and thick snow they floundered tragically and made a mockery of prior calculations. Ponies sank to their waists, the motor vehicle collapsed in snow, but the dogs pattered daintily across most surfaces. Peary's reports of their success in the Arctic seemed justified by the way Shackleton's dogs acted. Yet he was not flexible enough to alter his plans in the light of the evidence: 'I knew from past experience that dogs would not travel when low drift was blowing in their faces.' Ironically on one occasion, when a party made the journey to the old *Discovery* hut, they were followed by some of the puppies. The dogs went all the way, ate a meal and fell asleep. Shackleton could not take puppies farther, nor heed the example of the dogs' spirit. When he went on, he shut the puppies in the old hut, with biscuit, meat and snow: 'Their anxious barks and whines followed us as we moved southwards.'

The special character of Shackleton's expedition lies in things that may be intimately related: the remarkable physical achievement in penetrating so much farther south; and the close-knit human atmosphere that Shackleton created. Whereas Scott had had his men live on the *Discovery*, in quarters that were shaped by naval considerations of rank, Shackleton had the shore party housed in a specially made hut. Thirty-three feet long, nineteen feet wide and eight feet high, the hut was made in London and shipped south in sections that could easily be bolted together. Thus fifteen men spent the Polar winter in the same hut with some forty square feet each. Seven two-men cubicles were measured out, with a separate space for Shackleton himself. The boundaries were marked off with wires and sheets hung from them. By this means the hut offered a version of privacy – or, in Shackleton's words, a chance for the men to 'sport their oak' – but gently insisted on the shared experience.

One need not call Shackleton a democrat to show that his expedition was un-British with men of different sorts and ranks required to mix together. The leader's own background permitted no undue pomp, while his style of leadership depended on treating people alike. He never cut himself off from the rest of the expedition, and he sited the library in his own cubicle so that anyone had a pretext for calling on him. The men ate together, and meal-table conversations involved academics and sailors alike. Similarly no one was excused from the chores of housework. We have only to compare such circumstances with Scott's expedition to feel the novelty of Shackleton's approach. Today it may not seem remarkable that men so far from civilization, and living amid such dangers, should exist on an equal footing. It remains the case that Scott carried with him to the south some of the social reservations and distinctions that marked his England. So far from home, they looked less reasonable than usual. The matter cannot be measured, but it is at least possible that the two ways of living led to differences of morale and purpose.

Shackleton's plan to go south was for four men to set out with four sledges and ponies and food for ninety-one days. He took Adams, Marshall and Wild with him and allowed a daily ration of 34 oz. This was 0·7 oz more than the *Discovery* expedition had enjoyed, but Shackleton arranged his diet so that it contained substantially more biscuit. Noticing with the *Discovery* that biscuits were often in fragments when unpacked – with the loss of so much in crumbs – Shackleton had thicker biscuits made, toughened with plasmon, that a man could hold and bite at without the thought of losing morsels in the snow. In other respects Shackleton followed Scott's diet: Danish pemmican, tea, cocoa, sugar, chocolate and cheese.

Yet food was short from the beginning. Shackleton's long trek was a nightmare of raging appetite and diminishing allowance. There can be few human ordeals as depleting as man-hauling in sub-zero temperatures. The effort cried out for food as fuel. Yet to carry enough food makes the struggle to move heavy sledges almost impossible. On his return Shackleton discussed food in the language of a gourmet. This flowery style does not obscure for long the agony of hunger and the constitutional contradiction of having to pull harder on shorter rations:

Our cuisine was not very varied, but a voracious appetite has no nice discernment and requires no sauce to make the meal palatable: indeed, all one wants is more, and this is just what cannot be allowed if a party is to achieve anything in the way of distance whilst confined to man-haulage. It is hard for a hungry man to rest content with the knowledge that the particular food he is eating contains so much nourishment and is sufficient for his needs, if at the same time he does not feel full and satisfied after the meal and if, within an hour or so, the aching void again makes itself felt, and he has to wait another five hours before he can again temporarily satisfy the craving.

On the evening of 29 October 1908, the day before the Polar party set out, as they sat talking after dinner, the low sun came through the hut's ventilator and cast a halo on the picture of Queen Alexandra which slowly slid across to the companion portrait of the king. These men could not resist such an omen of good luck, and set out to do their duty by king and country. When we ask the imponderable question – Why did they go? – an unfashionable but idealistic answer – For the king – should not be lightly dismissed. Within the next decade millions gave up their lives in the mud of northern Europe and would have no more persuasive motive.

By early November they were held up by blizzards so that Shackleton lay in his sleeping bag reading *Much Ado About Nothing* and making the first calculation that ninety-one days' food could be made to last 110 days – in the event, they were away 118 days. Already they were cutting rations and hoping that a day's enforced idleness required less food. In other words, for most of the journey, the four men had less food than the *Discovery* sledge journeys had had. Yet by mid-November, on the Barrier, Shackleton rejoiced that they were doubling or even tripling the daily distance he had made with Scott and Wilson. In fine weather this must have been a heady time for Shackleton, proof of his own soundness and promise of the ultimate goal.

They were past 80°S almost a month earlier than the *Discovery* journey. But the ponies were lame or troublesome and the effects of isolation were beginning to be felt. Shackleton was reminded once of *The Ancient Mariner*:

'Alone, alone; all, all alone, alone on a wide, wide sea' and then when the mazy clouds spring silently from either hand and drift quickly across our zenith, not followed by any wind, it seems uncanny. There comes a puff of wind from the north, another from the south, and anon one from the east or west, seeming to obey no law, acting on erratic impulses. It is as though we were truly at the world's end, and were bursting in on the birthplace of the clouds and the resting home of the four winds, and one has a feeling that we mortals are being watched with a jealous eye by the forces of nature. To add to these weird impressions that seem to grow on one in the apparently limitless waste, the sun tonight was surrounded by mock suns and in the zenith was a bow, turning away from the great vertical circle around the sun. The circles and bows were the colour of the rainbow.

Six days later they were farthest south, 82°18½'S, and in sight of 'great snow-clad heights' ahead. As the ponies wilted, the strain on the men became greater and their appetites increased. They marched in the sun chewing lumps of frozen horseflesh, the ponies at last paying their way. By the first week of December they had the additional struggle and uncertainty of finding a way up the Beardmore Glacier. Food and distance obsessed them. Going uphill they were forced to relay, and did no more than three miles on one day. By 17 December they were on the plateau. Ration cuts had left them with five weeks' food and another 300 miles to the Pole. Christmas meant thoughts of home and one of those bizarre Polar feasts on food deliberately saved to mark the festival. As well as pemmican hoosh, they had a plum pudding, some brandy, cigars and a spoonful of crème de menthe.

They talked together and agreed to a further reduction of the regular ration: seven days' food would stretch to ten: 'Ah, well, we shall see all our people when the work here is done. Marshall took our temperatures tonight. We are all two degrees sub-normal, but as fit as can be. It is a fine open-air life and we are getting south.' There, in one line, is the strange mixture of travelling and mysticism, as if south were a state of being.

By the end of the year Shackleton had recognized that they could not get more than seventy miles from the Pole, with the chance of a desperate sortie from that base. They were suffering from headaches and nose-bleeding and Shackleton's temperature was down to 94°. In this distress Shackleton calmly balanced the odds: 'God knows we are doing all we can, but the outlook is serious if this surface continues and the plateau gets higher, for we are not travelling fast enough to make our food spin out and get back to our depot in time. I cannot think of failure yet. I must look at the matter sensibly and consider the lives of those who are with me.'

Their strength now was so diminished that a load of 70 lb weighed on them as much as 250 lb had done three weeks before. The steepness of that decline shows how far they had become emptied out versions of men, gradually but surely killing themselves. Shackleton estimated that at least 40 oz was necessary for the Polar ration, whereas they were then consuming not much more than 25 oz.

On the night of 6 January, at 88°7'S, they planned one more day going south, but a blizzard kept them in their tents for two days and on the second day there were seventy-two degrees of frost. On 9 January they got as far as 88°23'S. They hoisted their flag and stared through binoculars at the still hidden south: 'There was no break in the plateau as it extended towards the Pole.' They had done all they could and turned back. But let there be no doubt that Shackleton could have reached the Pole. He did not go that far because he saw it as too great a risk. Not that he was by any means confident of returning safe from 88°23'.

One worry was that they had only their own tracks to guide them to their dumps of food. If a blizzard had smoothed away their footprints they might miss a depot.

As they went north, through January, Shackleton's own health suffered and by 21 January he was too weak to put on harness. Yet it was on this return journey that they proved themselves: on 25 January, for instance, suffering a variety of ills, they did twenty-six miles on two cups of tea, three biscuits, a pot of hoosh and two spoonfuls of cheese per man. Short of every depot they were running out of food; to have missed one would have been fatal, and they once marched for twenty hours simply to reach more food.

The sledge was breaking up, they fell asleep in harness, there was the constant agony of hunger and Wild had dysentery from pony meat. Yet there could be no easing. Shackleton's calculations had been precise, and regular daily distances were vital to keep them fed. By 4 February all of them had dysentery and Shackleton had serious doubts about their chances. The entries in his journal are brief, tense and bleak: 'Dead tired. Short food; very weak.' They were down to five biscuits a day and half a pannikin of the pony meat that was upsetting their stomachs. To add to this, they thawed out a frozen block of pony blood.

The fifteenth of February was Shackleton's thirty-fifth birthday and the others gave him a cigar made from pipe tobacco and lavatory paper. Next day they were so weak that lifting bags was nearly beyond them. On the march the harness ground on their shrivelled stomachs. Yet by 21 February they were compelled to march in a blizzard: 'Our food lies ahead, and death stalks us from behind.'

Then at last they found the tracks of men and dogs and scattered remains of food left by depot-laying parties. It had been desperately close, and they had come back with nothing but themselves, the knowledge of having gone farther south than any other men and the memory of their last view of the still vacant white of farther south.

7
Preparing for
Terra Nova

The news of Shackleton's journey washed remorselessly over Scott. Once or twice he was even jostled by the crowds that came to greet his former subordinate. Then the two men shook hands and glared smiles across the distance of a few feet in a cheerful din that prevented them hearing one another. Shackleton inevitably glowed, rested and attended to the messy affairs of his brother. He had looked forward to recognition, and in the space of nine months his achievement brought him banquets and receptions, the aura of a popular hero, an undiminished notoriety in establishment circles, fame, money, a knighthood* and successful authorship of his own book, piercingly titled *The Heart of the Antarctic*, as if to remind other travellers of the interior they had missed.

Shackleton's expedition had been so independent that the sentimental press acclaimed its sturdy enterprise as typically British. The popular newspapers were quick to adopt Shackleton: he was not tied down to official patronage or gentlemanly tact. The aura of a privateer could easily be attributed to him, and Shackleton himself was a willing interviewee, alert to the provocative remarks journalists could exploit. In being the most dashing and glamorous of

* This from the king who was so anxious to conceal the connection between his own brother-in-law, the Duke of Argyll, and Shackleton's brother.

all the Antarctic travellers, his expedition did more than any other to make the South Pole the object of a race. Scott, for one, was swept up in Shackleton's momentum, but the man most roused by it may have been Amundsen. The sound of hurrying footsteps is always heard by others who want to be first.

Shackleton had turned Antarctica into a competition and stripped away many of those solemn motives that explorers offered. Scott, although earlier regretting the way Shackleton had dirtied the wholesomeness of the south, must have felt those few remaining miles to the Pole as an almost ridiculous challenge. Any further expedition would need to go all that way merely for the inner core of the journey. There seems not much doubt that expeditions with so tenuous a remaining task began to dislodge public interest from the claims of national prestige that travellers urged. We have only to think of the withering interest in the Moon once dull man had trudged about it, to see how far Shackleton had dissolved the mystery and emphasized the uniqueness of the Pole. Those who followed him must be honest about racing, concoct elaborate schemes of scientific research or go for the sake of travel. Amundsen was the blatant racer, Shackleton the habitual journeyer, and Scott the anxious seeker after seriousness and value.

The news of Shackleton's penetration reached London in March 1909. The Scotts had been married only a few months; Kathleen had just become pregnant and her husband that winter had suffered one of his worst depressions: 'I can't describe what overcomes me. I'm obsessed with the view of life as a struggle for existence, and then forced to see how little past efforts have done to give me a place in the struggle. I seem to hold in reserve something that makes for success and yet to see no worthy field for it.' Scott told his wife that he longed 'to be up and achieving things for your dear sake'. His melancholy may have clutched at the idealism of his energetic wife as a means to rise above itself. Yet marriage had not dispersed his dark moods. That feeling of having buried in himself the instinct for success is something Scott described very calmly. But it gave him more than ordinary frustration. It may be the gathered inhibition of the child, the caution of a natural hesitater, and the sour dislike of his own bad luck knocking against the urge to be glorious. Heroism was diminishing as a cult in Scott's lifetime. Many people were suspicious of its motives or scornful of its benefits. But in the dying age of any great idea may be found its greatest adherents, and Scott's struggle for existence needed some unavoidable combination of physical ordeal and imperious duty. It was not in him to take the initiative: thus, launching himself at the Pole was something he had to do discreetly. But he was made to command a great defeat, and if orders had decided that it should be at the South Pole he would have marched there singing. Who knows how typical the character is, yet most Englishmen have met the like of Scott: men of sad aspect and clipped utterance, who wait to be told what to do and then release a startling energy in doing it.

When he was at sea Scott kept several of his wife's statuettes in his cabin: lean, wilful, intensely romantic figures, such as a facile, earnest and rather doctrinaire girl in search of art might have derived from Rodin. In Kathleen Scott's sculpture and Edward Wilson's paintings there is the same slightly shrill insistence on purity and idealism. They are both narrow artists whose dilemma before experience had driven them into an inspirational assertion about life. The complexity of experience is dodged in both of them, and strident ideals are glorified. The work is far from unimpressive, and to the inhibited Scott it must have been a wonder that his wife could create with such freedom and vigour. The daily presence of Kathleen's figures may have made Scott a little more confident in expressing those romantic desires he nurtured. Of all the things that had happened to him, the most brimming with destiny was the phenomenon of his wife's full-blooded artistic nature. How could Scott realize that her art was as tense and protective as his sense of duty?

Certainly Scott was no longer alone. He had someone to talk and write to; any decision had a wife's support and a magnificent woman not to be let down. Kathleen uncompromisingly adopted his cause and disparaged Shackleton's. On some morning in that winter of 1908–9 the Scotts had received a letter from Shackleton's party in Antarctica that included nothing except a blank sheet of paper. There are several plausible explanations. Polar expeditions did have a mailing list of friends and notables deserving the rare Antarctic stamps, and such envelopes often contained no message. But it is possible that, out of mischief, Shackleton sent Scott a letter without words – to announce that the Pole was still vacant, or even as an insolent winding up of the McMurdo Sound dispute. The original intention is less important than the way in which the Scotts regarded the letter as a tasteless joke. Years later Lady Scott came upon the envelope while sorting through papers to give to Frank Debenham and said, 'Oh, there's that silly thing Shackleton sent to Con'. That was the widow still in charge of her husband's papers, the survivor of a national hero, who passes through bereavement to be manager of his reputation. It is natural in those circumstances for the widow to evolve in her own mind an orthodoxy about everything that concerned her husband. But with the Scotts that interpretation had begun before he died.

It is difficult to know when a man as volatile and fitful as Scott decided to go south again. Some maintain that a return had been his persistent goal since 1904. That may gloss the real indecision of the following years. I suspect that marriage urged him on and that Shackleton's glory nettled him. But, in so formal a man, I doubt if Scott's mind was made up until the day he announced it – 13 September 1909 – and then it was locked to the journey.

Nevertheless the summer of 1909 must have been a time of great turmoil for Scott. On the one hand he could not shirk welcoming Shackleton. As of March 1909 Scott was restored to London as Naval Assistant to the Second Sea Lord. There seems to have been no collusion in this move, but the Admiralty may have been providing Scott with a better opportunity to assemble another expedition. The story goes that, on 14 June, the day Shackleton arrived back in London, Scott happened to be in the offices of the Royal Geographical Society and allowed himself to be persuaded to join the welcoming party at Charing Cross Station. There was a handshake and time for a few words before Shackleton and his family were driven through the cheering crowd in an open carriage.

A few days later Scott presided at a Savage Club dinner for Shackleton, and on 28 June the Royal Geographical Society met to welcome him in the Albert Hall. Such occasions were the establishment's accolade for explorers, and since Scott was never to be present at his own eulogy it may be interesting to examine one such occasion. It was a meeting for the Society, but open to the public, so that popular applause fell down from the upper tiers of that pompous but intimate cavern. Proceedings were opened by the president, Leonard Darwin. He told the gathering that they were there to rejoice in the safe home-coming of Shackleton's men and to hear of 'the highest latitude ever attained by any human being'. Then comes the ambivalence of a royal society that muddles fact and inspiration:

We are not yet in a position to express final opinions on the scientific results of this expedition; but, as far as can be judged, they reflect the highest credit on all concerned. As to the latitude reached, it has been the policy of our Society neither to promote nor to reward either mere record breaking or any mere race to either pole because there is no reason to suppose that any especial scientific interest attached to that particular spot on the Earth's surface. But it would be mere cant not to acknowledge that we are all proud of the fact that it is one of our countrymen who at the present time has made the nearest approach to a pole of the Earth.

But as the president of the Royal Geographical Society came nearer to introducing this man who, on the one hand, must await official approval for his science and yet, on the other, had filled the Albert Hall with citizens whose notions of geography might be sketchy, so he plunged into comparison to make Shackleton's southern journey convincing. The explorer might be a little chastened to discover that the remote is only real if it can be likened to the familiar. It is an odd aspect of human inquisitiveness that it must often think in metaphor and not on the nature of things. Darwin asked his audience to imagine a journey begun in London and going north to Edinburgh (Shackleton's former home representing the farthest south Scott had reached), to Inverness and then on over the North Sea, 240 miles farther than John o'Groats. All that way, and all that way back. And did any voice float down from the upper level of the Albert Hall, wondering 'Who wants to walk across the North Sea?'?

Shackleton followed that bracing simile with a clear factual account and several photographic illustrations. At which the president returned to remind the audience of how little Mr Shackleton had said of his own courage. This kindly ritual would have allowed the assembly to cheer and Shackleton to flush. 'But', Darwin went on, 'mere courage is almost useless without the knowledge and the imagination necessary to enable the explorer both to realize risks in advance and to make full use of the opportunities afforded for observing facts. Long study in advance is absolutely essential, whilst actual previous experience is of enormous assistance. Not the least of Mr Shackleton's merits as a leader was, I believe, the care he took to make the utmost use of the experience he had previously gained when serving in the National Antarctic Expedition under Captain Scott.'

In truth Shackleton had survived despite learning so little from the earlier expedition. Did no explorer ever listen to such homilies and realize, 'My God, that's the very opposite of the truth. We meekly copy one another'? Or was scientific inquiry actually stifled by formal politeness? Darwin's reference to Scott was made partly so that Scott should have the honour and test of proposing a vote of thanks to Shackleton. Scott said that Shackleton could not have had a keener listener than himself. He added that 'this magnificent work of his crowns a great attack on the South Pole, and it is extraordinary to think with what speed that attack has been pushed forward'. Scott then extended the laudatory occasion to Clements Markham with the remark that the mountain named after him was still 'the highest and most dignified peak in that chain of wonderful mountains which flanks the road to the South Pole'. The vote of thanks, Scott suggested, was almost superfluous: 'the applause which has greeted Mr Shackleton's lecture must convince him how much we appreciate his work'. But he ended with his own decent and reserved tribute. There is no snideness here; it is an epitaph Scott himself would have hoped for: 'We honour him for the manner in which he organized and prepared his expedition, for the very substantial addition he made to human knowledge, but most of all because he has shown us a glorious example of British pluck and endurance.'

Many who were at the Albert Hall that evening foresaw a natural, companionable rivalry between Scott and Shackleton. The public mood easily anticipated a race, and the mandarins of geography argued about its desirability. Yet, even at that stage, it was not clear that Scott had made up his mind. He may still have had to be prompted or trapped into action, and it may have been a relatively minor incident that carried him over the feeling that Shackleton had left too little to be done.

On the day after the Albert Hall meeting, Sir Clements Markham was called on by Teddy Evans. Evans was twenty-eight, a lieutenant in the Navy, and the eager bearer of 'a written scheme for an expedition which he was to command'. If Evans had stayed up all night conceiving and writing out his plan, it would have been entirely in his character. He was a fulsome, bursting young man all his life. Men made fun of his high spirits and shallowness behind his back; Scott would die leaving a disapproving stain on Evans's shining rectitude. He easily sounds like a caricature, and yet he is one of the most consistent of Scott's men, the least inhibited believer in the ardour that gripped them all.

He was a romanticizer, and did not always remember the truth about himself. Later in life he found unexpected fame as a Labour peer created by the government of 1945. At the same time he wrote stories for boys and breathless surveys of Polar heroism. In the years after the Second World War he was out of his element, but he had always been a little too extreme for company. He was a Londoner, born in 1880, the son of a barrister. He liked it to be thought that he had knocked around as a child and known the rough parts of London. This is probably exaggeration, but he did not get on well with his parents and may have been neglected. At the age of eleven he was expelled from Merchant Taylors' School for an unknown offence. He went to a school for troublesome boys in Surrey and in 1895 he joined the *Worcester* as a naval cadet. He was already abnormally energetic, cheerful and headstrong: zest blazed from his face, and one teacher had told him to stop trying to be a pirate.

Yet the Navy could provide a respectable way of swash-buckling. Cadet Evans was a small youth made into a Hercules on the *Worcester*. And, when he was not doing athletics, drill or navigation, he might be a rapt, attentive member of a throng of cadets listening to lectures by Albert Armitage or Clements Markham. When Evans later wrote yarns for boys, he was carrying on a tradition built into the Navy's own method for making officers. Evans joined the *Hawke* in 1897 as a midshipman and, on Crete, fell seriously ill from drinking goat's milk. Illness threatened his very soul; subsequently health for Teddy Evans was always a feature of identity. Those who knew him main-tained that it was after that illness that he developed the habit of spectacular, foolish feats of strength. One trick was to pick up a fellow-officer, holding the seat of his trousers in his teeth. This grotesque vigour thrilled Evans, so that it is all the more important that he 'failed' physically on the journey south in 1911. There is a comparison with Shackle-ton worth making, in that both men put great store by their durability and yet faltered in that very respect in Scott's service.

The comparison is more striking if one realizes that Evans's first voyage to Antarctica had been as second officer on the *Morning*, the relief ship that brought Shackle-ton back to England in 1903. When Markham had been cautiously mounting the relief operation, the twenty-two-year-old Evans had called on him twice and, on the second occasion, taken Markham for a stroll in Hyde Park the better to explain his case. Markham was never averse to promenading propositions and Evans won his place by tying a cloth around the waist of the *Morning*'s captain, Colbeck, and letting him dangle a moment from his teeth.

It is likely that Evans had long talks with Shackleton on

that return voyage and, in Evans's relations with Scott, it may be significant that he had known the rival first, and been impressed by him. That is no wonder, since Evans was always a louder, less substantial version of Shackleton. In 1904 Evans married a New Zealand girl, Hilda Russell, with Scott present at the service as he made his return from the south. He spent the next few years stationed in England, and would have volunteered to go with Shackleton had he been able to afford it. Instead he won the Shadwell Prize and cultivated a pleasantry for mess guest nights when he would grab the material of someone's trousers and rip out the seat with one tug. Perhaps such men are destined for the south. In Evans there is that point where gusto topples into unsociability, and his Polar career needs to be seen in the context of those who admired his unequivocal gusto and those who thought he was an unbridled puppy.

However, in approaching Markham, he played no small part in Scott's expedition. If Scott felt jostled by Evans, that is one more instance of hesitation drawing Scott into greater difficulties than he expected. Supposing that Shackleton's speech at the Albert Hall did inspire Evans, he reacted with honesty, believing that nothing more was required than 'a dash for the Pole'. That still looks a reasonable opinion, and Evans may have been the very man to lead a dash.

Markham temporized and had Evans back to lunch on 8 July, at which occasion the older man 'persuaded him to go to Scott, and to be perfectly frank and above board with him. The proposal was most fortunate. Scott and Evans at once agreed to join forces, Scott to command and Evans to be second.' Yet this settlement was to prove a fraught convenience. Evans made Scott feel vulnerable and thus stole some of his shy initiative. Events showed that Evans was not the ideal second-in-command to Scott: the two

men were never close, and Scott's journal is irritated by
Evans's shallow vitality. From the beginning Scott may
have resented Evans's pushing approach to Markham,
while Evans must have been perplexed by Scott's ponder-
ously thorough expedition, rather than a sprint force
dedicated to reaching the Pole. No faction gathered around
Evans, yet in subtle ways the *Terra Nova* expedition
suffered from the unease between leader and second-in-
command. Furthermore Evans probably usurped a position
Scott had half-promised to Reginald Skelton, a proven
success on the first trip. Skelton had even been working for
Scott in the design and building of new motor sledges, and
he felt aggrieved that Evans could have prevailed on Scott
to omit him. Skelton wrote to Scott, 'Hang it all, judge the
case fairly,' and Scott may have treated Evans coldly for
having put him in so awkward a position.

But Scott's dilemma was that of a methodical, cautious
man who had been overtaken by events. His contradictori-
ness lay in the way the direct Evans could have thought
Scott was abdicating from his own right to Antarctica,
while Scott himself felt that he could take his time over it
without yielding or altering an indistinct feeling of destiny.
In 1909 Evans was precipitate; he may have acted to force
Scott's hand and secure a place for himself. But in 1907 he
had written candidly to Scott, asking to be his navigation
officer when he went south: 'I promise that you will have
no keener officer and no one will work harder than I shall.
I am tremendously enthusiastic, Sir, about Antarctic
exploration.'

By the summer of 1909 Evans's enthusiasm gripped
several explorers all over the world; there were rumours of
French and American moves to the south; and, without
any news of it, the beginnings of a Norwegian plan to
scoop the South Pole. But the exploration establishment
was unnerved by the vulgarity of a race, and by so bare-

faced a pursuit of the ultimate speck on the globe. Circumstances had made Scott the establishment's explorer and in
the echo of Shackleton's applause he had damping advice
from his natural patrons. Sir Lewis Beaumont wrote to
Leonard Darwin, the vice-president of the Royal Geographical Society, responding to the president's alarm that
Antarctica might become a place for sport: 'I have thought
carefully over what you told me of the Scott–Shackleton
difficulty and I cannot think of any better way for the
Geographical Society to deal with it . . . than to reply as you
said you thought of doing, that is, that the Society could not
encourage or support an expedition merely intended to
reach the Pole, but as individuals the members of the
Council could not help hoping that it would be reached by
an Englishman!'

That clash of scientific detachment and outright chauvin-
ism is typical of the Royal Geographical Society's role
in this story. Beaumont was adamant that Scott should
not be seen to compete, yet it is clear that he wished Scott
could win. Such tortuous support must have contributed to
Scott's own hope that he might achieve without the
indignity of taking part. Beaumont therefore urged Scott
the more strongly towards the tendentious justification of
'a scientific expedition primarily, with exploration and the
Pole as secondary objects'.

Yet that policy could expose a naval explorer to establishment criticism. After the *Discovery* expedition, for
instance, Scott had been subjected to long, niggling
reproach from several scientists over the reliability of some
of his work. Even as Scott mounted his second expedition,
the first was dismantled by Charles Chree, president of the
Physical Society, and Napier Shaw, director of the Meteorological Office. Chree went so far as to announce that any
other expedition should be in the charge of 'a physicist of
resource and ripe experience', someone who would not be

'overshadowed by the doers of exploits which appeal to the popular imagination'.

Shackleton was the victim of a more insidious under-mining. Some of the London authorities on Polar travel were casting doubt on whether he had gone as far south as he claimed. The suggestions are obscure and seldom identified, but clearly some people were implying that Shackleton and his party had doctored or bungled their observations so that they could say they had been within a hundred miles of the Pole. One such sceptic was Clements Markham, who may have been a more strenuous critic as his own protégé, Scott, prepared to go south. To discredit Shackleton would place more value on Scott's second journey.

On first hearing of Shackleton's achievement, Markham had asked to be put down as proposer for a medal for Shackleton. He accepted Shackleton's estimate of the distance done and added: 'It seems to me that my theory of the Antarctic lands will turn out to be the correct one.' But, not long after, Markham flowered with doubts, expressing his hostility towards Shackleton and an old man's fear that a once earmarked prize might be passing out of his reach. There is a sad combination of pride, spite and prejudice in this letter to Darwin that fits ill with the longing of men in the south to do momentous, clean and exhausting things for the sake of England, science and their souls:

As I am responsible for having started all this Antarctica business I think it right that I should send you a note of what I think of recent developments.

Shackleton's failure to reach the South Pole when it could have been done by another, and is really a matter of calculation, rather aggravates me. They will rouse ignorant admiration if the trumpets are blown loud enough, which they are sure to be. But I cannot quite accept the latitudes. For 88.20 they must have gone, dragging a sledge and on half rations, at the rate of 14 miles a day in a straight line, up a steep incline 9,000 feet above the sea, for 20 days. I do not believe it.

However, I have nothing more to do with it now. I am getting out of touch with new people, and deafness is beginning to come on, so I intend to retire from the Council next year. I shall then have served for 48 years continuously without a break, which is a fairly long service.

The British Antarctic Expedition 1910 was officially launched on 13 September 1909, towards the end of a summer in which Scott had to deal with his new desk job at the Admiralty, the celebrity of Shackleton and the brash ambition of Evans, the reticence of the geographical establishment and his wife's pregnancy. There must have been moods in which the traveller in Scott felt attracted by the liberty of the south. Indeed the first news of Shackleton's success had come in February 1909, on a day when Scott and Tom Crean were on a train to London. At a station on the way Scott got off the train to buy a paper, showed the report to Crean and said, 'I think we had better have a shot next'. But, in other moods, Scott seemed confused by the new status of Polar travel, by the increasingly naked appeal of that absurd dot at the end of the Earth and by the way in which the establishment felt inclined to leave such expeditions to independent commanders. Some writers have noted that Scott was master of his second journey, as if to be free of the mesh of committees that had tangled the first. That is a legitimate interpretation, but it is possible that Scott liked and needed official backing. So much in Scott was looking for approval, that he may not have had the confidence to enjoy standing alone. A great administrative burden fell on his shoulders on the second journey which often added to his melancholy and put his judgement under extra pressure. Financially the second expedition was always threatened by clouds of debt that were only removed by the impact of tragedy. Yet Scott mounted the most thorough and detailed expedition ever to go south, largely to persuade the world that his purpose was serious, scientific and inquisitive. That was an extra load, and in begging for funds Scott had to face several difficult questions on the actual necessity of a trip to the Pole. Only outline records survive of such moments at provincial meetings, but there is no account of an emphatic reply from Scott. The reason for that is worth considering. A Shackleton, one suspects, would have roused any audience with his mixture of heroics, patriotism and the feel of treading on untouched snow. An Amundsen would have courted the public's sporting interest and said 'Help me be first'. But Scott flinched from committing himself to competition and fell into the lengthy, involved and esoteric claims of science.

In July 1909 Scott and Shackleton exchanged curt letters, very different from the veiled frankness that had preceded Shackleton's departure. Scott wrote: 'I propose to organize the Expedition to the Ross Sea, which as you know, I have had so long in preparation so as to start next year . . . I should be glad to have your assurance that I am not disconcerting any plans of your own.' Shackleton sent an acknowledgement and conceded that 'it will not interfere with any plans of mine'. One may note in passing that he did not make any claim that the route he had pioneered up the Beardmore Glacier was his own reservation.

The special place Scott occupies in history derives largely from his coming second in a race imposed upon him. The public interest in Polar travel in 1910 was centered on the drama of a race that might demonstrate the honour and prowess of one nation or another. Nation and people alike were insecure enough to find comfort in such peripheral ventures. In a few years assaults and losses would be read in the same spirit – until their crushing reality sank in. Anyone less devotedly pledged to the service of his country than Scott, or less reserved about his own wish for glory, would have made support of a raid on the Pole as much a test of loyalty as politicians did the need for armaments in the years before the outbreak of war.

But Scott was too inflexible to woo the public. He wrote to Darwin in the hope that his venture would 'commend itself' to the Geographical Society and to members' chequebooks: 'At this juncture in the history of Polar Exploration I think it is absolutely necessary to continue those efforts which have given to this country the foremost place in Antarctic Research. I have undertaken the task of organizing an expedition and submit to you in brief the programme which I propose to adopt.

'I believe that the main object, that of reaching the South Pole, will appeal to all our countrymen as the one rightly to be pursued at this moment, but the plan which I present provides also for the scientific exploration of a considerable extent of the Antarctic continent.'

The October issue of the *Geographical Journal* announced the expedition and told its members where they might send their donations. Yet the Geographical and the Royal Societies between them subscribed only £750. That indicates how far, in the early twentieth century, the funding of such enterprises relied, awkwardly and inefficiently, on institutions and individuals who were too poor, grudging or indifferent to respond. Polar travel drew its funds from a few wealthy men, from slender government grants, from news agencies and publishers, but hardly at all from large corporations, government research programmes or the general public. The various bases and establishments in Antarctica today are all paid for out of national defence or research budgets, and in Scott we see one of the last private adventurers struggling to raise money.

When the expedition published a prospectus, on 15 September, there was a greater attempt to address the public. This pamphlet began: 'The main object of this Expedition is to reach the South Pole, and to secure for the British Empire the honour of that achievement.' But such directness was soon lost in an explanation of the need for a second base in King Edward VII Land, and in the discussion of three means of transport – dogs, ponies and motor sledges.

Not only was Scott's expedition more wide-ranging and staffed than any other, it was conceived with a variety of bases, purposes and means of transport that added to the cost and made management more taxing. Scott's plan was for ponies to carry supplies to the foot of the glacier, for dogs to take over on the glacier itself so that 'a picked party of men and dogs will make the final dash across the inland sheet'. Nothing had been learned from previous expeditions; motor sledges were taken as 'a main agent or useful auxiliary to the transport plan'. This is the variety of indecision, and the reader will note that a party setting out with three means of power was gradually reduced to a fourth – man-hauling.

From September onwards, Scott became the prisoner of his own cumbersome plans. The expedition had offices at 36–8 Victoria Street, and an assistant paymaster, Francis Drake, ran the office, with George Wyatt as general business manager. Sir Edgar Speyer agreed to be treasurer and served on the one and only advisory committee, which also included Darwin, Markham, Beaumont, Sir George Goldie and Lords Strathcona, Howard de Walden and Goschen. Essentially, however, every decision was Scott's, just as he had the burden of a dreary winter going round the provinces hoping to do more than cover his expenses.

At the outset, on 16 September, he wrote to Edward Wilson asking him to organize the scientific staff for the expedition. Wilson was still engaged on Lord Lovat's survey of diseases afflicting the grouse, though the end of that project was in sight: in all it occupied Wilson five years, during which he dissected over 2,000 birds. He only finished his report on the *Terra Nova* between England and South Africa. It is a sign of Wilson's placid nature that he could move from so deliberate and narrow a piece of research to a dramatic but perhaps no more relevant disaster. Temperamentally, he had pledged himself to Scott in declining Shackleton's invitation. 'Scott is a man worth working for as a man,' he wrote to his father. 'No one can say that it will only have been a Pole-hunt, though that of course is a *sine qua non*. We *must* get to the Pole; but we shall get more too, and there will be no loopholes for error in means and methods if care in preparation can avoid them. I can promise you it is a work worth anyone's time and care and I feel it is really a great opportunity.

'We want the scientific work to make the bagging of the Pole merely an item in the results.'

The *Terra Nova* had thirteen on its scientific staff if one includes Wilson and Edward Atkinson, a naval surgeon who served as parasitologist. Not all these men were pure scientists, but the size of the staff is an indication of Scott's determination that this journey should have academic respectability. He could easily have taken fewer and saved money on men and the equipment many of them required. At the same time the strong body of young scientists materially affected the atmosphere of the expedition, arguably warmed and intrigued Scott himself and emerged with a body of data and theories that may not have been strikingly useful but which represent one of the first exhaustive scientific expeditions in this century. Amundsen's intrusion pushed Scott farther into the role of scientist, – witness the determination of the last party not to abandon their load of rock samples. The scientific staff may have contributed to failure for Scott in confusing issues, but at another level the *Terra Nova* party expressed man's diligent wish to learn more.

The credit for that lay with many of the scientists, with Scott and especially with Wilson who chose most of them and took care of them in the south. The benign concentration of several men at work in the field – albeit a field of austere, frigid rigour – owed much to the considerate, unobtrusive way in which Wilson shepherded men and their disciplines and acted as an intermediary for them with the naval members of the expedition. Without the constant accessibility and kindly explaining of Wilson, naval officers might have treated scientists with a scorn born of insecurity and ignorance.

As meteorologist, the *Terra Nova* had George Simpson, a somewhat dry, solemn man, a little older than most of the other scientists, who would be called 'Sunny Jim' in the game of nicknames that quickly united the company. As a young meteorologist, Simpson had almost made the *Discovery*. He had been very disappointed when, as he felt, Scott took advantage of a doubtful medical report on Simpson in order that another, favoured, applicant should take preference. But the rival had subsequently had to drop out and, when Simpson visited the *Discovery* shortly before it embarked and told Koettlitz that there was no longer any question about his physical condition, the *Discovery* surgeon stamped his feet and said 'Damn! Damn! Damn! Why weren't we told this before?' However the omission of Simpson occurred, the *Discovery*'s lack of an authoritative meteorologist was not forgotten. When, in 1908, from India, the percipient Simpson sent a piece of embroidery to the Scotts as a wedding present, Scott was delighted to hear of him again and confessed the difficulties he was having with Napier Shaw over the weather report of the first trip: 'It is full of inaccuracies and insupportable theories and I have been forced to demand an official investigation by the

Royal Society. I anticipate the necessity of publishing some startling errata. It's a pity that some of your Indian efficiency cannot be imported into the London office.'

Before his posting to Simla, Simpson had had spells in Gottingen, Norway and at the Meteorological Office. He had an excellent, sound reputation and must have been encouraged by Scott's letter. When he heard Scott's announcement a year later, he asked a friend to speak to Scott for him and wondered whether the Government of India would give him leave of absence. Scott accepted Simpson without an interview and in January 1910, when Simpson came to London, the two men visited the India Office and settled the terms of Simpson's release. More than any other man, Simpson was a professional scientist, devoted to his research and excused most sledging work. That such a man worked well and happily – even if he occasionally irritated and was sometimes teased – is a tribute to the workmanlike attitude that prevailed. Simpson's diary contains this estimate of Scott as a patron of his scientists:

One thing which never fails to excite my wonder is Capt. Scott's versatile mind. There is no specialist here who is not pleased to discuss his problems with him and although he is constantly asserting that he is only a layman, yet there is no one here who sees so clearly the essentials of a problem. What is more he seems to know the terms and their meanings as used in most of our special work. He is constantly stating new problems and he seldom comes in from a walk without having made some useful observations. I must say he often sees things which have a bearing on my work which I have passed over without noting their import. Today he called me to describe how he had seen certain snow drifts in positions which did not agree with our general wind directions. He has a thorough grasp of the meteorological conditions, both from a practical and theoretical outlook.

Simpson immediately began to prepare equipment, and

further cluttered the Victoria Street offices. He was there, working on a stove to heat his future magnetic hut, when Griffith Taylor and Charles Wright came to London for an interview. They were Cambridge colleagues, Griffith Taylor an Australian geologist aged thirty, Wright a Canadian physicist aged twenty-three. One Saturday in December they were having tea in Wright's rooms at Caius College and agreed that they would both like to go. That evening Griffith Taylor attended the Philosophical Society dinner and was encouraged by several professors to approach Wilson next day. They bumped into one another – both Caius men – and Wilson gave Taylor a recommending letter to present to Scott. While Griffith Taylor was walking in the Alps, Wright wrote to Scott on his own behalf and at Wilson's suggestion. Wright was told that a physicist had already been appointed, but when Griffith Taylor returned Wright persuaded him that they should walk down to London from Cambridge and arrive on Scott's doorstep in a demonstration of their fitness. With hard-boiled eggs and chocolate, they set out at five in the morning and arrived twelve hours later. Taylor was duly confirmed and Wright learned that his predecessor had failed to pass his medical. The two young scientists were enlisted by Scott and given an £8 allowance to purchase travelling gear. As they left, they saw 'a huge petty officer' – Edgar Evans – sorting sledge equipment and already experimenting with ways of packing.

It is said that the *Terra Nova* party was chosen from over 8,000 volunteers, but no records survive of who was turned down or on what grounds. Both Griffith Taylor and Wright believed that Scott simply endorsed Wilson's original selection. In one way this policy bore fruit: the total contribution of the scientists was outstanding, not just in terms of academic work, but in sledging, marching and sustaining morale. In addition many of the young men who went with the *Terra Nova* were to enjoy distinguished careers, launched by their privileged experience of Antarctica. Yet, in most cases, the men enlisted recall a selection process of not much more than one long talk. We know neither how many of the 8,000 were interviewed nor how thoroughly Scott and Wilson looked into the claims of applicants. It is doubtful if either had the time necessary, and likely that the party was assembled out of a mixture of whim, instinct and expediency. There is only one known and notable exclusion: Julian Huxley was not taken as biologist. There were very few unmitigated mistakes in selection. Yet there is hardly a man on the party who some-where, in the deleted passages of Scott's journal, does not earn a waspish rebuke. Anxiety made Scott discontented and, for every confident claim of a united party, his journal gives way to brooding doubt over an individual. Many scientists found Scott hard to approach and, just as Wilson had chosen them, so undoubtedly he gave them encourage-ment and advice and filtered their views and feelings back to Scott.

Four other academic scientists were selected: Raymond Priestley, who had been on Shackleton's expedition, was now at Sydney University, and Scott enlisted him on his way south, along with another Australian geologist, Frank Debenham. There were also two biologists, both from Plymouth Marine Laboratory: Dennis Lillie and Edward Nelson. Lillie was twenty-six, from Birmingham and Cambridge universities, a rather frail, child-faced man who had earnest faith in reincarnation and who struck Scott as a potential crank. Nelson was a year older, also from Cambridge. He was wealthy and Wilson estimated that one day Nelson would own half the Shetlands. Nelson was one of the few scientists who had an undistinguished expedi-tion. Scott thought him idle and might have paid earlier attention to his wife's opinion that Nelson 'spends all his time on shore being a man about town, which makes him look exceedingly tired'. This is not to suggest that Nelson was a rake or especially depraved. But it gives a hint of how far Scott's men were deliberately not of the modern, sophisticated world. In many of them there was a gentle preference for the country and for less exploited times and ways.

There were five other men included under Scientific Staff. Another of Shackleton's party, Bernard Day, was employed to maintain and be responsible for the motor sledges. These ponderous, delicate toys made Day one of the more subdued and unhappy men in the expedition. Cecil Meares was more sociable and a man with several close friends in the group. But he remains a mysterious figure. He was a much travelled man, a jack of several trades and master of none. With more edge or nerve he might have been an adventurer. As it was, he was a wanderer – 'he has no happiness but in the wild places of the earth' wrote Cherry-Garrard. It is odd that Scott's sense of scientific purpose could still select a romantic drifter. At this distance it is not clear why Scott entrusted him with purchasing dogs and ponies in Siberia, independently bringing them to New Zealand to join the *Terra Nova* and with overall charge of the dogs during the expedition. Meares had worked with dogs in the Kamchatka area, and he chose animals that had been used on postal sledges crossing the frozen sea of Okhotsk. He also hired a young Russian, Demetri Geroff, who had worked with dogs, as well as a groom, Anton Omelchenko. With little or no English, these two Russians lived in the men's quarters and are rarely referred to in any of the journals. Meares came to New Zealand with nineteen ponies and thirty-one dogs, the main elements of Scott's advertised transport plan. That both failed cannot be blamed entirely on Meares, yet Scott trusted the selection to a man of whom he knew very little. Subsequently some have suggested that Meares picked up the nearest dogs at hand, that no survey of different breeds was made and that the ponies and the dogs on Scott's expedition were fatally in the hands of animal-lovers without thorough knowledge of using draught animals in extreme conditions. At the very least it is difficult to see Meares as an expert in the way that, say, Simpson was clearly a coming authority in his discipline. Yet in no other area was there greater need of experience and knowledge.

It is a further insight into the haphazard planning of the *Terra Nova* expedition that the animals were provided in so offhand a manner while Scott had the acumen to enlist a brilliant photographer and a man who ensured that the expedition would be conveyed to a large public. Previous expeditions had taken photographs, and even men known as photographers. But Herbert Ponting was a leading figure in his field, and, although this is not often acknowledged, his film of the expedition deserves a place in any history of documentary cinema. His film is not intimate or nearly as spectacular as his finely composed still photographs, but the film speaks of cold, isolation and the desperate efforts of men to be brave. Ponting took pictures of icebergs, caves and the ship at anchor that have all the misleading elegance of still photography. His movie, however, goes beyond prettiness and sometimes achieves a real poignancy in the dark, huddled figures against an inhuman white background. There are raw truths evident in the film, yet the mood of the expedition was such that Scott himself regarded Ponting as the illustrator of an inspirational adventure. Kathleen Scott remembered that her husband had hoped Ponting would ensure 'that the youth of the Nation should be conversant with such adventures as Polar expedition, as this would help to stimulate "a fine and manly spirit in the rising generation" '.

Ponting was older than most of the men on the *Terra*

Nova and, in Scott's estimate, the most widely travelled. He had already published several books on exotic parts of the world illustrated with his own photographs – splendid, picturesque, accomplished, the works of a man who liked to be thought of as a 'camera artist'. Thus, in his stills especially, photography often imitates the specious grace of late Victorian painting. Ponting was an aesthete, and something of an exquisite among so many seamen. But there was a rugged side to him. He had ranched and mined for six years in the West and his travelling had taken him twice round the world, to Japan and most of the Orient. He had also worked as a war correspondent during the Russo–Japanese and Spanish–American wars. It had been in 1907, on the Trans-Siberian railway, that he had read Scott's *Voyage of the 'Discovery'*. Two years later, in the autumn of 1909, Ponting met Scott in London and said that he would be delighted to photograph a second expedition 'if equitable arrangements could be made'. There spoke the professional, for in hiring Ponting, Scott was advancing on the delicate problem of how far dispatches and pictures from the south were the property of men or agencies in the communications business. Ponting struck a hard bargain, just as Scott was obliged to come to terms with one or other news agency. This meant that other members of the party were not free to send reports or pictures wherever they liked. This did not rankle with many, though Griffith Taylor – a budding journalist – had some arguments with Scott. It serves to remind us that the discoveries of explorers are not free; they are invariably licensed out so that the expedition may be paid for.

In March 1910 Scott and his wife went to Norway together. They met Nansen, who was deeply affected by Kathleen and apparently became the more attached to Scott for that reason. Nansen wished to recommend dogs and skis to Scott; equally he may have foreseen the

Englishman's polite but sceptical response. The larger purpose of the trip to Norway was to watch testing trials for the new motor sledge built by the Wolsley Company. Reginald Skelton and Bernard Day were also present at these tests. Day assured everyone that the difficulties evident on anything other than hard, packed snow would be put right in time. Skelton was less optimistic at the recurring need for repairs in mixed conditions.

Scott purchased his skis in Norway and, when Nansen saw the fifty-odd pairs that the English were taking, he expressed his approval and added that now the English wanted an experienced skier who could make the equipment useful. Nansen suggested a good young Norwegian and, when Scott reacted favourably, he recommended Tryggve Gran, only twenty-one, a handsome, rather arrogant man of wealthy background and a leading ski-jumper. In part Gran's role was to act as ski instructor. But he paid his own way and became one of the characters on the expedition, a thorn in Scott's side, a source of amusement to many, the helpless representative of a nation that had chosen to compete with the English, and one of the longest-lived survivors of the party. Gran's recollections of the expedition are profuse and contested, as if his colleagues could never forget the fanciful boaster he had been. But Gran was an observant outsider, and it is intriguing to note his description of the Scotts' departure from Norway, with Kathleen leaning over the side of the ship and crying out to the quay: 'Be sure, we are soon back in old, wonderful Norway!'

Gran's knowledge of ski was hardly scientific; nor was it adequately applied on the expedition. The last member of the Scientific Staff was also something of a joke among the other scientists. Yet Apsley Cherry-Garrard was to be a prominent member of the party, the most thorough and inspired writer to describe the expedition, one of those who engaged in 'the worst journey in the world' and, arguably, the most lastingly affected by the tragedy. Cherry-Garrard was taken on out of emotion, friendship and good grace, so that he appeared at first to be a supernumerary. But in the end he is Galahad to Scott's Arthur, the truest of Scott's men.

Cherry-Garrard was born in 1886, the son of an eminent major-general and a Bedford doctor's daughter. The family was wealthy and had two large homes: Denford Park, near Hungerford in Berkshire, and Lamer Park at Wheathampstead, Hertfordshire. The young Apsley was an eager athlete, thwarted by short-sight. He went to Winchester and then Oxford, where he read Classics and Modern History and rowed in his college's winning crew in the Henley Grand Challenge Cup in 1908. There could be no purer instance of the young Edwardian equally fulfilled by learning and striving.

Apsley was cousin to the publisher Reginald Smith, and in 1907 he met the Wilsons and Scott at Smith's house in Kirriemuir. Cherry-Garrard noted of this meeting: 'When I first met Wilson, it was certain that he and Scott were going South again if possible: they wanted to finish the job. I do not know whether Scott would have gone again without Wilson.' There is at least a hint there that Wilson's commitment to Lord Lovat's grouse survey was a factor delaying Scott. At first that seems far-fetched, but it helps us to measure the depth of Scott's reliance on Wilson.

The urge to volunteer was born then in Cherry-Garrard and his first serious letter came to Wilson in October 1909 from Australia. Wilson was already fond of Cherry-Garrard and must have urged his candidacy, but was compelled to say: 'Scott thinks that it is just possible that when we have filled up the actual scientific staff with the necessary experts in each branch, there may still be a vacancy for an adaptable helper, such as I am sure you would be; ready to lend a hand where it was wanted. Only I must frankly say that as it is a matter of real importance in these Shore parties to reduce numbers to a minimum, the reverse may be possible and there may be no room for any but the absolutely necessary Staff.'

By April 1910 Cherry-Garrard was back in England, reinforcing application with the offer of £1,000. Still he was turned down. But the young man insisted that his donation stood, whether or not he was accepted. Wilson wrote back, himself touched and trying to convey the impact of this altruism on Scott. Cherry-Garrard had not calculated that effect, but it had identified him as the very breed of man Scott admired, and might have been himself if born wealthier. Wilson's letter discloses how far he wanted Cherry-Garrard as at least one more man who might be close to Scott:

He says he must satisfy himself by a talk with you that there is no misunderstanding on the subject before coming to a deter-mination, otherwise he feels you might both be in something of a false position. I believe he is right, and the time has come when you and he must understand one another. I can tell you one thing, however, and that is that he very *much* appreciates the motive which induced you to send your subscription in-dependently of your chance of being taken. That is an action which appeals to him, not because of the money for which he cares very little, except impersonally, in so far as it helps the Expedition to be a success – but because he knows what to expect of a man who felt it was the right thing to do.

I know Scott intimately, as you know. I have known him now for ten years, and I believe in him so firmly that I am often sorry when he lays himself open to misunderstanding. I am sure that you will come to know him and believe in him as I do, and none the less because he is sometimes difficult. However you will soon see for yourself.

As men were chosen for the expedition, Scott laboured over gathering money. £1,000 from Cherry-Garrard was a substantial donation, some 5 per cent of the initial funds raised from individuals. It was the amount subscribed by Lord Strathcona and Sir Edgar Speyer, by Llewellyn Wood Longstaff and the government of New Zealand. That Longstaff should have given so much less for this second expedition denotes either hard times in Hull or a vast moderation of enthusiasm. The Royal Geographical Society gave £500; the Royal Society offered half that sum. Markham gave £100 and then was instrumental in acquiring the surplus of £670 left over from the *Discovery* expedition. As the total refused to go high enough, a circular was sent to 3,272 fellows of the Geographical Society; 212 responded and contributed just over £1,000.

All through the winter of 1909–10 Scott toured the country doing his best to raise money, to win a government grant and to hold off bills as long as possible. Of all the British expeditions, the *Terra Nova*'s was most troubled financially. It sailed uncertain as to whether the men could be paid, and even in the Antarctic Scott was tormented by rising costs, contingencies and the meagre flow of new money. The expedition remained in debt until its tragedy sprang the release on British pathos and nearly overwhelmed the survivors with money.

The ordeal was not one that suited Scott. By nature he was neither a debtor nor a borrower; by temperament he was an awkward pleader. When he came to purchase the *Terra Nova* from Bowring Brothers of Newfoundland, he made a down payment without knowing where the balance would come from. In a car Scott roamed the north of England, speaking whenever he could. The results were very mixed. From Manchester he got £2,000; but at Wolverhampton he had to be content with £25. This suggests fitful publicity, an uncertain sense of suitable venues and a growing dismay on Scott's part that must have impeded his practical preparations. In several places he was

questioned critically: about the utility of another expedition
and the possibility that the unemployed were more
deserving of charity. Early in 1910 the government allowed
£20,000. But the total was short of the £40,000 that was the
first, inadequate estimate of what would be needed. Cardiff
was generous – £2,500 at first, and then another £222 at a
luncheon activated by Teddy Evans, and finally 500 tons of
coal as a parting gift. In summary, yet one more expedition
was funded in spurts, without any large public support but
with a modest pay-off from the state and a few gifts from
individuals. Regarding the accounts, one must realize that
Scott invested nearly everything he had – perhaps as much
as £3,000 – enough to make him the largest individual con-
tributor.

The government grant that Scott had for the *Terra Nova*
was as large as Shackleton's total budget. The expense of
Scott's second expedition owes a lot to the high number of
men involved. This was so that the ship could go back and
forth, and so that there could be two separate shore parties.
But altogether Scott planned for thirty-three officers,
men and scientists to go ashore, with thirty-two staying on
the ship.

Among the men, Scott re-employed not only Edgar
Evans, but Crean, Lashly and Williamson. He had three
other Navy lieutenants: Victor Campbell, Harry Pennell
and Henry Rennick. His wife's brother, Wilfred Bruce, a
Merchant Navy lieutenant, was in the ship's party. There
were also two naval surgeons: Murray Levick and Edward
Atkinson. There is too little space to deal with these men in
detail, but two others, accepted by Scott, were leading
figures in the expedition and men who would die with
him.

Henry Robertson Bowers was born in Greenock,
Scotland, in 1883, the son of a merchant skipper who was
also a fellow of the Royal Geographical Society. The father

died when the boy was four and he formed a bond with his mother as close as that between Scott and his. He was educated at Sidcup and Streatham before, aged fourteen, he became a cadet on H.M.S. *Worcester*. He passed out in 1899 and became a midshipman in the Merchant Navy. In 1905 he was assigned to the Royal Indian Marine Service as a sub-lieutenant and he had served in the east for nearly five years before Markham's strong support got him on the *Terra Nova*, without his ever having met Scott. Yet sheer ability made Bowers perhaps the most dynamic man on the journey. Some have alleged that, as Teddy Evans disappointed Scott, so the leader came to rely more and more on Bowers as his master of supplies and planning.

Bowers was self-consciously ugly. He endured jokes about his nose and his dumpy figure – 12 stone and five feet four – but was sensitive enough to have been wounded by them. There was a clash in Bowers between earnest spiritual reflection and a brisk, businesslike way with the world's affairs. In and around Burma Bowers had become a scourge of pirates and an emphatic believer in the inferiority of Oriental peoples: he was especially disapproving of 'so-called democratic ideas' falling among the 'blighters' and was convinced of the inherent virtues of being British. The language here is jingoistic, and the complacency hard:

Now the artisans and cheap-labour specimens have come out here and said to the coolie – whose very existence depends on our occupation practically – 'You're my equal, why are you salaaming? Get up and say you won't work for less than 1/– a day.' No longer is the Sahib what he was, no longer do they respect the nation, who – by the Grace of God – licked them times without number at odds of 1 to 100, and gave them peace, famine relief, protection, and a degree of happiness thrown in.

I love my country, and trust that I shall not be found wanting when the day comes to act. That dear old country – I wonder if a

1, 2. Two portraits of Robert
Falcon Scott, the first in 1904
as a Royal Navy Captain, the
second in 1909-10, at his desk,
planning the *Terra Nova*
expedition. Although
clearly the same man, the
contrast of a splendid uniform
that must be filled and a tired
manager is very evident: the
longer one looks the greater
the gap between the
two seems to be.

3. Ernest Shackleton in 1907 in London before going south: a passionate stare from a depressive, sensual face, uneasy in town clothes.

4. Sir Clements Markham in the assured pose of a patron of travel.

5. Kathleen Scott.

6. Edward Wilson in 1911, tubercular as a young man in London, but in the south always seeming ready for more.

7, 8. Wild, Shackleton, Marshall and Adams on their return from 'farthest south' – savage, tanned scarecrows. And in London, later that year, men in street shoes and polar bear furs advertising an exhibition of Shackleton's photographs.

9. **Teddy** Evans on the *Terra Nova*.

10, 11. Ponting at his most picturesque: a study of the *Terra Nova* in McMurdo Sound.
And (above right) Keohane, at the end of the polar night of 1911, completing his model of
the ship he trusted would return.
12. (Below right) Bowers, with some of the stores he looked after.

13, 14. The hut at Cape Evans. Inside, it might be trench quarters or a prisoner-of-war camp. This shows 'The Tenements' with Cherry-Garrard, Bowers, Oates, Meares and Atkinson in their small spaces.

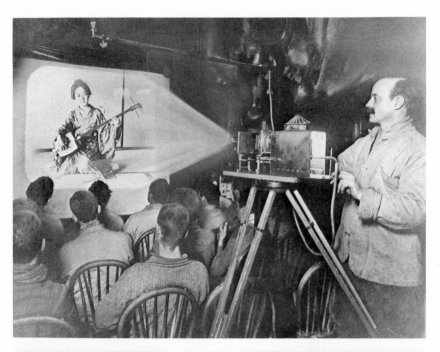

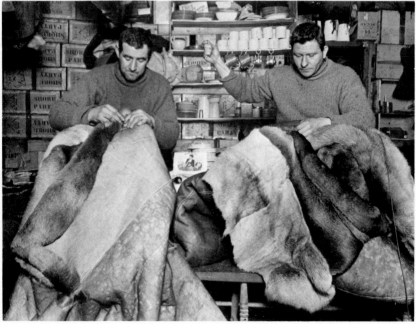

15, 16. Ponting enlivens the winter with an illustrated lecture on Japan. Crean and Edgar Evans repair sleeping bags.

17, 18. Scott in his den: writing, with pipe in hand, seacoat on the bed, and a gallery of pictures of his wife and son.

19. Apsley Cherry-Garrard, his eyes white where he has worn goggles, his nose burned by sun or frost.

20, 21. Before and after the mission to Cape Crozier. On setting out, Bowers, Wilson and Cherry-Garrard pose for a flashlight in the polar night. On their return, visibly exhausted, they pause in their first meal for an awed record of the change in them.

22. Oates.

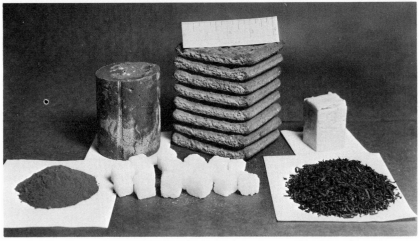

23, 24. The cook, Clissold, making rhubarb pies in the galley of the hut. Some of these photographs were taken with subsequent advertisements in mind. But the still life of a man's daily sledging rations only indicates disaster: from left to right – cocoa, pemmican, sugar, eight biscuits, cheese, tea.

25, 26. Man-hauling on the polar plateau ; and, at the Pole, a photograph by Bowers of Scott, Oates, Wilson and Evans dismayed by Amundsen's abandoned tent.

27, 28. Roald Amundsen, and the statue of Scott, by his wife, in Waterloo Place, London.

fraction of its inhabitants appreciate its worth, or does it require a probation of long absences to show one that that little island is – under *any* circumstances of weather or anything else – the best, the very best place on God's earth.

God in that context sounds like a colonial administrator in a Somerset Maugham story dreaming of his next leave. Bowers's views are extreme, even in the conservative company of Scott's men. But there is another side to him. God was not a hollow cliché for Bowers. Instead he had worked his way towards a naive view of the spirit that is manifested in his behaviour in the south. Bowers wrote long, introspective letters from India to his mother, and one contains this account of the journey of his soul. It is unlikely that he would have shared it with many people on the expedition, but Bowers was close to Wilson and there we may assume a special affinity and tent conversations long into the night:

Have been reading a lot and thinking a lot about things. This life at sea, so dependent upon nature, and so lonely, makes one think. I seem to get into a quagmire of doubts and disbeliefs. Why should we have so many disappointments, when life was hard enough without them? Everything seems a hopeless problem. I felt I should never get out, there was no purpose in it. One night on deck when things were at their blackest, it seemed to me that Christ came to me and showed me why we are here, and what the purpose of life really is. It is to make a great decision – to choose between the material and the spiritual, and if we choose the spiritual we must work out our choice, and then it will run like a silver thread through the material. It is very difficult to express in words what I suddenly saw so plainly, and it is sometimes difficult to recapture it myself. I know, too, that my powerful ambitions to get on in this world will conflict with the pure light that I saw for a moment, but I can never forget that I did realize, in a flash, that nothing that happens to our bodies really matters.

Bowers, Scott and Wilson were found, months after their deaths, starved and frozen. The last words of all three spoke calmly and happily of the companionship they had known and of the way it subdued terrible suffering. Bowers took pride in physical strength, and may have been the most hard-tested of all the men on the *Terra Nova*. Yet his dismissal of physical significance is touching and persuasive. We believe in Bowers's faith and can see how far it motivated most of the men with Scott. Bowers had spent years in steamy heat and all the while delighted in the remote prospect of one day living in great cold. From a distance he had followed Shackleton's journey: 'I thought it splendid. My only regret was that I was not one of them. If only they will leave the South Pole itself alone for a bit they may give me a chance.' It is no wonder that Scott chose Bowers, unseen and unknown, when the sub-lieutenant could have written something that sounds like Scott, desperate in case his destiny might be stolen.

Another point in common between Scott and Bowers was the obligation they felt to widowed mothers. Scott's marriage reassessed the role of his mother, but never diminished it. Bowers's mother was his most important human reference and, as with many adventurers and military men, he was torn over the way he so often left her alone: 'I do not wish to defend my action, but whenever I thought of Mother I used to say to myself "No! I can't do it." Even after I went to the *Worcester* I used to lie awake at night and vow I could never go to sea.'

Something of the same relationship features in the life and the going south of Lawrence Edward Grace Oates. Oates was born in 1880, in Putney, a suburb of London, but his life was rooted at the family home, Gestingthorpe Hall, in Essex. His father died while Oates was a boy and his mother became the firm guide of his life, even if Oates was seldom emotional in his attitude towards her. In most things, except the treatment of horses, he was exaggeratedly terse. He seems to have cultivated a worldly indifference, as if it were gentlemanly. It leaves an odd, vulnerable dryness in his letters, not very appealing, but not convincing either. Oates's reputation hangs on the sacrifice of his death, and he is widely regarded as an exceptional devotee of duty. However, his early life shows a very different, dissatisfied man for whom the south may have been all the more appealing as a thorough alternative to wasting and apathy.

Oates was educated at Eton and failed to get in to Oxford. Trinity College told him: 'Your papers are considerably below our standard, and I do not think it would be worth your while to stand again in September.' Thus he went into the Army, in the 6th Inniskilling Dragoons – 'the best Heavy Cavalry regiament [sic] in the British Army which is saying a good deal when it has to compeat [sic] with the Greys & Royals'. Horses were his passion and he was forever asking his mother for an advanced or increased allowance to buy a polo pony or a good saddle.

He went to South Africa and in March 1901 was wounded seriously in a fight with Boers. This left him with a limp and a left leg shorter than his right. It is an open question how far this troubled him in the Antarctic. Thereafter Oates was stationed in Ireland, Egypt and India, unhappy with the Army, his postings and a deeper sense of listlessness. In Ireland he hunted and owned a few steeplechase horses – 'hunting is the only thing makes life endurable'. As the British Army slowly yielded to reform, Oates was a sardonic observer of a vain attempt at improvement: 'A circular memo came round from the Army Council saying the shortness of candidates for the cavalry was critical and ordering more discomforts to attract the "poor man with brains", the thing they have not yet grasped is that the man with brains knows too much to join the service.'

Stagnation was unremitting: on the one hand, Oates loathed his routine, but he was cynical about any chance of improvement. He was required to go to Cavalry School and while there complained to his mother: 'Why I go on soldiering is an absolute mystery to me. I am beginning to think I am not quite all there.' He went to Egypt but thought Cairo spoiled by Americans; Jerusalem struck him as seven-eighths humbug. In India he was Master of Hounds at Mhow, but only the news that Scott liked his application managed to lift the veil of tedium. Once accepted, he wrote cautiously to his mother, saying he had never thought he would be chosen and hoping that the £1,500 it would cost was not too much. Oates, like Cherry-Garrard, paid £1,000 to go south. He told his mother, 'It will help me professionally as in the Army if they want a man to wash labels off bottles they would sooner employ a man who had been to the North Pole than one who had only got as far as the Mile End Road.'

Oates was known for silence on the expedition, and it is instructive to see how much bitterness lay beneath it. He seems an unhappy man, scornful of most things – including marriage and himself – and only enthusiastic about horses. Yet is there not something of the cult of the gentleman amateur in Oates – polo-player, master of hounds and steeplechaser – being hired to care for Siberian ponies in the Antarctic?

8
Going South

The race to the South Pole is an event poised at the threshold of modern times. Today space capsules can orbit the Earth in hours; telecommunications have crowded our experience with virtual simultaneity. Yet the two ships that went south from northern Europe in 1910 took seven and five months to make a landfall on Antarctica, and their awareness of one another was restricted to the arrival at civilized ports where cables were waiting. The drama of the race is accentuated by this prolongation and by the way decisive news was for so long unavailable. A decade later, radio communication and air transport had shattered the framework in which Scott and Amundsen went south. Thus, with the last great exploration of the Earth, we coincidentally lose the sense of parts of the world and pockets of life being inaccessible. But, for many of Scott's men, the chance to be out of the reach of sprawling, interfering civilization was very appealing.

Not that everyone involved was indifferent to returning or unable to think a few years ahead. In his last month in England Scott was rushing between the office, the dock where the *Terra Nova* was being loaded and a succession of dinners and receptions. At one such occasion he spoke of the coming crisis in Europe and the need for defensive readiness. Shortly before departing he visited the offices of the *Daily Mail* and asked informed men if war was likely.

The editor, Thomas Marlowe, replied that the opinion of experts held that by the summer of 1914 there might be a state of hostility. Scott considered and said: 'By then I shall be entitled to command a battle cruiser of the Invincible class. The summer of 1914 will suit me very well.' We do not often hear so calculating a careerist in Scott. But in hindsight the remark is tragic, for few wars were less suited to the professional preparedness of fighting men than the war that began in 1914. An Oates in India, Teddy Evans rousing seamen, or Scott passing through a fog of manoeuvres, might all be restless for action, but only because of their very restricted, conventional idea of what hostility would be. In one glimpse of Scott looking ahead, we discover how settled he was in something before the modern age.

On 1 June 1910 the *Terra Nova* edged away from its moorings at London Docks. There were many guests aboard, as well as those like Scott and Ponting who would not sail on the first legs of the voyage but join it later, in South Africa or Australia, allowing them time for pressing business affairs. Ponting congratulated Scott on the send-off and wondered what the return would be like, with the Pole as a trophy. But Scott assured Ponting that 'he cared nothing for "that sort of thing"; that he would willingly forego all acclamation both now and later; that all he desired was to complete the work begun on his first expedition seven years ago, reach the goal of his hopes, and get back to his work in the Navy again.'

That night the *Terra Nova* anchored at Greenhithe, near the *Worcester*, the training ship of Bowers and Teddy Evans. A dinner was held on board and, at 10.30 p.m., Scott, Kathleen and other guests were rowed ashore. The youthful Markham made do with a bunk in Evans's cabin and next day joined in a visit for breakfast to the treble enthusiasm of the *Worcester*. Markham was not easily persuaded to go home. He stayed aboard until 4 June and only disembarked at Stokes Bay. Nearly two weeks after leaving London the *Terra Nova* reached Cardiff, to take on its coal and attend the Lord Mayor's reception.

That evening was a lively one. Cardiff had been generous to the expedition, partly because of Teddy Evans's connections. The day of the reception visitors – at 2s. 6d. a head – added to the confusion on the packed ship, where the men had already given up some of their living space to make room for more equipment. Scott came to Cardiff for the night and wandered into a row between the two Evanses – Teddy and Edgar – both of whom must have been eager to make a mark in Cardiff. According to Edgar's niece, P. O. Evans drew Scott's attention to the fact that the wrong skis had been brought – so much for Nansen's satisfaction. Since Teddy Evans would have been in charge of loading, some blame may have fallen on him. At any event fresh skis were ordered and Edgar Evans was apparently made responsible for them.

At the banquet the Welshman Edgar Evans sat proudly between Scott and the Lord Mayor. But this celebrity, and the prospect of years away, set him drinking so that six men had to carry him back on board the ship afterwards. This seems to have fostered the acrimony between the two Evanses, and one senses the frustration of the second-in-command who shared the name of a man a good deal more experienced in the Antarctic than he was himself.

The *Terra Nova* quit Cardiff on 15 June and pushed out into the Atlantic towards Madeira. They stopped there a few days, time for some of the company to go ashore and take tea in the flower garden of Reid's Hotel, time for the men to play football with the team from the Telegraph Company and for a few visitors to look over the ship. One of those recalls a great array of razors down below, which led to the comment from one of the officers that they did not intend to go unshaven, like Shackleton's party. Such dedication to smartness only revealed how unexpectedly severe the Antarctic would be for some.

On the way to Cape Town Evans and Wilson shared the command and the company adjusted itself to the mixture of bravura and reserve. Already friendships were forming. Bowers thought Wilson 'a real Christian – there is no mistaking it – it comes out in everything . . . the perfect gentleman – the most manly and the finest character in my own sex that I have ever had the privilege to meet'. Furthermore Wilson, who was preparing a report on the men for Scott, found Bowers 'a perfect marvel of efficiency – but in addition to this he has the most unselfish character I have ever seen in a man anywhere'. Cherry-Garrard, in the words of Simpson, 'accompanying us without any special vocation', had come with an abundance of gifts and impressed himself upon Griffith Taylor with a pair of Jaeger socks. Gran was already known for stories about himself, his travels, his ski cups and his alleged success with young ladies. Oates had made it clear that he liked to be left alone: Wilson called him 'extraordinarily silent and laconic'. Although Teddy Evans cannot have been the most attractive of men to Wilson, he still bowed before the lieutenant's breeziness: 'Evans is the most boisterously good-tempered individual imaginable. I never knew anyone so persistently high-spirited, and we are all infected with his noisy good-nature.'

Relative outsiders, such as Simpson and Oates, give us some idea of the schoolboy version of the Navy that Evans maintained and which was tempered after Scott joined the party. Simpson was rooted in another, academic world, and he noted the cramped quarters, the readiness of officers to join in manual labour 'no matter how hard or how dirty it may be', and the atmosphere of a school outing:

Sometimes, especially at dinner, our spirits run so high that we should be taken for a party of school boys rather than a party of men engaged on work which has the attention of the whole of England. The usual form of our madness is the singing of songs & choruses at the top of our voices followed by cheering and other meaningless noises.

Such merriment often led to battles. One evening Wilson, Campbell and Cherry-Garrard defended the nursery against the rest of the wardroom. It went on for over an hour, with clothes being torn from the backs of the fighters. 'Excellent fun and splendid exercise' Wilson called it, without any hint of perplexity at the horseplay of men set free to be boys. Oates thought it 'the rowdyest mess I have ever been in', and added: 'I wonder what some of the people at home would think if they saw the whole of the afterguard with the exception of the officer of the watch struggling yelling and tearing off each others clothes the ship rolling and the whole place a regular pandemonium. Evans is a splendid chap. He leads all the ragging himself but I should be sorry for the person who hesitated to do what Evans told him.'

Oates also observed, gloomily, that the *Terra Nova* had two speeds: slow and slower. There was another stop at South Trinidad Island when a large party went ashore in the mood of a natural history society, collecting birds' eggs, insects, botanical specimens. They picnicked, rambled, walked the dogs and had several adventures when some of them were marooned. It was early August already and, with 2,500 miles to Cape Town, Evans decided to curtail an itinerary of the other inviting islands. 'It is perhaps just as well,' Bowers wrote to his mother, 'I am longing to get to the Cape to have your letters and hear all about you. Except for the absence of news, life aboard is much to be desired. I simply love it, and enjoy every day of my existence here. Time flies like anything.'

But for Scott it dragged. His original schedule had been for the *Terra Nova* to make the Cape on 2 August, and he duly arrived there with Kathleen and the wives of Wilson and Evans the following day. But the ship did not reach Simonstown until 15 August and Kathleen observed how anxious he became, fearing in one moment that the heavily laden ship had foundered and in the next wildly speculating about whether a replacement could be bought. Scott lectured while he waited and went to seek funds from the government in Pretoria. This brought forth £500 and some newspaper criticism that Scott should have approached the diamond industry instead.

The *Terra Nova* remained in South Africa for three weeks. This time was occupied with negotiations for more funds, the shifting of stores and a round of social invitations. Yet, for an expedition already behind schedule, it might have been a briefer interlude. The voyage south falls farther and farther behind time and must be seen as the first hint of prevailing slowness, or of being behind planned dates, that goes right through to the end.

Perhaps Scott foresaw this trend and hoped that his presence on the way to Australia would speed progress. It may also have been his revised intention to get some closer knowledge of the members of the party. At any event he now sent Wilson on ahead with the ladies and announced that he would himself join the *Terra Nova*. Bowers was thrilled to have the commander aboard and noticed an inspiring directness in Scott that was not always his and which may have been a diffident leader's attempt to make a good impression: 'There is not one of us whom he does not take a personal interest in. He took me by the arm when he came aboard the other day and began, "I say, old chap. . . ." He will take nothing but a straight answer to his questions and if the job is yours you've *got* to know all about it . . . It will be good to have him with us as a passenger. . . . But losing "Our Bill" [Wilson] is a great blow to all of us. It will be terrible without "our Bill" – at least we feel so – as he was always the balancing point in the men.'

Teddy Evans was also upset and jumped to the conclusion that he was being blamed for slowness. Here was another unfortunate source of friction between leader and second-in-command, but one that points to more serious problems: that Evans was insecure; and that the sailing rate of the *Terra Nova* had not been properly tested or calculated in advance. Furthermore this discord was played out between the two wives. Hilda Evans was demure, and Kathleen Scott outspoken; the one therefore would have had to endure charges that her husband was being 'petty' and probably carried them back to Evans in hurt dismay. These ladies kept company with the expedition as long as they could in a spirit of romantic loyalty, yet nothing suggests that Kathleen was discreet or detached and the boss's wife may have been a figure of commanding and reckless influence.

The *Terra Nova* left Simonstown on 2 September, only eleven days before it was supposed to reach Melbourne. And as Scott sailed slowly east, on 6 September, the *Fram* slipped into Madeira. It stayed four days and was off again and, after it had gone, its commander's brother, Leon Amundsen, sent an economical cable to await Scott in Melbourne: 'Am going south. Amundsen.'

That is one of the more famous cables in telegraphic history and it can hardly be denied that it had a flourish that stared brazenly in the face of ethical qualms. There is no reason now to be incensed by the heat of Anglo–Norwegian rivalry. Yet the cable is unmistakably Amundsen: it speaks of his strengths and weaknesses; it heralds his triumph, for it was the exact stroke of a man who believed he would win; it also grows out of the tiny crack of uneasiness that even Amundsen felt. In terms of drama it raises an episode in the

history of exploration to an emotional level that affects anyone who knows the story. It was a warning to Scott that he
grasped more than a year later. But it was also the surety
that men would never forget Scott. He would have made an
anonymous winner; nothing caught or fulfilled his destiny
better than that he should lose. Amundsen did him that
unintended service and gave him a few months in which he
was the unalloyed Scott, a tragic hero. Whereas Amundsen
is never more than a robust and simple-minded victor, an
explorer who made manifest the tedium and insignificance
of going south. Scott went south to realize himself in
disaster, whereas Amundsen went for no other reason than
to rush back and boast that he had been.

In the years after the *Belgica* voyage Amundsen was
obsessed with another geographical will-o'-the-wisp, the
north-west passage. Laboriously, he put together such an
expedition, using a ship named the *Gjoa*. Like Scott,
Amundsen was plagued with the difficulties of raising
money. But, while Scott persevered with accounts,
promises, debts and guarantees, Amundsen could take the
law into his own hands. In June 1903, when an angry
creditor gave him twenty-four hours to pay, Amundsen
'resolved upon a desperate expedient' that foreshadowed
his actions in 1910. With his crew of six he boarded the
Gjoa by night and set out for sea: 'When dawn arose on our
truculent creditor, we were safely out in the open main,
seven as light-hearted pirates as ever flew the black flag.'

The *Gjoa* went on a long and elaborate journey during
which the Norwegians lived among the Eskimos. Eventually they came through, having charted an intricate
passage that maritime civilization has ignored. Nevertheless the human risk was very great, and Amundsen's
personal need to discover all-important. When the last
great effort was rewarded, his reaction was primitive and
overwhelming and shows the man's coarse vitality: 'My

nerve-wracking strain of the last three weeks was over. And with its passing, my appetite returned. I felt ravenous. Hanging from the shrouds were carcasses of caribou. I rushed up the rigging, knife in hand. Furiously I slashed off slice after slice of the raw meat, thrusting it down my throat in chunks and ribbons, like a famished animal, until I could contain no more. Appetite demanded, but my stomach rejected, this barbarous feast.'

Amundsen was never merely a discoverer. He needed to communicate what he had done to the outside world, and as soon as the *Gjoa* was through Amundsen left his men, 'wild with eagerness to get to a telegraph office and send the news to the world'. Ironically, at Fort Egbert, as soon as the telegraph began pounding out Amundsen's joy, the wires snapped in the cold and the rapt explorer was made to wait a week before congratulations came back from the outside world.

If we recall Scott's reticence between first and second expeditions, there is something childlike in Amundsen's unblinking, 'Having achieved the first ambition of my life, I began looking about for new worlds to conquer'. Appetite noticed first the North Pole and adopted this motto from Rex Beach: 'The deity of success is a woman, and she insists on being won, not courted. You've got to seize her and bear her off, instead of standing under her window with a mandolin.' There speaks the rapist, to be put beside the Scott who had once transcribed Browning's 'A Woman's Last Word':

> Let's contend no more love,
> Sigh nor weep
> All be as before love
> Only sleep.

Amundsen hired Nansen's old ship, the *Fram*, sought funds and put together plans to go round Cape Horn, up the western seaboard of America, through the Bering Straits and then drift over the point of the North Pole.

So he would have done, no doubt, but in April 1909 came news that the American, Admiral Peary, had at last reached the North Pole. This was before Shackleton's return from Antarctica, and five months before Scott gave official notice to the world of his going south. A careful reading of Amundsen's publications conveys the shock to his system of this forestalling and suggests that he was immediately hunting for an alternative: 'This was a blow indeed! If I was to maintain my prestige as an explorer, I must quickly achieve a sensational success of some sort. I resolved upon a coup.'

That passage shows how far Amundsen's special lust for popular glory required not just achievement, but achievement that in its manner and style commanded public attention. 'I resolved upon a coup' may be the unwittingly frank admission of a man who determined not just to go south but to do so with such secrecy that his appearance there was like the entrance of a long-lost son in melodrama. No doubt he reckoned the son would be greeted as a hero; in fact he appeared to much of the world a furtive opportunist.

To some extent Amundsen's plight was one with which Scott could have sympathized. He had been through the extended agony of raising funds for one expedition, the purpose of which had now been eliminated. Any explorer, much less an Amundsen, must have felt the urge to shift funds and enthusiasm to some other venture rather than meekly hand back the money. Yet, once Amundsen had fixed his attention on the South Pole, he would have realized the need to be discreet about these plans. Thus he was in a dilemma of rare delicacy; for something like a year he was bound to act as if the North Pole still concerned him, while actually devising a way in the opposite direction. The legend goes that secrecy was wonderfully maintained, yet an objective reader may suspect that several people must have known or guessed Amundsen's real intentions.

There is no clear indication of when he decided to go south, but I suspect it was as early as the spring of 1909, and largely under the influence of Shackleton's achievement: 'Sir Ernest Shackleton! – the name has a brisk sound. At its mere mention we see before us a man of indomitable will and boundless courage. He has shown us what the will and energy of a single man can perform.'

Suppose that, by June 1909, Amundsen had conceived the outline of a plan to go south with the *Fram*, within three months he had the added incentive of a race with Scott. For Amundsen, as for Teddy Evans, it was in character to decide to go to the South Pole overnight. Neither man was oppressed by the problems; both felt the ease with which it might be done. The gradual way in which Scott closed in on the same decision is filled with anticipation of obstacles. Amundsen's presence jolted Scott and became one more difficulty. Scott's going south undoubtedly stimulated the Norwegian. From the time of Scott's announcement, at least, Amundsen was determined to beat the Englishman south and to give him as little notice as possible of the existence of a race.

In Amundsen's account of the journey to the South Pole, he works hard to discount the moral objection he anticipates to 'shabby rivalry'. By necessity this defence must be looked at closely. First, Amundsen considers the position of benefactors who had given money for one expedition only to see it transferred to another. The response here is brisk but evasive: 'my mind was soon at rest. They were all men of position, and above discussing the application of the sums they had dedicated to the enterprise. I knew that I enjoyed such confidence among these people that they would all judge the circumstances aright, and knew that when the time came their contributions would be used for the purpose for which they were given.'

It is true that Amundsen was widely admired in Norway, but how credible is it that sponsors should sit back so trustingly when it was common knowledge that Peary had tidied up the North Pole, and that Amundsen was not a man to go over someone else's tracks? No one with a history of avoiding creditors so skilfully is ever given quite the trust Amundsen claimed for himself. I have no evidence to offer, but it seems plausible that Amundsen quietly approached his patrons in 1909 and confided in them. How else could he have been so sure of enjoying blind confidence?

Next, Amundsen attempts to convince Scott's indignant supporters of his own honourable actions. The justification must be quoted at some length and then analysed. It should be pointed out that this justification was written and published in 1912, when Scott was already dead, but before knowledge of that had reached the world. Scott died in fearful cold towards the end of March 1912. Less than a month before, in Brisbane, the busy, deadline-conscious Amundsen began writing his triumphant account: 'Here I am, sitting in the shade of palms, surrounded by the most wonderful vegetation, enjoying the most magnificent fruits, and writing – the history of the South Pole. What an infinite distance seems to separate that region from these surroundings! And yet it is only four months since my gallant comrades and I reached the coveted spot.'

Amundsen's persistent haste, over the snow, and from expedition to manuscript to published book, was plainly intended to outstrip Scott in one more way – letting the world have Amundsen's story a year before Scott's came through. At the same time Amundsen could not have written with quite such relish had he known Scott's condition as he sat in balmy Brisbane. That he never guessed Scott's fate is partly because, for the Norwegians, Antarctica was not so dangerous a place. Nevertheless from Brisbane, or on the ship home, this was Amundsen's explanation of why he had waited a year to tell Scott they were going to the same place:

Nor did I feel any great scruples with regard to the other Antarctic expeditions that were being planned at the time. I knew I should be able to inform Captain Scott of the extension of my plans before he left civilization, and therefore a few months sooner or later could be of no great importance. Scott's plan and equipment were so widely different from my own that I regarded the telegram that I sent him later, with the information that we were bound for the Antarctic regions, rather as a mark of courtesy than as a communication which might cause him to alter his programme in the slightest degree. The British expedition was designed entirely for scientific research. The Pole was only a side-issue, whereas in my extended plan it was the main object. On this little detour science would have to look after itself; but of course I knew very well that we could not reach the Pole by the route I had determined to take without enriching in a considerable degree several branches of science.

There could not be a sharper illustration of the hypocrisy of Polar explorers. Amundsen chooses to treat Scott according to his pious defence of science – ignoring the candour of the appeal to the public – and yet cannot quite deny himself the happy bonus of a little science along the way!

Amundsen also claimed that he could not say anything in case press and public reaction 'stifled' his project. Yet surely the Norwegian press and those backers who trusted him would have been far happier with a declared race than with a bewildering attempt to follow Peary. No, the secrecy is explained by only one thing: the wish to race Scott with every possible advantage. Amundsen would be a more acceptable man if he had been able to admit that in

1912. That he could not, and that he turned Antarctica into the setting for melodrama, only shows his own shallow fierceness. This is not simply to fall into the traditional English disapproval of Amundsen. Instead it is my overall stance that Polar travel was materially futile, but in terms of imagination, spirit and character utterly compelling. It is Amundsen who is the evasive explorer, and Scott who emerges from the comparison as a figure of hurt, neurotic gravity.

In September 1909, Amundsen said, he worked out a thorough plan at his home, near Christiania. It predicted a return from the Pole to the base-camp in the Bay of Whales on 25 January 1912. In that forecast he proved exact, even if he may have loitered on the return to ensure exactness. He also planned to go due south from the Bay of Whales, thus pioneering a new route, and avoiding the path Scott meant to inherit from Shackleton – 'Without discussion, Scott's route was declared out of bounds.' More important, the traction power on Amundsen's journey would consist entirely of dogs.

Undoubtedly there was secrecy surrounding Amundsen's plans: anyone who knew of them could have spread the word. The visit of the Scotts to Norway early in 1910 must have given him an anxious time. It is also certain that Nansen was not aware of Amundsen's plans. Temperamentally he could not have known and kept silent to the Scotts. Indeed, reading between the lines, one detects a certain distaste in Nansen for Amundsen's uncompromising methods. One bulky object to be hidden was the hut that Amundsen would use as living quarters in the south. It was twenty-six feet by thirteen feet, and twelve feet high at the ridge, and Amundsen put it together in the grounds of his own house to avoid rumour and speculation. In many other respects he could disguise the real needs of Antarctica as those he might reasonably expect in the

Arctic. The hut did obtrude, since in the ice wasteland of
the north the ship was man's home.

By June 1910, the month of Scott's departure, the *Fram*
was ready to set out. But, of the men going, only Amundsen
and Captain Nilsen were aware of the real destination. Even
Helmer Hanssen, who had been with Amundsen on the
Gjoa, thought that he was on his way north. Hanssen came
aboard, one of twenty men, half of whom were only
engaged as far as San Francisco. They rigged out the ship
and then, to Hanssen's surprise, went to Amundsen's
house and loaded the prefabricated hut. Hanssen examined
the hut before it was dismantled and was puzzled by the
kitchen range and sleeping berths for nine men: 'The
house was to be an observatory, I was told. But I was very
doubtful whether such a large elaborate building would be
of any use in the drift ice. I thought our plan was to drift
across the Arctic Ocean and I told Captain Nilsen that no
power on earth would get me to sleep in that house, built
on drift ice. But Captain Nilsen suddenly disappeared and
after that he did not seem to want to talk any more about
this house.'

On the evening of 6 June – as the *Terra Nova* entertained
guests off Portsmouth – a farewell supper was held in
Amundsen's garden. Auspiciously departure was set for the
next day, anniversary of the formal dissolution of union
between Sweden and Norway. The astute publicist had
ensured that the surprise he would cause in Norway could
be interpreted as a flamboyant patriotic gesture. The *Fram*
went on exercises for several weeks, to Scotland and back
to Bergen, so that the men could become familiar with the
ship. Then it slipped back to Fredricksholm and took on
board ninety-seven dogs from Greenland.

The real voyage began on 9 August amid an atmosphere
of growing disquiet in the crew. The hut had bewildered
Hanssen. No one could guess why the dogs were taken on

so early when Alaska could provide as many as were
required. Furthermore the decks were cluttered with
timber that California possessed in ample supply. Amundsen
noted that the men's faces 'began to resemble notes of
interrogation'. Nilsen was endlessly questioned. So much
on edge, Amundsen took two others into his confidence –
Prestrud and Gjertsen – and was delighted when they both
agreed to go along with the new plans.

They reached Madeira early in September. Amundsen's
brother, Leon, was waiting there. Leon was not an explorer,
but an accomplished businessman who acted as manager to
the expedition and handled many matters that were too
subtle for his bold brother. For instance, when Scott had
sent Amundsen a pendulum marking their proposed
journeys to the opposite ends of the earth, it was Leon who
decided that it would be most politic not to acknowledge
the gift. Leon was in Funchal, Madeira, with the Norwegian
consul, Rocha Machado carefully preparing to divulge his
brother's intention to the world. The *Fram* took on fruit,
vegetables and water and Machado arranged a festival for
the Norwegians.

They stopped at Funchal four days and then put out to
sea again. On the sultry afternoon of 9 September, in
Funchal Roads, Amundsen called every man on deck. Leon
and Nilsen stood beside him and there was a large map of
the southern hemisphere on display. Quickly and simply
Amundsen told them that he planned to go to the North
Pole by way of the South! Hanssen recalled: 'He said he
had deceived us and also the Norwegian nation. But that
could not be helped. He suggested that we should all be
released from our contracts when we got to San Francisco,
and be given free passage home. Anyone on board who
didn't want to go to the South Pole was at liberty to
leave the ship right away and go back to Norway with
Amundsen's brother.'

It is hard to believe that objectors would have been taken to California, and not dumped ashore in Madeira. Every possible pressure had been put on the men to accept, and for many of them there cannot have been too much difference between one Pole and another. Still Amundsen paced the deck nervously and watched the expressions of surprise, but 'before I had finished they were all bright with smiles. I was now sure of the answer I should get when I finally asked each man whether he was willing to go on.' The roll was called and every man said 'yes': 'It is difficult to express the joy I felt at seeing how promptly my comrades placed themselves at my service on this momentous occasion.' The men were then told to go below and write a letter home conveying the altered plans. These letters were given to Leon – he did not post them until he was back in Norway – who was then taken back to Funchal from where he sent the telegram to Scott, once the *Fram* was out of sight.

A month behind schedule now, the *Terra Nova* came in view of Melbourne on 12 October. Again she had been slow. Until a fierce storm near the end that might have carried away a mast, the wind had been moderate and the voyage uneventful. Scott's presence had stilled much of the more violent ragging, but he had taken every opportunity to judge the members of the party. Crossing the Indian Ocean, he published the names of the landing party. There was one notable alteration: Rennick was replaced by Bowers. This was no discredit to Rennick. Instead it showed the deep impression made on Scott by Bowers's capacity for organization. Although his career in the Indian Marine had given no hint of it, Bowers had developed into a meticulous quartermaster, one of the most useful talents Scott required and one that he might have made sure

of before leaving. In landing on Antarctica, and in the preparation for most sledge journeys, Bowers's calculations
and supervision of supplies were instrumental. No one was
as thoroughly promoted during the expedition as Bowers,
and perhaps no one so grew into being himself. In all this,
Bowers remained as popular as he was efficient, and not
even Rennick bore him the least grudge.

Wilson, Kathleen, Oriana Wilson and Hilda Evans were
all in Melbourne awaiting the *Terra Nova*. If there ever
seems the faintest trace of dullness in Wilson, Kathleen may
have discovered it. The force she exerted on Scott shows
itself in that she may sometimes have troubled his best
friend. As the *Terra Nova* approached, Kathleen prevailed on
the others to take a launch and meet Scott at sea. Wilson
thought it too dangerous in heavy seas, but could not resist
Kathleen's determination. They pitched around, with
Scott's wife becoming increasingly unpopular until 'at last
we got close to the beautiful *Terra Nova* with our beautiful
husbands on board. They came and looked down into our
faces with lanterns.' Kathleen alone boarded the ship and
later admitted: 'The relief at getting back to sane folk who
understood me was more than can be written about.' How
much did this 'vagabonding' adventurousness inspire
Scott? Was there ever a moment when the tomboy
wondered whether a woman could go all the way south?

The *Terra Nova* stayed only a few days in Melbourne
before going on to New Zealand under Wilson and
Evans. Scott came ashore in Australia for what Evans
called 'yet another begging campaign'. But before the ship
sailed the officers and wives were entertained by Admiral
Poore – all except Oates who was so devoted to rough
Polar clothes that he had nothing to wear for dinner. Poore
was delighted to see Evans again, who had once been a
midshipman under him, and thought Scott 'a nice straightforward, pleasant *gentleman*'. He inspected the *Terra Nova*

and asked a veteran petty officer – Evans or Crean – how he liked going back. The reply was cool and understated, in the spirit of the leader: 'Oh, I don't know, sir; I thought I'd like to see the end of it.' Simpson noted dourly that the inspection had delayed them one more day.

Scott had hoped for another £5,000 from Australia, but got only half that amount. He did more lecturing, despite his persistent worry that there was 'nothing to give me confidence of being heard'. Everyone was impressed by the assistance and encouragement of Professor Edgeworth David who had been on Shackleton's expedition and yet thought it natural to recruit Debenham for Scott and give him every benefit of his experience. Generosity always touched Scott and he wrote of David in breathless admiration: 'He is wonderful – full of fine enthusiasm – inspiring in efforts to help – palpably honest & sincere – simply and openly religious – a great heart carried with great dignity – a really splendid personality.'

The news of Amundsen does not appear to have ruffled Scott's businesslike surface. He was interviewed in Australia and spoke openly of the dangers – 'We may get through, we may not. We may lose our lives.' – without referring to the Norwegian. Already late, and committed to diverse plans, it would have been difficult and undignified for Scott to summon a sprint. In February 1911, in his journal, he spelled out an attitude of lofty silence towards Amundsen that had probably formed in Melbourne: 'His proceedings have been very deliberate and success alone can justify them. That this action is outside one's own code of honour is not necessarily to condemn it and under no condition will I be betrayed into a public expression of opinion.'

On 28 October the *Terra Nova* sailed into Lyttelton Harbour where it was to spend a further month in repairs, equipping, loading and the task of making farewells. In

New Zealand Scott was able to settle many matters with his agent there, J. J. Kinsey – 'He is a good creature in spite of his pervading personality and his somewhat braggart manner.' This was the final assembly place for the party. Ponting arrived on 25 October, Scott and Kathleen a day later, the latter temporarily tamed by sea-sickness. Meares and Bruce were waiting with dogs and ponies after an involved journey that must have wearied the animals: they had come by ship from Vladivostok to Kobe, then by way of Hong Kong, Manila, New Guinea, Rockhampton, Brisbane and Sydney before a last steamer to Lyttelton. There had been a variety of hot, cramped ships and several compulsory inoculations for the animals. This regime, or their natural fierceness, had made many of the animals unapproachable, and Scott wrote to his young niece telling her that 'the people who don't know them have to be careful not to go too close or they would get bitten'.

Oates was preoccupied with building stalls on the deck of the ship and fretting over whether the ponies would fit into them. Bowers was endlessly shuffling stores to achieve a tighter, secure fit. A temporary office was opened near the cathedral in Christchurch where Griffith Taylor saw piles of letters from the public asking for autographs, penguin eggs and rocks. Every possible ton of coal was being taken on, but funds were dangerously low until a young Australian, Samuel Hordern, saw fit to match his government's £2,500.

Inevitably, as the last of so many departures drew nearer, emotions ran high. The cluster of women seethed in a rivalry of feelings. There had been a steady animosity between Kathleen Scott and Hilda Evans, as if the two wives competed at hating to surrender their husbands. All along Teddy Evans's position as second-in-command was being eroded and this may have been exacerbated on 26 November when Edgar Evans went on another drunk.

Scott 'spoke straight' with the petty officer and said he had disgraced the ship. Evans was told to take the train to Port Chalmers and join the ship after he had had time for sober contrition. But two days later, as the *Terra Nova* made ready to leave, Scott found Teddy 'much excited with very vague and wild grievance'. Oates claimed that Kathleen and Hilda had had a fifteen-round row and the tempestuous Mrs Scott put this derisive comment in her diary: 'All went well, till on the wharf we met the Evanses, both in a tearful condition. Apparently she had been working him up to insurrection and a volley of childish complaints was let fly. Such as that Con had cut his wife's dance, and many others too puerile to recount, and therefore he must retire. Their tantrums spoilt the day and prevented us from being happy. If ever Con has another expedition, the wives must be chosen more carefully than the men – better still, have none.' Oates remarked drily that the party had been affected by this 'coolness' and trusted that it would not linger on in the hut in the south.

Finally, on 29 November – six weeks late – the *Terra Nova* headed south, laden down perilously, the decks almost jammed with equipment, forage and pony stalls. The wives were in tears, or staring out to sea white-faced. Yet, in later years, Kathleen Scott's recollection was gilded and framed like a Victorian genre picture: 'In agonies and ecstasies of reciprocated love I followed my husband. With a queer elation and serenity I said goodbye to him as his ship left New Zealand for its long voyage to the South. I watched his face radiating tenderness as the space between us widened, until I held my memory of that upturned face, but held it for a lifetime.'

Other views were mordant and practical. Oates wrote to his mother as he did whatever he could for the ponies and voiced more fully than anyone else the question of where the Norwegians might be. Every delay had pained Oates.

Scott's Men

Not all of Scott's men were as disinclined to race as the leader; nor did Amundsen's tight-lipped tactics seem too alien to the morose 'soldier' become a deckhouse groom:

What do you think about Amundsen's expedition. If he gets to the Pole first we shall come home with our tails between our legs and no mistake. I must say we have made far too much noise about ourselves. All that photographing cheering, steaming through the fleet, etc. etc. is rot and if we fail it will only make us look more foolish. They say Amundsen has been underhand in the way he has gone about it but I personally don't see it is underhand to keep your mouth shut. I myself think these Norskies are a very tough lot. They have 200 dogs and Yohandsen is with them and he is not exactly a child. Also they are very good ski-runners while we can only walk. If Scott does anything silly such as underfeeding his ponies he will be beaten as sure as death.

9
Life in the Antarctic

In this chapter, without doing violence to the chronological narrative, I would like to explore the society of men who lived in the Antarctic. What interests me is the everyday atmosphere behind the achievement and tragedy: the character and mood of men willing to go away from the busy world to live together, in hardship and community, to measure themselves against a receding wilderness. What simplicity the life offered! What conviction seems to radiate from the men. Yet how near they now seem to a futile and fatal pursuit.

The Polar night had once overwhelmed men's spirit. Nothing of that calamity befell Scott's party. On the contrary, snug in their hut throughout a Polar winter, ingeniously busy and resourceful, endlessly playful and humorous, they seem a charmed group, a Navy ship happily becalmed, but with provisions enough to last out eternity. This is not to patronize Scott's men, only to suggest that they were a decent, enterprising but never intimate company, the model of desirable society for reserved officers and gentlemen.

It is part of that attitude to admire common sense and avoid emotion. Cherry-Garrard attempts to be matter-of-fact in recalling the hut, but does not keep a note of fond nostalgia from creeping in. The hut was somewhere a variety of men could live together without revealing themselves; it was based strictly on order; it established amiability but seldom anything deeper than that. The hut shows us the comradeship and the limits of Scott's men, and one needs to hear the passionate understatement in Cherry-Garrard's memory: 'Whatever merit there may be in going to the Antarctic, once there you must not credit yourself for being there. To spend a year in the hut at Cape Evans because you explore is no more laudable than to spend a month at Davos because you have consumption, or to spend an English winter at the Berkeley Hotel. It is just the most comfortable thing and the easiest to do under the circumstances.' It is a delightful trick – but a trick nonetheless – that makes such strenuous extremism seem natural and sensible.

As the *Terra Nova* lurched south, Scott admired the tight fit, everything crammed to the last inch that Bowers had been able to contrive, ship and contents as solid as a handshake. Sea-sickness affected some of the men and the animals were miserable on deck with no room for exercise. Below decks too it was 'a squash', but the more congenial for that. On the ship, as in the hut later, meals were ritual occasions in the day, when men sat with elbows tucked in, sharing in the formal arrangement and the banter, and in the unwritten faith that privacy would not be invaded. 'Merry are the meals we have in the wardroom,' wrote Griffith Taylor, impressed by four big feeds every day. The steward would appear some forty-five minutes ahead of time with the call 'Table, sir!' which warned the officers and scientists to clear away what they were doing and set digestive juices working. The settled framework is evident in all accounts, and it is as reliable as that at a grand hotel, in a sanitarium or on board one of Her Majesty's ships. The menu may have been monotonous – soup, mutton with potatoes, beans or kale, plum-duff, roly-poly pudding or apple pie – but the servings were large and the food wholesome. And afterwards there was singing, a toast to 'Wives and Sweethearts' and even an impromptu concert on piano, banjo and mandolin. It is the ideal mess life, adaptable to peace or war, and it is convenient as a way for men to live in a group without intruding on one another or falling into soul-searching.

The traits most respected in this community are hardiness, team-spirit and moderation, all of which require a routine to sustain them and keep off anything that smacks of wildness, intuition or obsession. It is a scale that prefers physical ordeal to intellectual inquiry. Thus it is not accurate to see Scott's men as hampered by problems of weather, existence and food. The physical severity actually brought out the best in them. The threat to survival delayed an examination of the quality of life. Such men are deeply conservative, hopeful for a reliable order in things that they are striving to protect against vague but constant perils. There is another point of view – that the existing order may not always be worthy – but it is rarely evident among Scott's men. Thus they see character in overcoming material threats: effort and labour become shining features of human integrity. For someone as timid as Scott, British Antarctic exploration reaffirmed a stable way of life, increasingly a phantom in Britain itself. The years in the south were also a time of labour disputes, unrest in Ireland, suffragist hunger strikes, the final humiliation of the House of Lords, the beginning of decline for the Liberal Party, a Royal Commission on divorce, the simultaneous fame of Elinor Glyn and E. M. Forster and the opening of the Diaghilev ballet in London.*

* This has to be only a sketch of England's history. But the state of the country at the time need not be left out of account as a factor contributing to the journey south. The interested reader is recommended

That would suppose a reluctance in many of Scott's men to face the tumult in the years 1910–14. This escapism could make a virtue out of overt, manageable tasks, as if to say that less soluble dilemmas did not exist. For instance, after one very taxing night on the voyage south, Bowers wrote, 'Under its worst conditions this earth is a good place to live in'. He seems to be saying that, even in the most trying circumstances, life is bracing. Yet it does not wrench the words out of the context in which Scott's men lived to wonder whether they sometimes found fulfilment in the most terrible physical conditions. Then Antarctica is the one place where life is bearable.

The adventure Bowers was describing might have destroyed the expedition, and substantially reduced its means of transport. A storm came up and the leakage in the *Terra Nova* proved more than pumping could contain. The water level rose in the stokehold, the sleeping quarters were awash and then the furnaces were put out. The overladen ship was surely sinking, with coal sludge choking the pumps. A pony died and a dog was swept overboard. In desperation a plan was agreed to cut a hole in the engine room bulkhead so that the small, agile Bowers and Evans could crawl into the pump-well and clear away the slurry. Bowers later described the height of the crisis in a way that shows us Scott and the other men at their best. More than that, the danger seems to permit a freedom not felt at other times:

Captain Scott was simply splendid, he might have been at Cowes, and to do him and Teddy Evans credit, at our worst strait none of our landmen who were working so hard knew how serious things were. Capt. Scott said to me quietly – 'I am afraid it's a bad business for us – What do you think?' I said we

to pursue George Dangerfield's *The Strange Death of Liberal England* (London, 1966) which shows how uncomfortable England was in the years before 1914 for anyone threatened by change.

were by no means dead yet, though at that moment, Oates, at peril to his life, got aft to report another horse dead; and more down. And then an awful sea swept away our lee bulwarks clean, between the fore and main riggings – only our chain lashings saved the lee motor sledge then, and I was soon diving after petrol cases. Captain Scott calmly told me that they 'did not matter'. – This was our great project for getting to the Pole – the much advertised motors that 'did not matter'; our dogs looked finished, and the horses were finishing, and I went to bale with a strenuous prayer in my heart, and 'Yip-i-addy' on my lips, and so we pulled through that day.

Once that crisis had been overcome, the *Terra Nova* fell into the pattern of delay that had beset it ever since London, and which only now seemed to worry Scott. The ship worked under sail and steam, but Scott was anxious to give the wind every chance in order to protect his limited stocks of coal. His notebook has many calculations about how far the coal could last and how much was consumed in raising steam. For nearly three weeks the ship was caught in the pack ice, with Scott agonizing over whether to raise steam or trust to the drift a little longer. In that time they averaged eighteen miles a day and used up over sixty tons of coal. Such delay devoured resources, inevitably increased the costs of the venture, further reduced the constitution of the animals and began to foreclose operating options. Under such pressure another pattern emerges: of a harrowed commander trying to conceal his feelings from a merry company. Throughout December 1910 we can hear two voices in Scott's journal: the cheerful, forthright address to the men, and the inner nagging of a worrier going over his problems. Here is the conflict, in the space of two days:

December 22: There is not a vestige of swell, and with the wind in this direction there certainly ought to be if the open water was reasonably close. No, it looks as though we'd struck a streak of real bad luck; that fortune has determined to put every difficulty in our path. We have less than 300 tons of coal left in a ship that simply eats coal. It's alarming – and then there are the ponies going steadily down-hill in condition. The only encouragement is the persistence of open water to the east and south-east to south; big lanes of open water can be seen in that position, but we cannot get to them in this pressed-up pack.

December 23: Very little can happen in the personal affairs of our company in this comparatively dull time, but it is good to see the steady progress that proceeds unconsciously in cementing the happy relationship that exists between the members of the party. Never could there have been a greater freedom from quarrels and trouble of all sorts. I have not heard a harsh word or seen a black look. A spirit of tolerance and good humour pervades the whole community, and it is glorious to realize that men can live under conditions of hardship, monotony, and danger in such bountiful good comradeship.

There again is a glimpse of sublimity in the capacity of men to weather adversity; and again it is as if man could attain no higher state, in Scott's opinion. It is not too far from some monastic scheme, that a man's integrity and quality may manifest themselves in physical durability and the faith that remains cheerful under all stress. The creed is robust, anti-neurotic but depending on a graspable order that has never been under such withering scrutiny. The real feelings of men may be evaded by the creed's willing adoption of social or military ranking. The greatest test Scott could have submitted to would have been to talk candidly and intimately with other men. He was excused that test by virtue of being commander. Thus a Bowers could see Scott's perplexity but could not interfere in it: 'Capt. Scott, who has to face all the anxiety and worry of things, but never shows it, is splendid; he is geniality itself, and you could not imagine a more congenial leader or one that inspires more confidence.' We think of Wilson as Scott's closest companion, but the distinctions of command and the ultimate craving for discretion kept them apart in the last resort. Wilson was not an initiator, not a man to act on his thoughts. He was detached, kindly and responsive. Thus he would take up a man's cause, as tactfully as possible, if asked. Left to himself, he became the absorbed mystic. In the days of Scott's fraught discussion with himself on where to land, Wilson wrote this to his wife:

I simply love the Crow's Nest – my private chapel. I have spent the happiest times you can possibly imagine there . . . alone with God and with you . . . and nothing above but the sky and snow-squalls, and nothing below but the sea and miles of ice. I have an excellent reason for being up there, for I am making pencil sketches, and no one wonders why I am there so often, and the pull of the rope always warns me when anyone is coming . . . I feel as much at home there as in a church.

The ship broke through the pack, but was unable to make a landing at Cape Crozier without great risk and difficulty. Scott admitted 'Reluctantly and sadly we have had to abandon our cherished plan'.* They therefore rounded Ross Island and headed into McMurdo Sound, past Shackleton's base at Cape Royds to another cape which Scott 'rechristened Cape Evans in honour of our excellent second-in-command'. There was a good landing place and a sheltered position for the hut and, on 4 January 1911, the *Terra Nova* made fast with ice anchors. Scott was still wondering how secure the ice was and how easy communications would be with Cape Royds and the old *Discovery* hut. The site was safe but it gave a slow, problematic start to every sledging journey south, so that no party ever set off with a swift, immediate penetration of the Barrier. But only time underlined that handicap. After a prolonged

* The perplexities of landing did not teach Scott belated sympathy for Shackleton's dilemma. On the march, however, Scott always compared the two journeys.

voyage, and so many anxieties, Scott took heart from the fine weather that greeted them at Cape Evans:

After many frowns fortune has treated us to the kindest smile – for twenty-four hours we have had a calm with brilliant sunshine. Such weather in such a place comes nearer to satisfying my ideal of perfection than any condition that I have ever experienced. The warm glow of the sun with the keen invigorating cold of the air forms a combination which is inexpressibly health-giving and satisfying to me, whilst the golden light on this wonderful scene of mountain and ice satisfies every claim of scenic magnificence.

The unloading was difficult, exhausting and largely the responsibility of Bowers. A party of men lived on the ice in a tent in order to erect the hut more quickly. By 7 January Scott was encouraged by the emergence of a solid building: 'The station is beginning to assume the appearance of an orderly camp. We continue to find advantages in the situation; the long level beach has enabled Bowers to arrange his stores in the most systematic manner. Everything will be handy and there will never be a doubt as to the position of a case when it is wanted.' The persistent appreciation of tidiness gives a hint of how much disorder would disturb Scott.

The hut when finished was fifty feet long and twenty-five feet wide. There was eight feet clearance at the eaves, and sixteen at the ridge. The building material was wood, but thorough insulation was employed everywhere. On the side walls there was double boarding on either side of the frames, with seaweed quilt linings between them. The roof had two layers of matchboarding, then a thickness of rubber and cork insulation, more seaweed, another layer of matchboarding and finally more rubber and cork. On the floor there were two layers of boarding separated by felt and seaweed and, inside the hut, heavy linoleum. Volcanic dust was piled all round the base of the hut to exclude draught.

Then, against the south and east sides, the pony forage was stacked up, and on the north side the ponies themselves were stabled.

The company moved into the hut on 17 January and were 'simply overwhelmed with its comfort'. There was a stove at one end of the hut and the cook's galley at the other, so that a temperature of 52°F was maintained – much less than modern central heating allows, and low enough to demand jackets and jerseys inside the hut, but adequate, and to be compared with an outside temperature that regularly reached −45°.

On that first day in the hut Scott took a decision characteristic of his expedition, but one, apparently, that he had not foreseen. The industrious Bowers was marking out cubicles 'as I had arranged, but I soon saw these would not fit in, so instructed him to build a bulkhead of cases which shuts off the officers' space from the men's, I am quite sure to the satisfaction of both'. Thus the hut was made into two rooms, the one approximately twice the size of the other. Scott and fifteen scientists and officers lived in the larger of the two, with nine men in the other.

Today it seems a bleak adherence to distinctions of rank and society that twenty-five men at the end of the earth, depending upon one another for survival, should be separated by a wall made of packing cases put up at the last moment in a hut that was planned to be open. That does not mean that, in 1911, it would not have seemed as reasonable and proper to the majority, as it did to Scott. We may be tempted to interpret the barricade as a sign of Scott's social limitations, but no one else on his expedition raised a similar objection. It was clear to everyone involved that naval practices obtained wherever possible, and more than half the party in the hut were Navy men perhaps disconcerted by undue tendencies towards openness. Thus Scott talks of the wall or barrier being a bulkhead, pretending they are still in a ship. Nor is it any proof of democracy (let alone evidence that democracy is beneficial) if twenty-five men live together in one hut, sharing in as many things as possible.

But one fascination of Scott's men is that they lived in that hut shortly before the sense of democracy became imperative in Britain. In examining their use of distinction, there is no reason to criticize them, but there is some hope of discovering more about how they thought and what they believed was important. Scott's action is offered as much for the benefit of the men as for that of the officers and gentlemen. In fact there may even have been a conference on the matter between Scott and the officers who led other long-term parties on the expedition. Six men made up the eastern party: Lieutenant Campbell, Dr Levick, Raymond Priestley and three seamen – Abbott, Browning and Dickason. During their ferocious ordeal they spent some months in a cave only twelve feet by nine, and yet this is how Priestley described the allotting of territory within the cave:

Soon after we abandoned our tents and moved into the cave, Campbell did one of these things which seem strange at the time of their doing and will probably seem stranger still to anyone who was not with us, but which made, in the end, all the difference in the world to our compatibility and contributed enormously to the good fellowship and the understanding that prevailed between all of us to the end.

With everyone assembled and wondering what he was up to, Campbell, using the sole of his boot, drew a line down the center of the cave. Pointing to the area occupied by the enlisted men, he said, 'That becomes the messdeck.' Pointing to our side, he said, 'This will be the quarterdeck. You, Priestley, will have a simulated rank as a commissioned officer in His Majesty's Navy. Once each week, I shall inspect all quarters. As on board ship, everything that is said and done on the messdeck will be the responsibility of the men and it shall not be heard or paid attention to or interfered with by any of the officers who reside on the quarterdeck. And the opposite shall prevail. The men shall not hear anything that is said by the officers.'

Commander Campbell knew that our enlisted men had come up from the ranks in the Royal Navy. They had been in it since they were young boys, and he knew they would feel uncomfortable with too much familiarity with the officers and the loss of the sense of belonging to the messdeck. From that day onward, each of us knew exactly where he stood and this contributed enormously to our tranquility.

The expressions of satisfaction are all from officers or gentlemen, and so often they are made with a candour and a lack of subtlety that fails to see how far a passing remark reflects a state of mind – 'From that day onward, each of us knew exactly where he stood and this contributed enormously to our tranquility.' But there are a few demurring voices, and some arguments that must be set against the decisive kindness of Scott and Campbell. Charles Wright has pointed out that in the second winter at Cape Evans, when Dr Atkinson, a naval surgeon, commanded the group of men who waited to discover the fate of the Polar party, 'there was no actual or imaginary line of demarcation . . . I think it worked very well indeed within our party of thirteen and *might* have worked in the first winter, though not so successfully'. Shackleton observed no strict division of class, and Amundsen's party lived on equal footing. That equity had nothing directly to do with Norwegian success in getting to the Pole first; but it did represent the common purpose in Amundsen's party and the shared sense of a proper way to proceed. The barriers in Scott's group may not have accentuated rifts and differences, but perhaps they were the outward demonstration of doubts.

There is, if nothing else, a contradiction between the partitioned hut and a tent routine on the march that observed no such differences. Some of Scott's men have dismissed the idea that, among the final five, Edgar Evans was socially uneasy or lacked for his own company. But, if Evans was as relaxed as ever, then how far was Scott really catering to the sensibilities of the men in building a packing case wall? The men are silent on the point, just as they were trained in the Navy to do as they were told. In which case, it is no wonder that they conformed as tranquilly to Atkinson's open plan as to Scott's partition. Moreover the wall then becomes the sign of a certain vulnerability among the officers, and in Scott especially. In this respect it is worth noting that Scott isolated himself from the other officers, as much as he separated the officers from the men. When Campbell and Priestley speak warmly about how 'each of us knew exactly where he stood', the implication must be drawn that Scott was unusually insecure about his position and authority.

Campbell's instruction that conversations were not to be heard across the line is very like the tact that existed between masters and servants. As such it may be regarded in two ways: it is mannerly, considerate and civilized; but it has the daunting impact of a wall. It is true that any Navy ship in 1911 would have distinguished men from gentlemen more thoroughly than was ever possible in Scott's hut. The navies of most countries would still insist on such distinctions today. Through more than four years of trench warfare there were the same invisible gulfs between ranks, as effective as wire, mud or no man's land. But it is Scott's preconception that forces us into treating his expedition like a military operation. In many respects it aspired to be more: an inquiry into natural phenomena; an attempt to find peace away from the discord of Europe; and, not least, in Scott's eyes, a search for single purpose and social cohesion. No one speaks more movingly of the bonds between the men than Scott; yet he quietly clung to some policies that make his optimism always a little suspect:

The spirit of the enterprise is as bright as ever. Every one strives to help every one else, and not a word of complaint or anger has been heard on board. The inner life of our small community is very pleasant to think upon and very wonderful considering the extremely small space in which we are confined.

The packing cases also reinforced some of the expedition programmes. Once the Polar night had closed in, the enlisted men had much less to do than the scientists and officers. The scientists seldom entrusted their delicate machinery to others, and they insisted on taking all readings and soundings themselves. Griffith Taylor noticed the way in which the seamen were given an odd privilege in having fewer duties than the officers:

It must have been a topsy-turvy experience for them to see the weary watchman – who was always one of the officers during 1911 – nodding or shivering over the stove, while they snugly slept through the night.

Occasionally, if the unfortunate officer fell over the fire-irons, or otherwise disturbed the 'mess deck', the sailor men would permit themselves the luxury of caustic remarks behind their curtains – well knowing that the chance of scoring off a member of the 'afterguard' would not occur in a less socialistic community.

There were now three huts within a few miles: Shackleton's at Cape Royds, the old *Discovery* hut and the most recent at Cape Evans. Scott's men visited the other two and were intrigued or disturbed by the frigid dereliction that so nearly mimicked their own warm hut. The detritus and leavings of prior expeditions could impress subsequent parties with the fleeting impact man made in Antarctica, though it did not always remind them that their own base would one day be a frozen relic of habitation. But, even in the matter of excursions to the former hut, we can see a difference between Scott and some of his young colleagues.

Wright and Griffith Taylor went on an expedition to Shackleton's hut that Scott later scolded them for. They remarked on the quantity of rubbish around the hut and found a letter from Professor David pinned to the door 'in case the *Nimrod* is lost on her return voyage'. Taylor had been David's pupil and was tickled to find the redundant note. He gave it to Scott for historical interest, never guessing the impact that Scott's last writings would have when retrieved months after his death. The two young men forced a way into the hut and found it intact, with every sign of how hurriedly Shackleton's party had left. Books were on the floor and socks rigid on a line. 'At the back was a tray from the oven with a batch of scones just cooked, and a loaf of bread. I lifted the latter, and the whole outer surface peeled away, leaving a ball in the middle.' But there were many edibles remaining: bottled fruit, plum pudding, sardines, pickles, onions and sausages. Scott later visited the hut and found 'a good quantity of flour and Danish butter and a fair amount of paraffin, with smaller supplies of assorted articles – the whole sufficient to afford provision for such a party as ours for about six or eight months if well administered. In case of necessity this would undoubtedly be a very useful reserve to fall back upon. These stores are somewhat scattered, and the hut has a dilapidated, comfortless appearance due to its tenantless condition.'

That was written in May 1911, by which time Scott's respect for a tidy Antarctic home and his near contempt for Shackleton had already coincided in an unhappy visit to the old *Discovery* hut. Shackleton's men had occasionally used the hut for shelter but, whereas the *Nimrod* hut had been left properly sealed, Scott's hut had been abandoned with an open window so that the interior was now packed with ice and snow. 'It is difficult to conceive the absolutely selfish frame of mind that can perpetrate a deed like this,'

Scott wrote in his journal. Ten days later there was an attempt to dig out the hut, but the snow was frozen hard. Again Scott's journal seethed against Shackleton in a passage that was deleted before publication:

Everyone was disgusted with the offensive condition in which the hut had been left by its latest occupants. Boxes full of excrement were found near the provisions and filth of a similar description was thick under the verander [sic] and some in the corners of the hut itself. Its extraordinary to think that people could have lived in such a horrible manner and with such absence of regard for those to follow – It seems evident that in no case can we inhabit our old Hut.

Within a month of the unpleasant findings at the *Discovery* hut Scott's men had more shattering news. Towards the end of January the *Terra Nova* prepared to sail north for the winter, depositing Campbell and the eastern party on its way. Scott was by now greatly impressed by Pennell, who would be in charge of the ship: 'They have behaved like bricks and a finer lot of fellows never sailed in a ship. It was good to get their hearty send-off.' The *Terra Nova* sailed east and, on 3 February, rounded the western headland of the Bay of Whales to find the *Fram* at anchor there.

The Norwegian ship had come south without stopping anywhere other than Madeira; it had made its way in some ten weeks less than the *Terra Nova*. *Fram* only crossed the Antarctic Circle on 2 January 1911 and sighted the Barrier nine days later. It took two weeks to unload and build the hut on a site, called Framheim, just over two miles inland. The Norwegian base was constructed on Barrier ice, but Amundsen was confident that there was solid rock beneath it and that the location was not hazardous. On 28 January his land party of nine men had taken up residence in the hut.

The British were astonished by the actual ship which they had only seen in illustration from books. Priestley, who was on the *Terra Nova*, wrote later, 'I think that at that time no member of the ship's company had any idea that we had any rivals in this portion of the Antarctic, though most of us knew that Amundsen intended to try for the Pole'. Amundsen had made his landing provocatively near Scott's, in an area where the British plans had talked of operating, and in such a place that the two paths to the Pole would be dramatically similar and nearly parallel. Within the context of Antarctic geography, Amundsen had put himself in the next lane to Scott, and not, as some of the English party had anticipated, in an opposite part of the continent. But not every one of Scott's men even knew that the Norwegians were mounting a simultaneous expedition. The telegram at Melbourne had not reached all members of the close company. Petty Officer Frank Browning wrote in his diary: 'The discovery of the *Fram* in this quarter was a surprise to all; of course we had heard rumours of other expeditions, one from Japan, but we thought the Norwegians were going North.'

The meeting was carried off as politely as possible on both sides. The *Terra Nova* dropped anchor alongside the *Fram* and Campbell went on board to meet the lone watchman. Amundsen and the rest were at Framheim, and when they arrived with empty sledges next morning they were as surprised as the British had been. The two nations were together half a day. Campbell, Pennell and Levick were invited to take breakfast on the *Fram* and Amundsen and two other Norwegians went to lunch on the *Terra Nova*. In addition the men were at liberty to look over one another's quarters. There were many piquant moments. When Amundsen complained of lack of news Browning gathered together a bundle of newspapers and magazines from the *Terra Nova*. The English offered to carry any

Norwegian mail, but Amundsen said he was too busy to write at the moment. Helmar Hanssen remembered that, on board the *Fram*, some of the English seamen were taken to the saloon for aquavit: 'While they were drinking some of our men came into the saloon, and the Englishmen were afraid they were officers and did not want to be seen standing about drinking. It was explained to them that on board the *Fram* the officers lived forward, and the crew aft, and that each man had his own cabin. This impressed them so much that they did not believe it was true.'

There seems to have been no outward animosity, though both sides must have been alert and tense. Tryggve Gran was not present at the meeting, but he may have gathered this conversation from subsequent meetings with some of the other Norwegians. Apparently Campbell was the most defensive of the Englishmen, and when Amundsen asked him how the motor sledges were faring at Cape Evans Campbell replied – with less than truth – that the sledges were remarkable and probably, at that moment, well on their way towards the Beardmore Glacier.

When the English left, the Norwegians found that they had contracted irritating nose colds. The effect on Scott's men was profound. They had all been impressed by the Norwegians as 'men of distinctive personality, hard, and evidently inured to hardship, good goers, and pleasant and good-humoured'. Amundsen's inquiry about the motor sledges may have been only a pleasantry or a cool tease from a man who had probably gathered his own reports of the trials held in Norway. Of more significance was the lesson the English learned from the quality and quantity of the Norwegian dogs. Priestley had been an impressed spectator of a performance from Amundsen himself that may have been calculated to deplete English morale:

I think that no incident was so suggestive of the possibilities latent in these [dog] teams as the arrival of Amundsen at the side of the *Terra Nova*. His dogs were running well, and he did not check them until he was right alongside the ship. He then gave a whistle, and the whole team stopped as one dog. With a word of command he inverted the empty sledge and came on board, leaving the animals to themselves; and there they remained until their master had finished his visit. They were all exceptionally strong-looking brutes and completely under control; and when dogs are good they have no compeers as draught animals under Polar conditions.

The *Terra Nova* went back immediately to Cape Evans and left a message that Scott received on 22 February as he returned from his depot-laying journey towards next summer's southern advance. We have a good insight into the first reaction of the main party in Cherry-Garrard's temper. At first they were 'furiously angry, and were possessed with an insane sense that we must go straight to the Bay of Whales and have it out with Amundsen and his men in some undefined fashion or other there and then'. A more astute man than Scott might have done that and seriously embarrassed Amundsen with a proposal for collaboration. With two ships to employ, a pack of dogs and all Scott's alternative transports, with an assault team set on the Pole and a band of scientists, much could have been done by an Anglo–Norwegian party employing two bases. All Amundsen's opportunism could have been pierced by a subtle proposal; the pressure of the race might have been drained away into the snow. That it was not suggests that Scott was as implacable a non-sharer as Amundsen, and that he was not fully alive to a rare opportunity for science.

Cherry-Garrard harked back to that confused myth of Polar priority to explain English feelings: 'We had just paid the first instalment of the heart-breaking labour of making a path to the Pole; and we felt, however unreasonably, that

we had earned the first right of way. Our sense of coopera-
tion and solidarity had been wrought up to an extraordinary pitch; and we had so completely forgotten the
spirit of competition that its sudden intrusion jarred
frightfully.' In that mood there must have been some in
the party – Teddy Evans and Oates, perhaps – who would
have done everything possible to make a race of it still, who
would have responded to the challenge. Yet Scott, once his
anger had gone down, chose to ignore the Norwegians:
'One thing only fixes itself definitely in my mind. The
proper, as well as the wiser, course for us is to proceed
exactly as though this had not happened.' That is inflexibility merging with hurt dignity. A wiser, less predictable
commander might have amended his plans, especially as
Scott foresaw that, with so many dogs safely landed,
Amundsen had a striking advantage and a shorter distance
to the Pole. It is worth stressing that, whatever his opinion
of dogs, Scott had little doubt about what Amundsen
would manage with his. Scott talks of the 'excellent'
Norwegian plan for running dogs, and the advantage they
had over ponies in starting earlier in the season. At the
least this adds confusion to Scott's own attitude to dogs and
makes us more aware of his loathing of having to ill-treat
them.

An adroit attempt to join forces would have been alien to
a man with so little cunning. Yet, aware of his own
disadvantages, Scott elected to take part in a race while
trying to persuade himself that he was acting independently.
Had Scott possessed the judgement of Amundsen, he might
not have risked and lost the lives of five men. On the other
hand, he would have had to find an appealing alternative,
for his debtor expedition was trapped by its promise to go
to the Pole. That Amundsen made no gesture of companionship is understandable: he was a competitor aware
of his favourable circumstances. For Scott to have united

the two expeditions might have avoided tragedy and would have been an intriguing demonstration of collaboration for the rest of the world. But he did not, and thus two paths converged on the Pole, cutting a slice of cake out of Antarctica.

In one sense it is admirable that Scott was not swayed by Amundsen's presence. It showed steadiness of purpose. Yet, psychologically, it was easier for Scott to act as if nothing had happened. It did save him from reappraisal and improvisation; it also allowed him to overlook the deeper ambivalence in his own approach to the Pole. That tragedy ensued cannot be blamed wholly on rigidity, but it has something to do with it, just as minds made up saw no alternative to the destructive patterns of frontal assault in the First World War. In Scott's day firmness was admired in a commander; today we hope for more inventiveness.

It is interesting to note that, even years later in his book, *South with Scott*, the rather patronized Teddy Evans described the impact of Amundsen with a readiness for changing plans that seems never to have dawned on Scott: 'We spent a very unhappy night, in spite of all attempts to be cheerful. Clearly, there was nothing for us, but to abandon science and go for the Pole directly the season for sledging was advanced enough to make travelling possible after the winter.' Nothing of Scott's plans for the winter seems to have altered, however, and, before examining the British party in their hut through the Polar darkness, it is worth a glimpse of how Amundsen prepared. With the Norwegians there was stringent simplicity and no compromising of the central task.

They lived together, without any difference in leader and led, save for an unquestioning respect among the men for

Amundsen's prowess and his own domineering wish to be the centre of attention. Still, everyone was on first name terms, and practical jokes and cheeky remarks could be directed at Amundsen. After their very thorough preliminary work in laying bases, the Norwegians rested. Amundsen allowed no nightly weather readings, in case anyone's sleep was disturbed, and put as little physical strain on his men as possible while employing all manner of games to keep them mentally alert. During the winter they cared for the dogs and gradually eliminated excess weight from the sledges, so that their unloaded weight came down from 80 to 28 kilo. That is remarkable adaptation and needs to be remembered when the British cry out at the terrible dead weight of their sledges. The Norwegians fed well but plainly: for breakfast hot cakes, jam, bread, butter, cheese and coffee; for lunch seal meat, vegetable and tinned fruit; and in the evening more fresh seal meat, whortleberry jam, cheese, bread, butter and coffee. This kept them fit, and there are claims for the special efficacy of Norwegian whortleberries. But the Norwegians who went to the Pole were required to expend so much less energy that it is impossible to make a close comparison of diets. It is more important that, as they sledged south and back again, the Norwegians killed and ate their dogs without qualms.

We know much more of the British winter, for there were more men there, many of whom kept journals that found a way into print. There may be another reason for the British dwelling more on their life together, which is that it was more important to them than a necessary period of waiting was for the Norwegians. The journals of Scott's men resound with happy tributes to fellowship. As the party celebrated Midwinter 1911, making a tipsy Christmas out of it, Scott wrote: 'If good will and happy fellowship count towards success, very surely shall we deserve to succeed. It was matter for comment, much applauded, that there had not been a single disagreement between any two members of our party from the beginning.'

What pressures and tensions must there have been in a group of men that permitted no disagreements? Or had Scott's fulsomeness forgotten many of his own doubts in the warmth of Midwinter festivities? A great dinner was held that day, with bunting in the hut and a Union Jack down the centre of the table on which champagne, sherry and punch bottles rested. They had seal soup, roast beef with fried potatoes and Brussels sprouts, plum pudding and mince pies, followed by all manner of delicacies – a savoury made from anchovy and cod's roe, crystallized fruit, chocolate bonbons, almonds and raisins. There were toasts and speeches, after which Ponting showed them his photographs of the expedition and home-made music started some of the men dancing with one another. It was a happy day for the cook, Thomas Clissold, and, as he and many others had had too much to drink, so, according to Teddy Evans, 'Clissold so forgot himself as to call Scott "Good old Truegg". Truegg was the composition used by us for cooking in various ways omelets, buttered eggs, puddings, and cakes of all kinds, and, although it was a great boon to the Expedition, we had by this time tired of it. Still, we used it as a term of endearment, but nobody in his sober senses would have dreamt of calling our much respected Commander "Good old Truegg"; the brandy punch must have been responsible for Clissold's mixing up of names!'

One feels for Clissold if that brief shedding of his inhibitions could so easily be explained away. It may be that Scott loomed over the expedition no more forcefully than any Navy captain in his ship. But he was an unusually shy, yearning man, torn between generosity and reticence, between good nature and an overbearing emphasis on self-respect. Anyone drawn to Scott must be saddened that he arranged the expedition in such a way that no one was ever tempted to break down his defences. Freed of them, he might have fallen into a benign ease and maturity.

But Scott lived on his own. He had a private room, or cabin. There was his bed, with his old naval overcoat for an eiderdown, a table and chair, and, on the wall, pipe racks and photographs of Kathleen and his son Peter. Ponting took a photograph of Scott in his room, working on his diary and, at first glance, it is a picture of a writer rather than an explorer. The library is in Scott's cabin and one can see how anyone hesitating to come in and choose a book would be sensed and admitted with a word or two, without dislodging Scott from his work. Shackleton kept the library in his room to waylay others with stories and jokes. For Scott, it was more a matter of the convenience of a writer not wishing to be far from a library. Ponting, who was in some ways closer to Scott than other subordinates could be, observed him shrewdly: 'He had kept much to himself during the winter. He read a great deal – generally books on Polar exploration, relieved by an occasional novel. He worked a great deal on his plans for the future; he wrote much in his diary, and smoked incessantly. Almost invariably he took his exercise alone.'

For very few of the party was such solitariness possible. There were many natural alliances that made for friendly bickering within the hut. Scientists could find themselves surrounded by naval officers; and colonials sometimes teased British stolidness. Atkinson, Oates and Meares were companions, the first two both temperamentally quiet, the latter drawn to them by their interest in animals. Gran and Teddy Evans struck up a friendship that began with their surveying work but flowered in the kinship of two adventurous boasters. Griffith Taylor had a sharp, witty tongue and he wrote several articles for the revived *South Polar Times* that played upon the temperamental groupings in the hut. They do not survive literary scrutiny, but they reflect the superficial distinctions between men that became running jokes in the hut. Thus there were schoolboy gangs – Ubdugs and Bunderlohgs – often based on nothing more substantial than the side of a hut to which chance had directed a man. Campbell's insistence on a line was borne out in the hut where the men in one cubicle fell into cultish, light-hearted rivalry with those in another.

Some deeper differences revealed themselves, though never in passion or acrimony. Perhaps men in groups need to make light of their beliefs if they are to go on living together. Cherry-Garrard, Bowers, Oates, Atkinson and Nelson were all innately conservative, though none of them may ever have voted that way. While the colonials, in contrast, could easily seem radical, and Griffith Taylor was called – in fun and high exaggeration – Keir Hardie. But the civilized world faced many issues to divide conservatism and liberalism and on evening after evening those prepared to do so could stay up in contention. Griffith Taylor was a dedicated arguer and describes such evenings:

We could always rally a strong colonial contingent in the persons of Debenham (Australia) and Wright (Canada); and never have I had such amusing arguments (cags as we called them) as during the Antarctic night. Women's Suffrage I have known argued *ad nauseam* from dinner-time (7 p.m.) till midnight, when Nelson and myself were left still opposed, and still full of argument. Prayers for peace never deterred Nelson from preaching women's inferiority.

Boots were the arguments that usually drove him to seek his cubicle and sink to rest.

There are not many accounts of Scott wandering into such conversations, though he must have overheard them from his cabin. Nor did he easily join in the other commonplace pastimes, beyond taking lessons in photography from Ponting. There was a player piano and a gramophone donated by H.M.V. that must have played every record over and over again. The men played cards most of the time, but in the ward-room the favoured games were chess, backgammon, draughts and dominoes. Nelson was the champion at most games, perhaps the fruit of his time in London clubs. Scott did like chess, but was regularly beaten by Nelson and so took to playing with Atkinson, a man he could himself master.

Inevitably much time was devoted to reading. Oates had a small bust of Napoleon by his bed and was usually reading Napier's *History of the Peninsular War*. Cherry-Garrard had brought the complete Kipling, Day loved Dickens and there were factions to say that Tennyson or Browning was the finest Victorian poet. Reference books were always at hand to settle arguments and the many volumes of Polar history were studied, sometimes with ominous foreboding. In addition there was a supply of cheap editions of popular novels, leading to arguments about the 'depraved' tastes of individuals.

No doubt the winter would have passed well enough with backgammon, records and a programme of Edwardian romances, but Scott's regime was always more high-minded. Scientific work went on unabated and there were several demanding midwinter excursions. In the hut too Scott introduced a sense of purpose in a regular series of lectures: 'the people seem keen and it ought to be exceedingly interesting to discuss so many diverse subjects with experts'. The whole party were invited, though attendance was not compulsory. Most of the officers and scientists were faithful to them, out of genuine interest and a wish to support Scott's faith in education, but many of the seamen stopped coming after one or two. The lectures varied. Some were of riveting interest to everyone: for instance, Scott on his plans for the southern journey. Others were

widely accessible and amusing – Oates on horse management and Bowers on Polar clothing. Ponting gave an
illustrated talk on Burma and Wilson described Antarctic
flying birds. But others were of a more concentrated nature
that often led to elaborate discussion among the scientists
in which Scott manfully strove to keep up: 'To-night
Wright tackled "The Constitution of Matter" with the
latest ideas from the Cavendish Laboratory: it was a tough
subject, yet one carries away ideas of the trend of the work
of the great physicists, of the ends they achieve and the
means they employ. Wright is inclined to explain matter as
velocity; Simpson claims to be with J. J. Thomson in
stressing the fact that gravity is not explained.'

Suddenly the hut could turn into a university seminar
room. There were several brilliant men in the group, and
for those of more ordinary talent the lectures could be out
of reach. Furthermore Scott's diary often contained real
criticism of the performances, so that the younger men had
reason to feel that Scott employed the lectures as a test. For
instance, when Teddy Evans's turn came to speak on
surveying, the published diary says: 'He was shy and slow,
but very painstaking, taking a deal of trouble in preparing
pictures.' Whereas the original is much more disgruntled:
'He is painstaking but has not intelligence of a high order,
consequently his effort was laborious but uninstructive. I
had wanted a summary of general principles with or
followed by hints likely to be useful to our travellers in the
field. We got a halting disquisition on place construction.
Yet the boy tried his best, taking a deal of trouble in preparing pictures, etc.'

It is inevitable that the leader of an expedition should find
shortcomings in some members of the expedition. What is
instructive in this case is the extent of these faults, the way
they lead to something like grievance in Scott, his own
reluctance to deal with them openly and their subsequent

suppression when the diary was published. That last point is neither surprising nor sinister. Many of the comments could not have been decently printed in 1913 and Scott told Kinsey to 'be silent concerning any criticisms' his diary contained. Yet it is striking that there should be so many, and clearly the general estimate of Scott has never had to absorb these outbursts of dismay and irritation. Furthermore some criticisms only illuminate the haste or compromise of original selection. By May 1911 Scott had come to a conclusion about Evans that he could have reached earlier:

Evans himself is a queer study. His boyish enthusiasm carries all along till one sees clearly the childish limitations of its foundation and appreciates that it is not a rock to be built upon. He is altogether a good fellow and wholly well meaning but terribly slow to learn and hence fails altogether to grasp the value of any work but his own. Very desirous to help everyone he is mentally incapable of doing so. There are problems here for I cannot consider him fitted for a superior position. Though he is physically strong & fit for a subordinate one. It was curious to note how his value (in this respect) suddenly diminished as he stepped on shore.

Nothing suggests that Scott ever confronted Evans with his own reservations; instead, they rubbed on themselves in his own mind. Many of Scott's complaints were imprecise, emotional and hardly sustained by other opinions or history. Sometimes they sound like the attempt of an insecure man the better to define his own position. Thus on Nelson, Scott wrote to himself: 'Nelson is very quick & clever, the making of a man who might have gone far, but he is a skimmer, armed with superficial information on many subjects, profound knowledge concerning none. As a fact he will get nowhere in life. He is too typically "dilettantish".'

The sadness of such passages lies in the way they isolate Scott from the body of the expedition. Ponting remarked

how often in the winter Scott seemed to be worrying –
over funds, sledging rations or Amundsen – but hardly
guessed that sometimes the worries dwelt, secretly, on
members of the group. Ponting himself comes in for one
dainty rebuke: 'I've found Ponting is a very charming
character, generous, highly strung, nervous, artistic, but
the effects of his wrestling for existence with the material-
istic conditions in California and showiness has also had its
effect.' Ironically Ponting's greater familiarity with business
was one of the very things that might have alleviated Scott's
anxieties. Scott had often come to Ponting for advice – a
privilege only Wilson shared – so that the photographer had
'discovered how totally inexperienced Scott was in dealing
with the Press. He seemed to have little idea of the value of
photographs made at so remote a part of the earth.' Ponting
had urged Scott to be more shrewd, and the leader allowed
the photographer to negotiate for him when he made his
early return. Yet Ponting found that the expedition was tied
by, and made to suffer from, agreements Scott had made in
1910 and never mentioned to Ponting.

Thus Scott's criticisms – just or unjust – say as much for
his isolation as they do about the objects of attack. In some
cases they read irrationally, or as if based on something
more than a commander's objective estimate of his own
men. The clearest instance of that is his reaction to Tryggve
Gran, who is more remorselessly brooded over than anyone
else. Some reasons for this are clear: Gran and Scott were
temperamentally very different. Gran was also Norwegian,
and Scott was apparently having to subdue his hostility
towards another Norwegian, Amundsen. Gran was a
brash romanticizer, but to many others in the group he
was an attractive character, a source of amusement and, in
general, a valuable man. His chief reason for being there –
to teach the others to ski – may not have been a success, but
that cannot be blamed on Gran.

Scott on Gran is intemperate, suspicious and extreme –
moods otherwise absent in the *Terra Nova* expedition. One
can hardly believe all of this outburst, since it is not backed
up by other witnesses. Therefore one wonders what inner
pressures urged it. But at least in Scott there is the troubled
note of a complex, real man of hurt feelings and fine
ideals:

I sent Gran with Evans to take the sledge & lunch tent run.
Griffith Taylor & party en route to their second sledge were to
help up the hill. Before reaching the cap ridges Gran dropped
down suddenly declaring he had 'cramp' in both legs. He rose up
as I approached & commenced to totter about leaning on
Taylor. From this point I had scant patience & sent him back to
the Hut. When we returned in the evening I told Wilson &
Atkinson to examine him thoroughly. They could find nothing
wrong with him nor could they make head or tail the symptoms
he confusedly described.

Both doctors were convinced that there was nothing the
matter beyond some stiffness caused by the small sledge excursion of last week. I felt there was nothing for it but to tell the
young man exactly what I thought of him and I did so. At the
same time I directed him to keep clear of the fire and to go to
Pram Point the next day to fetch in more blubber. Yesterday he
started on this last mission keeping up the pretence that he
could scarcely walk. When he thought he was observed he
staggered about like a drunken man and as he passed the sledge
party at the top of the hill he seized the opportunity to totter &
fall prone. The whole thing was an elaborate pantomime to
extort pity. I'm afraid it got none. Later we watched the young
man descending Crater Hill. It would have been amusing had it
not been so terrible to see him playing the lame man when he
thought the sledge party might be looking yet walking on
briskly when he imagined himself unobserved. . . .

It was a terrible mistake to bring him but now he is here he
must work and I shall see he does so. But for all practical purposes he is useless to the Expedition and all that remains is to
rid oneself as far as possible of the nuisance of his presence. For

himself and for the contemptuous opinion which he has earned from every member of the Expedition he appears to feel no shame whatever.

The one member of the expedition who shows us such inner disturbance is Scott.

One of the most fascinating and disturbing traits in the British party is their clinging circumspection in such extreme circumstances. This is not to say that several men were not moved by the wilderness, the desolation and the natural evidence of human insignificance. Still the hut was a club; not a London club perhaps, but one that would have fitted any military establishment where club rules held. Of these rules, none was as profound, heartening or disappointing as the unwritten code that institutional hierarchy freed men from deeper philosophical thoughts on their station in life. But perhaps this sounds censorious or carping. Why should men not be jolly, decent and reasonable with one another near the South Pole? Of course they must be, but they might have been more, for surely life is not neatly wrapped up in those qualities? I have compared the Pole with the Moon, and there is another point to be added to that comparison. When Americans landed on the Moon, they sounded like the men they were: trained, eerily normal, undeviant, middle-class, healthy Americans. Therefore they were a little dull; and there was both charm and a deeper sense of valuable human ordinariness in their monotonous, cliché observations. But man has always nurtured the chance of poetry, and perhaps life on Earth now is so perilous that we needed to send a poet to the Moon. None went with Scott, but action itself, in the form of disaster, made a sort of epic poem out of the journey and has ever afterwards left the question of going south in our imaginations.

10

To Reach
the Pole

The task of reaching and returning from the Pole was brutally unsubtle. For it to be done, and recognized by the rest of the world, men – or at the least one man – had to set out from a base on the edge of the Barrier, go over the ice, then ascend the mountains and cross the Polar plateau. Eventually these men would have to decide when they were at the Pole and then stick a flag in the snow that they could round before making the same immense journey in reverse. By the straightest line, the distance from base to the Pole and back again was at least 1,500 miles; though no one could hope for straight lines showing the way. Sound navigation was as necessary as at sea, and for many days on the journey the level expanse of white resembled nothing more than a burnished ocean. Not that the surface would prove as smooth as glass. There was wearying variety. In some places there were concealed crevasses that might not bear the weight of a sledge or a man. Elsewhere the snow could suddenly change from a hard, flat basis aiding traction to slush or gravel that made the sledges ponderous. What looked like flatness from a distance sometimes turned into startling valleys and gradients, as well as the undulating sastrugi, a dune formation in the snow caused by prevailing winds and leaving ridges as much as a foot high.

This journey had either to carry all its food or leave stores on the way out that could be collected on the return.

Thus, immediately, the plans for such a journey have to calculate the length of time it will take, the number of men who will be needed and the burden of food and equipment required to sustain them. The time factor involves an allowance for so many days of blizzard when marching may be impossible, it must estimate the performance of whatever source of power is adopted, and it must remember the span of Polar summer in which travelling is favoured, and the onset of winter where falling temperature, darkness and storm quickly deplete man's energy and resolve.

It remains a long walk in the snow. No matter how carefully a Polar commander has recruited scientists and lectured on the contribution of his exercise to learning, he must recognize that the attention of his own men centres on the way, for something like five months, most efforts and resources will be concentrated on the long walk out and back. It is a journey stripped bare of subsidiary purpose; indeed, the travellers trust that there will be nothing at the Pole. If there is, they will only have to drag it back – be it a fossilized pterodactyl or the cultural emblem of a lost world. As the British came nearer, they strained their eyes to the south and eventually saw the black flag that Amundsen had left there. That curt sign of civilization must have been the most crushing sight of their journey.

I have said that getting to the Pole was brutally unsubtle, and I think that that is why Amundsen was there first. Scott was neither brutal nor unsubtle, and that helps explain why his plans for the journey were so flawed. All through the winter at Cape Evans, Scott was ruminating over his attempt on the Pole, and rehearsing every imagined contingency as he waited to sleep. Three hundred miles along the coast, at Framheim, Amundsen was passing a relaxed winter, his plans made. The Norwegian journey is quickly told, a tidy and emphatic demonstration of its own scheme, remarkable, but neat and single-minded. It was on the Polar journey that Scott's plans fragmented. But the broken pieces only reveal the contradictions, the noble mistakes, the wrongheadedness and the mystical heroism of his men. Already I have wondered whether failure did not fulfil Scott more than success. That does not imply that he consciously sought failure or death. The sequence of endeavour and disappointment was natural and uncontrived, and that is what gives it the impact of tragedy.

When Scott published his prospectus in September 1909, identifying the Pole as his 'main object', he acknowledged Shackleton's 'brilliant results' with ponies over the Barrier and outlined his own intentions:

The plan for the journey to the South Pole from King Edward VII land includes the use of the three means of sledge traction described – ponies will be taken in sufficient numbers to ensure a thoroughly adequate amount of food being taken to the base of the glacier. A dog team with a relay of men will transport the loads over the glacier surface, and a picked party of men and dogs will make the final dash across the inland ice sheet.

The use of the word 'dash' there is a concession by Scott to the public susceptibility to racing and to the enthusiasm of men like Evans. The same prospectus refers to the motor sledges, 'according to their proved capacity', and asserts that they will be used to the extent that their performance allows. Thus, in outline, Scott faced the prospect of coming on to the barrier with both dogs and motor sledges backing up the ponies. He had invested time, faith and money in the vehicles and, before setting out, his optimism reckoned that the motor 'bids fair to become the most promising means of polar transport.'

However, by early May 1911, when Scott spoke to the members of the party in the hut about his plans for going south, his mind had changed: 'I could not but hint that in my opinion the problem of reaching the Pole can best be solved by relying on the ponies and man haulage. With this sentiment the whole company appeared to be in sympathy. Everyone seems to distrust the dogs when it comes to glacier and summit.' Scott asked the men to think over the problem, 'freely discuss it, and bring suggestions to my notice'. Yet there is little documentary evidence of a policy or idea arising within the group and seriously influencing the expedition plans. Similarly, when Scott speaks of 'the sentiment' of 'the whole company' it is questionable whether this is a matter of open, informed discussion or of a band of deferential followers anxious to encourage their commander.

Already cold reality had struck at the motor sledges and the optimism that had attended them. At first they did well. Two out of three were landed from the *Terra Nova* and used to ferry supplies to the hut site. Day and Nelson drove them on several runs in which they carried $1\frac{1}{2}$ to 2 tons. Day bubbled and Scott wrote: 'One begins to believe they will be reliable, but I am still fearing that they will not take such heavy loads as we hoped.' Was there a turmoil of straining optimism and pessimism in Scott that he should yield to hope in taking three unproven motors and then quickly succumb to anxiety that he had erred? In two days there were troubles: the engines overheated and the clutches slipped. Then, on 8 January, what Scott called '*disaster*'. As the third motor sledge was lifted ashore, the ice proved too weak for it and the sledge plunged into the sea beyond recovery. Scott was not present at the loss, but according to Day: 'Before we loaded her the Owner* examined the ice & said it was firm enough. I must say it

---

* Scott was commonly known as 'the Owner' or 'the Boss' to men on the *Terra Nova* expedition. Such terms reflect the proprietorial effort he had made and the constant business-like risk.

certainly looked weak but it has done for some days & I went over the spot late last night with 2 Ton, 3 Ton.'

Day's diary presents a rather gloomy man who saw his own prospects in terms of the motors. Immediately after the loss he wrote: 'My chances do not seem to be too bright as it is & this has not tended to make them brighter.' Furthermore the chains that drove the sledges required wooden rollers that were splitting because of the hard ice. Day was short of spares and confessed 'I have still to break the news to the Owner. Its lucky he's not counting too much on them for the South I am thinking after all.'

In the event the motor sledges did no more than predict a time when more sophisticated, powerful machines might drive across Antarctica. The two remaining sledges were used on the first part of the southern journey and suffered every mishap indicated in their first few days ashore. Even the dedicated Day detected Scott's fundamental mistrust of the motors – 'He has watched them very carefully, like everything else, and did not think they would be of great assistance.' The explanation for the presence of the motors is that Scott himself never faced up to his own doubts. The inventor in him and the would-be scientist was very keen to adopt some novel enterprise, no matter that it obscured the need for clarity and singleness of purpose. If Scott had ever understood that, at best, motors were a far-fetched gamble, then he would have been one step nearer choosing between ponies and dogs. The variety of his transport only fostered indecision and the traits of sentimental prejudice between man and animals and man and motor. As late as September 1911, only six weeks before going south, Scott grasped the limits of the motors yet could not act upon the understanding. This passage from his journal shows how hesitation could be added to by a wish to prove his theory:

I do not count on the motors – that is a strong point in our case – but should they work well our earlier task of reaching the

Glacier will be made quite easy. Apart from such help I am anxious that these machines should enjoy some measure of success and justify the time, money, and thought which have been given to their construction. I am still very confident of the possibility of motor traction, whilst realising that reliance cannot be placed on it in its present untried evolutionary state.

The motors broke down long before the crucial stages of the Polar journey. It is harder to understand why, by May 1911, Scott should have mistrusted the dogs if he ever had the faith in them that the prospectus claims. Here we must make the comparison with Norwegian practice that Amundsen's success demands. It is probable that Scott's initial number of dogs, thirty-three, was inadequate for a full Polar march, and that he would have been better advised to find his dogs elsewhere. There is also the likelihood that Meares was not the man to put in charge of them. Amundsen believed in the superiority of Eskimo dogs, and it is significant that a short passage on the dogs in the official published report of the *Terra Nova* expedition claims that the two Eskimo dogs Scott had with him were the best of his bunch. Yet Meares had outlawed those two as being unmanageable and it was the cook, Clissold, who took the trouble to train them in his spare time.

Even before he knew of Scott's fate, Amundsen stressed the great difference in approach that the alternative attitude to dogs represented. Whereas British explorers imitated one another's errors, Amundsen looked at the various condemnations of dogs by Scott and Shackleton and still believed that the surface and conditions gave dogs an enormous advantage. Shackleton had made it clear that ponies could not be expected to get up the Glacier and Amundsen noted dryly that, once that stage is reached, 'men themselves have the doubtful pleasure of acting as ponies . . . It must be rather hard to have to abandon one's motive power voluntarily when only a quarter of the distance has been covered. I for my part prefer to use it all the way.'

Amundsen's plan was bold and uncomplicated – in British eyes; for his part, he looked on it as obvious. He would use dogs, in great number, on the Barrier, in the mountains and on the plateau, gradually killing off the pack and feeding the dead to the living. Thus there was no need to carry the loads of forage and grain required for ponies. Irrespective of opinions about the prowess of dogs, in terms of mathematical effectiveness they had an advantage that Scott recognized. In those notebooks where Scott did his calculations one finds this fascinating summary:

dog drags 80 and consumes 0·8 per 15 miles
pony drags 600 and consumes 10 lb per 15 miles
motor drags 4,000 and consumes 55 lb per 15 miles
dog – 80/0·8 = 100
pony – 600/10 = 60
motor – 4,000/55 = 73

It is arguable whether the three modes of transport can be so simply compared: in part such calculations are the notebook wisdom of a naval captain out of his element. Even so, it is worth seeing that Scott had a formula that indicated the adoption of dogs, just as he admitted Amundsen's favourable position as soon as he heard how many dogs there were at Framheim. It is not enough to say that Scott misjudged the value of dogs. The truth is more complex and human: he did not believe himself or his men capable of using dogs in the Norwegian manner. Amundsen himself guessed this handicap:

There must be some misunderstanding or other at the bottom of the Englishman's estimate of the Eskimo dog's utility in the Polar regions. Can it be that the dog has not understood the master? Or is it the master who has not understood his dog? The right footing must be established from the outset; the dog must understand that he has to obey in everything, and the master must know how to make himself respected. If obedience is once established, I am convinced that the dog will be superior to all other draught animals over these long distances.

Amundsen's insinuation is that an abiding national gentleness prevented the British from using dogs properly in the Antarctic. This would be very hard to prove, but some illustrations for it can be found. None of the British party was as used to driving sledge dogs as the Norwegians were; yet most of them would have had dogs as household pets since childhood. That entails several things. The British were hurt and perplexed by the savagery of their dogs. They often tried a disastrous kindness in dealing with them. Whereas Amundsen dominated his pack, the British may have looked for a relationship with 'man's best friend'. Scott was prepared to be sympathetic to the dogs when they were soaked on the deck of the *Terra Nova* going south – 'The group forms a picture of wretched dejection; such a life is truly hard for these poor creatures' – but felt alienated by their habits when tethered in the snow: '. . . with the dogs it's a very sickening sight. They are all very loose & appear ravenously hungry and in this state not a moment is lost after the passage of excrement before it is re-devoured providing the animals can get at it.'

The inability of the British to impose their will on the dogs was most damaging in the work of sledge-driving. Adroit command of a dog team requires either training or experience, and the British party had neither. Meares and the Russian, Demetri, trained the dogs on their own, but may not have achieved much. By the middle of March 1911 Scott was forced to write: 'Bit by bit I am losing all faith in the dogs and much in Meares. I'm afraid neither he or they will ever go the pace we look for. Meares is a real nice fellow but he hates exercise and doesn't inspire any confidence to see the thing through.' As with many of Scott's other suppressed critiques of his men, we cannot test the merits of this. However, on a South Polar expedition, how can one explain the way Meares was lazy but 'a real nice fellow', and Teddy Evans ceaselessly at work yet not up to par, without noticing some indistinct test of class or breeding? Still, the dogs were neglected and they were a source of trouble and distress to the men. Perhaps Meares deserves some blame, but then so does Scott for entrusting so vital an element of the expedition to a relatively un-known quantity.

As it is, the British experience with dogs was often one of sad, amused muddle. Wilson thought that the *Terra Nova* dogs were fitter and more responsive than those that had died with the *Discovery* expedition, but still his chief impression was that of someone always expecting to have to restrain a stampede or stop a fight. Wilson described how the appearance of a seal could always disrupt an orderly march on the depot-laying journey: 'One has to rush in amongst them with the whip, and then every dog jumps over the harness of the dog next him, and the harnesses become a muddle that takes much patience to unravel, not to mention care lest the whole team should get away with a sledge and leave one behind to follow on foot.' Wilson persevered with the dogs and came to love them. That tells us something about the sort of naturalist he was, just as this pleased account of devotion in one dog is a glimpse of British anthropomorphism and of ultimate reluctance to make the animals work to their limit: 'my old leader . . . never fails to come and speak to me whenever he sees me, and he knows me and my voice ever so far off. He is really quite a ridiculous "old man", and quite the nicest quietest cleverest old dog gentleman I have ever come across. He looks in fact as though he knew all the wickedness of all the world and all its cares, and as though he was bored to

death by both of them. I must get Ponting to photograph
him with me: he's a dear old thing.'

How many of Scott's men must have uttered that encouraging endearment to spaniels, retrievers and wholesome mongrels curled up on their hearthrugs at home?
This is not to deride or exaggerate the English affection for
animals. But it may help to explain the temperamental gap
that restrained them from subduing, driving and even
eating their sledge dogs. Scott once wrote in his journal,
with resignation and pity: 'Hunger and fear are the only
realities in dog life.' That he could not insist on both does
credit to his kindness, but makes him an odd Polar commander. Above all Scott was dismayed by the abrupt
changes of mood in dogs. A team could be reduced in an
instant to a flurry of snarling competitors. This account of
chaos may be all the more pained because Scott yearned so
much for a fully binding team in his men:

For instance, the dogs are as a rule all very good friends in
harness; they pull side by side rubbing shoulders, they walk over
each other as they settle to rest, relations seem quite peaceful and
quiet. But the moment food is in their thoughts, however, their
passions awaken; each dog is suspicious of his neighbour, and
the smallest circumstance produces a fight. With like suddenness
their rage flares out instantaneously if they get mixed up on the
march – a quiet, peaceable team which has been lazily stretching
itself with wagging tails one moment will become a set of
raging, tearing, fighting devils the next. It is such stern facts that
resign one to the sacrifice of animal life in the effort to advance
such human projects as this.

Nevertheless at the end of the expedition there were dogs
left and the feeling that they had not been used adequately.
Granted that Scott's men made mistakes with dogs, still
there seem to have been fundamental errors in the choice of
particular dogs, in the trust placed in Meares and in the
reluctance to respond to advice from either the Norwegians

or Peary, who had used dogs in the Arctic. It has been a British tradition to remark on Scott's soundness as a leader. Yet there are moments when he seems slow and obtuse. This passage from his journal comes not much more than a month after landing at Cape Evans and it amounts to a large confession of mistakes and disappointment:

The dogs are as thin as rakes; they are ravenous and very tired. I feel this should not be, and that it is evident that they are underfed. The ration must be increased next year and we *must* have some properly thought-out diet. The biscuit alone is not good enough. Meares is excellent to a point, but a little pig-headed & quite ignorant of the conditions here. One thing is certain, the dogs will never continue to drag heavy loads with men sitting on the sledges; we must all learn to run with the teams and the Russian custom must be dropped. Meares, is loath to run &, I think, rather imagined himself racing to the Pole and back on a dog sledge. This journey has opened his eyes a good deal and mine too. It is evident that I have placed too much reliance on his experience.

A similar but more distressing situation occurred with the ponies. Their failure was not simply a blow to the plans of the expedition, but a spectacle that upset the men and affected their own confidence. There is no question that all the animals suffered in Antarctica, but Scott's men suffered on their behalf. That sympathy is very appealing, but it may at times have been indulged and it shows a contradiction in men at the ends of the earth, compelled to be severe, but still clinging to softer ways. There is a harsh resilience, evident in the Norwegians, that Scott's men never possessed. It betrayed them, and it may sometimes bemuse or irritate their supporters, but it is essential to note the ways in which they never adapted to extremity, for such ignorance and complacency exposed them to the Polar wildness. Had they been shrewder or more knowing explorers they would not have uncovered as much of human nature as they did.

The ponies too had been gathered by Meares, and doubt-less wearied by the difficult journey from Siberia to New Zealand. There they became the responsibility of Oates. It is notable that that disenchanted soldier immediately changed when he had these animals to care for. If his life had been empty so far, the ponies gave him a purpose. As they declined, so Oates may have become an immeasurably more serious and troubled man. 'I don't know how long it is since I have been so anxious about anything as I am about these ponies,' he wrote to his mother as he supervised their loading aboard *Terra Nova*. Four ponies were housed on the deck and fifteen in the upper forecastle, but even at Port Chalmers Oates foresaw that any bad weather would undermine the animals.

The storms encountered going south killed the first two ponies and weakened the others. This started a tender agony in the men, who could only watch the plight of creatures naturally meek and always associated in England with children. Siberian ponies were tougher and less amenable than the Shetlands that used to carry every English child who wished to resemble the children of the royal family, but ponies were creatures of great sentimental charm. If it seems fanciful to stress their charm for men going on so rigorous an expedition, listen to Scott observing his ponies beaten by the weather on the *Terra Nova*:

... one knows that they must be getting weaker as time goes on, and one longs to give them a good sound rest with the ship on an even keel. Poor patient beasts! One wonders how far the memory of such fearful discomfort will remain with them – animals so often remember places and conditions where they have encountered difficulties or hurt. Do they only recollect circumstances which are deeply impressed by some shock of fear or sudden pain, and does the remembrance of prolonged strain pass away? Who can tell? But it would seem strangely merciful if nature should blot out these weeks of slow but inevitable torture.

Compare that with moments when Scott is describing his own depression, and one may appreciate how thoroughly he identified with the animals and how far his energetic enterprise was blunted by melancholy. When Amundsen spoke scathingly of the British having 'the doubtful pleasure of acting as ponies' that was an unusually penetrating analysis of national character. Like so many late Victorians, Scott's men were beguiled by the notion that animals – poor patient beasts – were refined ennobled versions of men.

On the ship, at Cape Evans and on the march Oates spent hours with the ponies attempting to improve their circumstances whenever possible and otherwise hoping to comfort them with his presence. Yet these were horses unlike any he had been used to, and when Oates lectured on horse management he could only compare the ponies with horses he had known – hunters, steeplechasers and polo ponies. Scott's report of that lecture hints at the awkwardness of a sea captain and a dedicated hunter having to find the best way for strange animals to pull great weights in appalling conditions:

Our trainer went on to explain the value of training horses, of getting them 'balanced' to pull with less effort. He owns it is very difficult when one is walking horses only for exercise, but thinks something can be done by walking them fast and occasionally making them step backwards.

Oates referred to the deeds that had been done with horses by foreigners in shows and with polo ponies by Englishmen when the animals were trained; it is, he said, a sort of gymnastic training.

But too many of Scott's ponies simply wilted in the conditions. Between landing at Cape Evans and 1 March three more perished from cold, blizzard and general debility. Many had poor, withered coats, and even full hair only served to hold snow that froze and chilled the animals. There were many complaints of bad temper in the ponies, which may have been the result of their wintry moroseness, but could support Wilson's feeling that Oates had 'had a great string of rotten unsound ponies thrown on his hands'. Wilson also thought that the harassed Oates had been criticized too much in what was a forlorn task. Then in early March two more were lost when an ice floe broke up. In the middle of April another died: eight gone out of nineteen before the Polar journey began. Only ten could be used on the southern journey and they were in persistent difficulty and hardship. The men who led them were fond attendants, and the animals must have benefited from this support. But the march was an ordeal for men and ponies, the latter always vulnerable to wind, blizzard and soft snow that sometimes came up to their bellies. The ponies, and the men's willingness to push the animals, stopped short of the Beardmore Glacier – their original target – and those remaining were slaughtered in desperation. Cherry-Garrard summed up the relief that came with that merciful dispatch: ' "Oh for the simple man-hauling life!" was our thought, and "poor helpless beasts – this is no country for live stock".'

Thus the dreadful, killing simplicity of man-hauling came as a great human effort that might obliterate the cruel demands made on helpless animals. Different schemes for the animals occupied Scott's thoughts at different times, but a careful observer of the British might have guessed that before the end they would opt for man-hauling, if only to settle their own confused thoughts and feelings. Before setting out from Cape Evans on the southern journey, Bowers wrote cheerfully to Kathleen Scott about the decision not to use dogs on the plateau:

Certainly to trust the final dash to such an uncertain element as dogs would be a risky thing, whereas man-haulage though slow, is sure, and I for one am delighted at the decision. After all, it will be a fine thing to do that plateau with man-haulage in these days of the supposed decadence of the British Race.

What marvels of endurance and hardship man can survive to avoid the charge of decadence. But how narrow a sense of decadence Bowers had if he felt that cold showers and hard slogging could dispel it. Decadence is a twentieth-century culture, and Bowers shows the inept defences against it of a man blithely unaware of its depths.

From Scott's point of view, one attraction of both the motor sledges and the ponies was that they would carry heavy supplies that could be dumped in depots across the Barrier to await the returning Polar parties. In all Polar journeys the greatest nicety arises in carrying supplies for the shortest distance possible. The ideal is to travel as lightly as is safe. But that depends upon picking up one depot after another, as rations run out. Thus, in advance, plans have to be made for a sequence of depots that commit the marchers to a necessary daily distance if they are not to starve. Bad weather can prevent marching and depots may not easily be located, so some margin for error has to be allowed. But the more cautious the party in carrying reserves of food the slower they will move – and the more food they will require. It is a vicious spiral: real security consists only in having immovable quantities of supplies.

The Norwegians at Framheim had ambitious plans for depot-laying, and if Scott had known how thoroughly they were carried out he could have had no doubt about Amundsen's advantage. Four of the Norwegians set out on 10 February with three sledges and eighteen dogs. Their target was 80°S, and they made it on 14 February, leaving there 1,500 lb of provisions. Six dogs therefore had dragged a sledge loaded with over 500 lb: the first two days they covered seventeen miles a day; then, as they settled to a rhythm, they managed twenty-five and twenty-three; free of their load they romped back, doing forty-three miles one day and sixty-two the next. If Amundsen had ever had any fears over the dogs, they were dispelled now: 'We went forward at a rattling pace; the going was perfect. The dogs' feet trod on a thin layer of loose snow, just enough to give them a secure hold.' The distance from Framheim to 80°S was some fifty miles less than that Scott had to cover from Cape Evans, but the British performance was in every way less spectacular.

Thirteen men set out from Cape Evans on 24 January with eight ponies and twenty-six dogs. On 17 February the party reached 79° 28½'S and there depoted 2,181 lb of supplies. 'It is a pity we couldn't get to 80°,' wrote Scott, 'but as it is we shall have a good leg up for next year and can at least feed the ponies full up to this point.' This depot was called One Ton Depot and that small falling short of 80°S would prove a harrowing deficit next year when Scott, Wilson and Bowers died only eleven miles south of One Ton.

The British had met all manner of obstacles and difficulty. Eleven dogs together found 500 lb a back-breaking load – 'they brought it at a snail's pace'. The ponies were sometimes pulling 800 lb each, but they had great trouble with their footing and often sank deep in the snow. Three days were passed waiting for a blizzard to subside, during which time Scott reassured himself with cosy thoughts of being in a tent:

What a wonderful shelter our little tent affords. We have just had an excellent meal, a quiet pipe, and fireside conversation within, almost forgetful for the time of the howling tempest without: – now, as we lie in our bags warm and comfortable, one can scarcely realise that 'hell' is on the other side of the thin sheet that protects us.

The lack of foresight must be remarked on. The British rarely exceeded twelve miles a day and often did less. The labour of the animals, the time the party took between waking and setting out, the daily mileage and the great time taken ought to have been a warning to Scott. Again we must note how often that anxious man gave way to optimism or complacency, and we must heed a verdict that Amundsen would later set down on the discipline of planning in Polar travel:

The reason for all this minute study, repeated experiment, and careful construction came out of my firm belief that the greatest factor in the success of an exploring expedition is the way in which every difficulty is foreseen and precaution taken for meeting or avoiding it. Victory awaits him who has everything in order – luck, people call it. Defeat is certain for him who has neglected to take the necessary precautions in time – this is called bad luck. Will power is the first essential of a successful explorer – only by the mastery of his own soul can he hope to master the difficulties placed in his path by opposing nature. Both imagination and caution are equally essential – imagination to foresee the difficulties, and the caution which compels the minutest preparation to meet them.

Scott came back from his depot journey to hear of Amundsen's establishment at Framheim. But, on the very day that Scott learned this, Amundsen set out on a second depot journey. This time eight men took seven sledges and forty-two dogs. Averaging some fifteen miles a day, they passed 80°S on the fifth day of travelling, and in another four days were at 81° where they built a depot of 1,200 lb. Five men went on to 82°S, which they reached in another five days and where they left another depot, chiefly dogs' pemmican, of 1,350 lb. The dogs were very tired, but on the return they did thirty miles and then two days of twenty-five before two dogs died and slowed the rate a little.

Amundsen was not done yet. In early April seven men took $1\frac{1}{4}$ ton of seal meat to 80°S. These preparations enabled him to launch himself at the Pole next year with the utmost velocity and confidence. Also he had proved the dogs, found their limit and given his drivers valuable experience. All manner of small refinements followed in the Norwegian method. Not only was the sledge weight reduced to less than a third. The tents were given an extra layer and dyed blue. Alterations were made in footwear, the dog whips were adjusted and there were modifications in ski bindings and dog harness.

The Norwegians had also appreciated that in several months' time it might be difficult to find a depot. Consequently they had taken the trouble to lay down an elaborate set of markings. Their depots were signalled with long bamboo poles and flags. But laterally, for five miles in either direction, flags were set up, 900 yards apart, in case the Polar party were off course. All this work would have been done by men on ski and needs to be taken in the context of their high daily average on the depot journeys. As a further safeguard the north–south path was also signed by beacons, as often as possible at visible distances. This meant that when the Norwegians started for the Pole, and on the last stages coming back, they had a way laid out for them, and less of the gnawing worry that they might miss a depot.

In comparison Scott's depot work looks sketchy and lethargic. If one doubts the fairness of that, the death of five men must serve as a reminder. But if one is inclined to see Amundsen's driving efficiency as symptomatic of a Nietzschean superman taming the wilderness, then listen to this confession of calculating dominance and set it beside the genuine distress that Scott suffered with his animals:

How hard and unfeeling one gets under such conditions; how one's whole nature may be changed! I am naturally fond of all animals and try to avoid hurting them. There is none of the 'sportsman's' instinct in me; it would never occur to me to kill an animal – rats and flies excepted – unless it was to support life. I think I can say that in normal circumstances I loved my dogs, and the feeling was undoubtedly mutual. But the circumstances we were now in were not normal – or was it, perhaps, myself who was not normal? I have often thought since that such was really the case. The daily hard work and the object I would not give up had made me brutal, for brutal I was when I forced those five skeletons to haul that excessive load. I feel it yet when I think of Thor – a big, fine, smooth haired dog – uttering his plaintive howls on the march, a thing one never hears a dog do while working. I did not understand what it meant – would not understand, perhaps. On he had to go – on till he dropped. When we cut him open we found that his whole chest was one large abscess.

The Norwegians passed the dark months of winter warm, comfortable and resting. They harboured their strength, remade their sledges and trimmed clothing and equipment to the lessons of the depot journey. Amundsen waited impatiently for travelling weather and 'the object I would not give up'. The British winter was neither as restful nor as concentrated. The diversity of approach and purpose in Scott's second expedition reaches one of its climaxes in the winter journey to Cape Crozier to collect the eggs of Emperor Penguins. This mission was largely quixotic in that no significant advances in embryology or evolution were derived from the eggs. Many would have wondered at the hazards and discomforts endured for so remote a prize. Amundsen would have been bewildered that the three men who went and lived in temperatures frequently below − 50°F for over a month were destined for key roles in the Polar party. Even Scott might have questioned whether

Wilson and Bowers – the men who died on either side of him – should have had the gruelling preparation of what Cherry-Garrard, their companion, humbly called 'the worst journey in the world'.

But the trip to Cape Crozier survives every expression of incredulity. Its waywardness embodies the unsophisticated altruism of Scott's men; its performance beautifully typifies the ideals they hoped to find manifest in one another; while Cherry-Garrard's description of the journey is a testament to the place of Scott's men in a more cautious world. The Cape Crozier excursion may or may not have affected the chances of Scott's last group surviving; surely no conscientious planner would have allowed it. That Scott did, a little grudgingly, permit the three to go, and was so unmistakably moved by their achievement, tells us something very valuable about his sense of fulfilment.

When Wilson returned from the *Discovery* expedition, he reported: 'The possibility that we have in the Emperor Penguin, the nearest approach to a primitive form not only of a penguin, but of a bird, makes the future working out of its embryology a matter of the greatest possible importance.' He outlined the chance that a three-man party might have in winter of securing eggs containing embryos. There would be dark, cold, wretched living conditions and the mass of crevasses at Cape Crozier. He summed up: 'The whole work no doubt would be full of difficulty, but it would not be quite impossible.' There is no doubt that this task held a major place in Wilson's plans from the moment he realized he might go south again; and he reckoned on Cherry-Garrard as a likely companion before the *Terra Nova* even left England. Scott was not quickly persuaded to allow the trip to Cape Crozier, and Wilson evidently had to press him and make the rash promise that he would bring the men back safely.

Wilson, Bowers and Cherry-Garrard set off on 27 June,

with Ponting attempting to film them by flash candle. They had two sledges and six weeks' provisions and a load of over 250 lb per man. 'This winter travel is a new and bold venture,' Scott wrote 'but the right men have gone to attempt it.'

Cherry-Garrard's book, *The Worst Journey in the World*, contains a long chapter on the Cape Crozier journey, which is the centrepiece of an enduring classic. Arguably, however, no one would so ardently have identified the special quality of the ordeal as Cherry-Garrard: he was emotional, valiant and yearning to be of service. At the same time there was a vein of incipient disillusion and fatalism in him, a feeling that the world was moving beyond the reach of good men, which increased as he grew older, and which makes for the gravity in his account of the winter journey. Without intent or trick, Cherry-Garrard's earnestness turns the story into a mythical quest in which embryos are a pretext for the dedicated honour of men at the end of their tether.

Thus, for my purposes, the physical nature of their ordeal can be conveyed fairly quickly. More time is needed to observe their reaction. Every eventuality exceeded anticipation. The cold was worse than they feared: not only did the temperature once go down to $-77°F$; in the unremitting darkness, cold took on a greater psychic intensity. All the old awe of Polar night invaded the men once they ventured out of the hut. When men die of exposure, we imagine that their bodies, their organisms, wither from the severity of weather; but it is the imagination and the spirit that also suffer, and how can they fail to feel daunted when the ordeal takes place by night?

It took nineteen days to go from Cape Evans to Cape Crozier, a distance of some eighty miles. The way was littered with obstacles and crevasses that had to be felt out in advance in the dark. The sledges were heavy. In summer it was a straightforward journey, but in winter extraordinary tortures were added to it. For instance, the temperatures were such that breath and all body moisture froze. Their clothes became heavier and by the end of the journey every man's sleeping bag had doubled in weight. On the march those bags rested on the sledge, rigid shapes with a gaping opening so that at night a man could at least commence the business of thawing his bag by thrusting himself into the starched cavity. Even human posture could be frozen. Terrible cramps afflicted all of them at night. One morning Cherry-Garrard came out of the tent, raised his head to the sky and found that he could not look down because his clothes and hood had frozen. Thereafter they took care to come out of the tent in a stance suited to sledge-hauling, otherwise they might have to pull in the grotesque postures of cripples and idiots.

At Crozier they built a crude igloo. They found the penguins and obtained five eggs. Two broke on the way back and they almost missed the igloo in the dark. There then comes a passage in Cherry-Garrard's book which is very expressive of the way, in 1922, he could see the Polar expedition in terms of the calamitous impact of war on European civilization:

I have heard tell of an English officer at the Dardanelles who was left, blinded, in No Man's Land between the English and Turkish trenches. Moving only at night, and having no sense to tell him which were his own trenches, he was fired at by Turk and English alike as he groped his ghastly way to and from them. Thus he spent days and nights until, one night, he crawled towards the English trenches, to be fired at as usual. 'Oh God! What can I do!' some one heard him say, and he was brought in.

Such extremity of suffering cannot be measured: madness or death may give relief. But this I know: we on this journey were already beginning to think of death as a friend. As we groped our way back that night, sleepless, icy, and dog-tired in the dark and the wind and the drift, a crevasse seemed almost a friendly gift.

They were dreading the return journey, no matter that it might take them home. Then, at night, a blizzard struck them and the tent – in which their gear was stored – was ripped from the ground. They gathered most of their things into the igloo, struggling against a wall of snow driven by the wind. Once carried away, they would have been as helpless as a scrap of paper.

Then the roof of the igloo went and the three men tried to sleep, huddled together with only a groundsheet as cover, and with no idea of how they would survive and return without a tent. At such moments, for Cherry-Garrard at least, there was temptation to give up the ghost. We have no better description from Scott's men of the belief that one is going to die and of the way in which it may be embraced. This is not necessarily the lasting frame of mind of Scott, Wilson or Bowers during their final days. But the hopelessness of that trio was only a little more marked, and the hunger that much more desperate, than that facing Cherry-Garrard, Wilson or Bowers. Cherry-Garrard wrote the book that Scott inspired: his most personal passages take urgency from the last pages of Scott's journal, just as Cherry's peace of mind seems never to have digested the tragedy of Scott or the tormenting feeling that he might have been saved:

Face to face with real death one does not think of the things that torment the bad people in the tracts, and fill the good people with bliss. I might have speculated on my chances of going to Heaven; but candidly I did not care. I could not have wept if I had tried. I had no wish to review the evils of my past. But the past did seem to have been a bit wasted. The road to Hell may be paved with good intentions: the road to Heaven is paved with lost opportunities.

The three of them returned, and perhaps there is not much more that anyone who was not with them can say. They did find the tent, still on its bamboo poles: only the weight of ice in the fabric had saved it. But, as Cherry admitted, 'The horrors of that return journey are blurred to my memory and I know they were blurred to my body at the time. I think this applies to all of us, for we were much weakened and callous.' They came in to the hut on the night of 1 August. 'They looked more weather-worn than anyone I have yet seen,' wrote Scott. Ponting was haunted by their expressions and reminded of Russian prisoners he had seen after the battle of Mukden – perhaps even the men whose passage Shackleton bartered for.

As they neared the hut, Wilson had wondered whether they should not go straight in, but live in a tent outside for a day or two, to adjust. Perhaps this was out of a sense that events had moulded them together in a way that would make them alien to others living in comfort. The terror and extremity had forged a bond, known only to people who have saved one another's lives or been ready to die together. When they were packing before the last march in to the hut, Wilson had spoken to the other two, quietly and no doubt while intent on fixing a piece of gear, 'I want to thank you two for what you have done. I couldn't have found two better companions – and what is more I never shall.'

The quest for penguin eggs had been Wilson's, and often in those five weeks he feared that he might have taken men to their death. He did not himself live to hear the sparse findings deduced from his eggs, and it was Cherry-Garrard who had the frustration of being told by the Natural History Museum in London that the eggs did not even exist or had been mislaid.* History therefore regards

* In *The Worst Journey in the World*, Cherry-Garrard gives a comic, but bitter account of official indifference to the eggs. The eggs were eventually passed on to Edinburgh University and Cherry-Garrard quotes a generous but inconclusive report from Professor Cossar Ewart of Edinburgh on whether feathers developed from scales.

that journey as being significant chiefly in demonstrating that men can suffer so much for so unlikely a cause. In some respects the winter journey is a rehearsal for Scott's Polar mission: the measurable achievement is less than the momentous impression of endurance. There is something not too far from exaltation in the way those three men rejoiced in what they had kept intact and proved for themselves amid the horrifying tempest. Cherry-Garrard, more than anyone else, appreciated and insisted on this ascetic joy of dignity emerging from pain and travail, and he makes it sound like a strange mixture of a school cross-country race and a mystical experience. He was the poet of the Cross among Scott's men, and his credo might have been acknowledged by most of them:

And we *did* stick it. How good the memories of those days are. With jokes about Birdie's picture hat: with songs we remembered off the gramophone: with ready words of sympathy for frost-bitten feet: with generous smiles for poor jests: with suggestions of happy beds to come.

We did not forget the Please and Thank you, which mean much in such circumstances, and all the little links with decent civilization which we could still keep going. I'll swear there was still a grace about us when we staggered in. And we kept our tempers – even with God.

II
The Race

Now the race begins; there is no other way to deal with it in the telling. At every point the simplicity of Amundsen's assault pierces that mistiness in Scott's mind. The context of two simultaneous ventures south reveals salutary warnings about Polar conditions, irony – that two parties should perform so differently, the grisly disparity of dates, speeds and targets and the final pathos of exuberance in one quarter and despair in another.

Amundsen was restless to be away. He had made his plans and every last refinement by 24 August, the third day in a row that Scott's men were confined to their hut by blizzard clouds of snow. The Norwegians were poised like athletes on the eve of a great contest. The extra toughness of the dogs was an advantage that compelled Amundsen to make an earlier start. Exploiting advantages was Amundsen's character, and thus he started too soon. His men were as anxious to go as he was: Helmer Hanssen acknowledged that 'our goal, and only goal, was to reach the South Pole'. Amundsen fretted as days went by towards the end of August and the temperature stayed at −40°F. 'It is not at all pleasant to hang about waiting like this; I always have the idea that I am the only one who is left behind, while all the others are out on the road.' The Norwegians wondered what Scott was doing, whether it was warmer at Cape Evans – 'you can take your oath they're not lying idle. Those boys have shown what they can do.'

The Norwegians made a precipitate start on 8 September, a day when Scott and Bowers were still embroiled in checking one another's figures for sledge weights. It was a Friday and some of those staying at Framheim warned against starting on a day overshadowed by Scandinavian superstition. (We must allow that, at the ends of the earth, in weather of crushing rigour, men may put on one boot before another as a licence fee to fate.) In three days they made forty-five miles, but then on two successive days the temperature fell below −60°F. The dogs flinched, compasses froze, and as soon as they reached 80°S the party hurried home with frost-bite, managing twenty miles in one day. It was still penguin-egg winter. The superstitious smiled and Amundsen was vexed, but in truth the performance was awesome. The dogs had reached 80°S, despite the cold, in five days. Two months later it would take Scott eighteen days to get so far.

The month that followed must have preyed on Amundsen, just as the false start could have been a threat to the morale of competitors. But on 19 October Amundsen set out in earnest with four companions – Hanssen, Wisting, Hassel and Bjaaland. They took four sledges, each one drawn by thirteen dogs. In advance, Amundsen had a meticulous schedule of how many dogs would go all the way and of when and where portions of his pack would be slaughtered for food. With such reliable depots they could start lightly loaded and cut the time to 80°S down to four days. Amundsen strode along beside the sledges on ski, but found that he could not keep up and so consented to be towed along. Thus all five of the Norwegians were being carried by the energy of their dogs.

At this very time Scott was slowly getting his motors in order and consumed with regrets that the weather was too bad to exercise the ponies: 'This is annoying, as just at present they ought to be doing a moderate amount of work and getting into condition on full rations.' Moreover, on the eve of departure, Scott was still preoccupied with the shortcomings of some of his closest followers. Scott's approach to the Pole was vague enough to be crowded with contingencies, every one of which needed its own set of calculations on weights, rations and days. There must have been nights when the columns of figures writhed over one another, like ski trails round the hut; and days when Scott admitted a little dismay to his journal: 'In the transport department, in spite of all the care I have taken to make the details of my plan clear by lucid explanation, I find that Bowers is the only man on whom I can thoroughly rely to carry out the work without mistake, with its arrays of figures.' Even the arrangements for horse forage had had to be taken out of Oates's head – where they were too much for him – and given to Bowers to ponder. Arguably no one knew more about the plans than the squat Indian Marine who still washed in the open every morning and increasingly impressed everyone as a cocky titan sparrow. Had something in Scott selected men unable to share his planning; or was he himself sceptical of plans that were not his alone?

Scott's thoughts before setting out were downcast. In hindsight it is easy to imagine he anticipated being beaten and 'the chance of finding our venture much belittled'. But then he reassured himself, 'It is the work that counts, not the applause that follows'. In that mood Scott could turn full circle. Looking away from the disappointment that he had so little mathematical help, he could survey the snow, inhale the air of comradeship, come back to the same men and see an idyllic band of brothers playing football for Ponting's film camera in the days before going south:

The study of individual character is a pleasant pastime in such a mixed community of thoroughly nice people, and the study of relationships and interactions is fascinating – men of the most diverse upbringing and experience are really pals with one another, and the subjects which would be delicate ground of discussion between acquaintances are just those which are most freely used for jest. For instance, the Soldier [Oates] is never tired of girding at Australia, its people and institutions, and the Australians retaliate by attacking the hide-bound prejudices of the British army. I have never seen a temper lost in these discussions. So as I sit here I am very satisfied with these things. I think that it would have been difficult to better the organization of the party – every man has his work and is especially adapted for it; there is no gap and no overlap – it is all that I desired, and the same might be said of the men selected to do the work.

It seems necessary to recognize that Scott had two distinct and opposite ways of looking at his expedition. His agonizing volatility could not digest the placid abilities and limitations in his cheerful band. The veerings of his opinions are the movements of nervous indecision put in total command. It ought to have been possible to admit that there were rifts and disagreements, none of which ever threatened the remarkable and devoted community that had been prepared for the ultimate ordeal. The day before going south Wilson wrote to his wife about his own role as peacemaker and soother. Apparently, as the great venture drew nearer, more and more people came privately to Wilson with grievances – 'My goodness! I had hours of it yesterday; as though I was a bucket it was poured into me.' In part Wilson knew that he was the listener others sought out because, like Brer Rabbit, 'I only listen to what people like to tell me here . . . and say nothing all the time, and keep on saying nothing which seems to encourage confidences'. He hoped that he might have channelled some of these grievances, and kept them from boiling over; alternatively, if he had spoken up more clearly, Scott might have taken heed. Scott's unapproachability is the tense reserve of someone who wants to be addressed and melted but who cannot take the first step. The saintliness that so many detect in Wilson is always quietist. And he too looked forward to the south with something more and less than Amundsen's impatience: 'Whether we reach the Pole or not I really care very little so long as we feel we have done all we could. I feel I am here for a better purpose than to merely get to the Pole.'

Scott's men moved off in stages: the motor party ahead, the larger group with ponies behind them. It was not long before the ponies too were broken into groups that advanced at different speeds. Meares and Demetri came last with the dogs, but soon caught the ponies. The motor sledges set out on 24 October, with Teddy Evans, Day, Lashly and Hooper. The main party with the ponies consisted of Scott, Wilson, Oates, Bowers, Edgar Evans, Atkinson, Wright, Cherry-Garrard, Crean and Keohane. Every pony had a leader – every man had his pony to care for – and most ponies had a pace and disposition of their own, so that disjointed progress soon reminded Scott of 'a regatta or a somewhat disorganized fleet with ships of very unequal speed'.

Immediately therefore first plans gave way to muddling necessity. Night marching was adopted in the thought that the ponies worked themselves warm in the coldest hours and then rested at the most pleasant time. This course had not been foreseen, and no one could be sure how far it really suited the ponies' constitution. Furthermore at night the surfaces for pulling were often more difficult.

At first the motors had done well, but on 4 November the main party came upon a dump of petrol and this bleak note: 'Big end Day's motor No. 2 cylinder broken.' In the motor party Evans had sympathized with Day's 'crushing disappointment', but already noted that on one day when he had to make a detour he had managed fifteen miles on ski while the motors did three. Behind them, and several days later, Scott recognized that 'the dream of great help from the machines is at an end! The track of the remaining motor goes steadily forward, but now, of course, I shall expect to see it every hour of the march.' Not until that breakdown were Scott's elusive feelings about the motors really trapped. The remote chance of their success had no more deserted him previously than the undertone of doubt about such a long shot. It is also instructive to see Scott, so early, going south with expectations of what ruin he may find ahead of him.

A day later the second motor suffered a similar fate and the motor party transferred their load to another sledge, put on harness and began to pull it themselves. Less than a hundred miles out Scott's men were man-hauling. This too was an amendment to the plans and one that would have serious consequences. Evans was not a motor man, and he may not have been at ease on the land, but he took the responsibility of the motors very seriously and 'determined that they [the motor party] should not be overtaken by the ponies to become a drag on the main body'. Thus four men – Evans, Day, Hooper and Lashly – began a process of self-exhaustion before any others; and Lashly, many have contested, was ideally suited to being in the final Polar party. But, taxed too early, he limited Scott's choice.

The ponies were fulfilling the daily schedule of ten miles, but whenever the weather deteriorated the animals suffered. Then, in shared response, Scott's men flinched: 'We men are snug and comfortable enough, but it is very evil to lie here and know that the weather is steadily sapping the strength of the beasts on which so much depends. It requires much philosophy to be cheerful on such occasions.' These men built snow walls for the horses at every camp but still, if it snowed the flakes penetrated their coats and prevented them from resting. For the moment, however, the surfaces were hard and reliable. Scott was regularly comparing his own progress with Shackleton's, and he allowed himself another dry dismissal of the men who had gone before him: 'In passing I mention that there are practically no places where ponies sink to their hocks as described by Shackleton. I imagine he confused hock & fetlock or wilfully exaggerated.'

By 11 November they met a surface of mixed sastrugi and soft crust with other areas of sandiness. The weakest horses could not do ten miles, though on the same day Scott's dogs managed twenty. They were already calculating how many days some horses had left, and wondering whether the bulk could reach the foot of the Glacier: 'I am anxious about these beasts – very anxious, they are not the ponies they ought to have been.' The weather was building up as another manifestation of Scott's bad luck, and march after march seemed 'horrid':

It has been snowing consistently for some hours, adding to the soft surface accumulation inch upon inch. What can such weather mean? Arguing it out, it is clearly necessary to derive this superfluity of deposition from some outside source such as the open sea. The wind and spread of cloud from the N.E. and the exceptionally warm temperature seem to point to this. If this should come as an exception, our luck will be truly awful.

They reached One Ton Camp on 15 November and gave the ponies a day's rest – on this same day Amundsen was at 85°S, more than 400 miles farther on. Ahead of them Evans was pushing the motor party hard and they were averaging fifteen miles a day – 'exceedingly good going' Scott judged from the notes they were leaving behind. Next day the ponies did over fifteen miles, but Scott was deeply suspicious of their breeding and age and lamented the frequency with which the ponies now sank halfway to the hock.

On 19 November they passed 80°S and two days later they came up with the motor party, who had been waiting six days for them. Scott discovered that these four felt very hungry; this was the first warning of the conspicuously extra demands imposed by man-hauling. The commander interpreted the evidence as justification for the small, extra ration he would allow on the summit – four ounces more of pemmican in an overall ration increase of just under two ounces. Yet something in Scott saw through this inadequate increase, guessed the implication of men seriously hungry after only three weeks' man-hauling and allowed that, even with the bonus, 'I have little doubt that we shall soon get hungry'.

Scott should not have forgotten that the gauntness he saw in the motor party came after almost a week's rest, spent waiting for the ponies and listening to Day reading from *The Pickwick Papers*. The dogs were still going well and Meares was openly looking forward to the killing of the first pony as a reward for his animals. The others saw the dwindling performance of the ponies in terms of the fond skill which had been sustaining them. Cherry-Garrard, years later, observed that they had done 192 miles in twenty-one days 'and formed a very good idea as to what the ponies could do'. The contrary is nearer the case: a temperate commander could have seen by 21 November that the full burden of the journey was now destined to fall on man-hauling, that that means of transport evidently demanded special feeding and that even a steady progress there and back was bound to leave the last party out on the Barrier dangerously late. In other words, the sequence of difficulties that confounded Scott and his four companions were already looming out of future's obscurity. Scott was a pessimist in most things, but he rarely saw the worst clearly.

The men were cheered that the 'crocks' among the ponies lasted so long; they nursed them, and, like anyone prolonging life, tolerated the slowing pace. The surface now was consistent: a crust of soft snow so that hooves sank in three or four inches at every step. The men were finding such walking arduous, and these were men in their first month out. As ever Scott vacillated. On 23 November his diary reads with a sort of incontinence of optimism and worry: 'Getting along. I think the ponies will get through; we are now 150 geographical miles from the Glacier. But it is still rather touch and go. If one or more ponies were to go rapidly down hill we might be in queer street.' 'Queer street' is an English middle-class phrase referring to peril; but it is generally used jokingly by people who have never known disaster. Still, it is an ominous phrase, no matter how lightly it is uttered. One wonders how searchingly Scott asked himself what he meant by it.

Next day the first pony was shot – 'it is wonderful to think that he has actually got eight marches beyond our last year limit and could have gone more'. Day and Hooper now went back; without the motors, of course, they would not have been there. On 27 and 28 November they had 'the most trying' and dismal days. The surface constantly impeded men and ponies and there were regular worried calculations as to whether pony forage would last as far as the Glacier. Another pony was shot on 28 November and Scott considered transferring the main loads to dog- and man-hauling, deciding against this in order to save the men. By 1 December Scott reckoned on three more marches to the foot of the Glacier, and reported that the experiment of putting snow shoes on a pony had helped. Next day he planned to kill ponies off for food and thought that they would make it if the weather held. Simultaneously he remarked bitterly that, on the same journey, at the same time of year, Shackleton had enjoyed splendid weather.

Then, early in December, Scott's dark luck was horribly confirmed. On 3 December he himself called it 'preposterous'. As they prepared to start the day's march a storm came on that delayed them seven hours. Then they started and marched an hour before 'The sun went out, snow fell thickly, and marching conditions became horrible . . . The changes of conditions are inconceivably rapid, perfectly bewildering.' The next day they did thirteen miles, but the barometer was showing great disturbance: 'Well, one must stick it out, that is all, and hope for better things, but it makes me feel a little bitter to contrast such weather with that experienced by our predecessors.' Were there ever times when the greater good fortune of Shackleton obscured the real danger creeping up on him?

They now had a fine view of the mountains that contained the Glacier. Bowers recognized the great luck Shackleton had had in coming straight to the mouth of the Beardmore, but still allowed that 'He must have been a stout-hearted fellow to have tackled such a place hitherto untrodden'. He also saw that on his left hand the line of mountains went sharply south – 'from that point the journey to the Pole would be very short. If Amundsen has got there all right and found a way up he should have a much shorter summit journey than ours. In fact if he has not met with adversity he should have reached the Pole by now. I hope he has not, as I regard him as a back-handed, sneaking ruffian.' As Bowers wrote, the 'ruffian' was already on the plateau, men and dogs easily covering twenty-five miles a day.

On the morning of 5 December the British woke to 'a raging howling blizzard' that was to keep them immobile for four days. Snow covered everything and excluded visibility. 'What on earth does such weather mean at this time of year? It is more than our share of ill-fortune, I think.' Confined to his tent and soon wretchedly caught in the slush of a thaw, Scott dwelled on the way fate had treated him. He wondered about his plight 'whilst others go smilingly forward in the sunshine', and concluded that no

foresight or procedure could have expected this predica-
ment. But who could reckon on stable or predictable
weather in Antarctica? Man's meteorological knowledge of
the area was still so meagre. One might as easily land in
Dallas, Texas, in July on a cool day and bank on cold
summers in Texas thereafter. In all the resentment at luck,
Scott never reflected that his southern journey was already
at a point where the risk was increasingly out of proportion
to the object.

As the storm went on, they called the camp, their thir-
tieth, the 'Slough of Despond', and the reference to pilgrims
on allegorical journeys matches this cry of the spirit from
Scott: 'The ponies look utterly desolate. Oh! but this is too
crushing, and we are only 12 miles from the Glacier. A
hopeless feeling descends on one and is hard to fight
off. What immense patience is needed for such occasions!'

By 7 December they were living in their tents but already
eating summit rations. Scott became more depressed,
staring at the wet green walls of the tent, listening to the
'everlasting patter' of the snow and seeing the despondent
faces of his men. Amid such dank dismay and with time for
further calculations, Scott seems to have considered no
drastic alteration to his plans. 'Resignation to misfortune is
the only attitude, but not an easy one to adopt. It seems
undeserved where plans were well laid and so nearly
crowned with a first success. I cannot see that any plan
would be altered if it were to do again.' Bowers sympathized
with Scott's anguish and was glad that the leader had
Wilson in his tent – 'he comes out best in adversity'. For
himself, Bowers practised massive stoicism, the epitome of
British team-spirit, subduing his own problems amid the
equal distress of others. It may not be the intention of such
commitment, but it does sometimes attend it, that the
policies of the team are not often examined: 'We are all in

the same boat, none of us is more wet than the next man, and I can endure what any other man can! That is my creed down here – if any voice is raised in protest it shall not be mine.'

They got away on 9 December on what was bound to be the ponies' last march. It was among the worst. The heavy snowfall made the surface so exhausting that no animal had the heart to lead for more than a few minutes. Cherry-Garrard remembered that march as a nightmare. The ponies had to be pushed, led, and hauled and beaten out of the holes they made in the snow. The men dared not stop for lunch, knowing the ponies would never start again. They stumbled into an area of pressure ridges and were forced to zig-zag. It was a march towards death, and men forced ponies to go seven miles in eleven hours. 'There was not one man there who would willingly have caused pain to a living thing. But what else was to be done.'

These men were already feeling the ache of cold, fatigue and hunger. They were afflicted with what they took for wretched luck. Their plans were not working well. Few of them cannot have wondered at some time whether they were being beaten by the Norwegians. These last days had piled a specially severe difficulty on the others. Their tender, honourable spirits were made to be cruel to helpless animals. They could not even like themselves as easily when they had to force a wretched pony forward again and again. On 6 December Teddy Evans surveyed the desperate ponies and the remaining task and wrote in his diary:

I think it would be fairer to shoot them now, for what is a possible 12 miles help? We could now, pulling 200 lb per man, start off with the proper Man-hauling Parties and our total weights, so why keep these wretched animals starving and shivering in the blizzard on a mere chance of their being able to give us a little drag? Why, our party have never been out of harness for nearly 400 miles, so why should not the other eight men buckle to and do some dragging instead of saving work in halfpenny numbers?

Evans and Lashly were still man-hauling, and going so slowly that that day they took fifteen hours to do their distance. Thus they came into camp late, missing the slaughter of the last five ponies. 'Poor beasts!' wrote Scott from 'Shambles' camp, 'they have done wonderfully well considering the terrible circumstances under which they worked, but yet it is hard to have to kill them so early.' Scott had persevered with the ponies, partly because he had elected to make them the mainstay of his transport and perhaps because he did not readily change his mind. But, for most of the men, the slaughter was a merciful relief. Wilson gladly accepted the shooting, and poignantly failed to see what it would mean for the future: 'Thank God the horses are now all done with and we begin the heavy work ourselves.' It was 10 December; the British were at the foot of the Glacier; they had three quarters of their entire journey still ahead of them, and they would have to do it all themselves on reduced rations. A brilliant commander would have turned back at that point; but Scott was more and less than brilliant. In four days' time Amundsen would be at the Pole.

If one now turns to the progress the Norwegians had made there is a spectacle of startling ease. To read and follow Scott is to become overawed by Antarctica and its obstacles. But beneath Amundsen's skis it seems a tractable, sunny prairie where men are always vigorous and assured. Yet it was the same place, at the same time, and the two paths came closer the nearer they got to the Pole.

By 31 October Amundsen was leaving 81°S; a week later he was pushing beyond 82° and finding a steady improvement in performance. His dogs – nothing but power and obedience – were getting stronger with exercise. The daily rate was pushed up from seventeen to twenty-three miles – an astonishingly casual amendment next to Scott's withering reduction. Furthermore the dogs moved at the rate of nearly five miles an hour, so that they had to work for not much more than five hours a day. The Norwegians had few worries beyond knowing how to pass the other hours of the day and the discovery that their paraffin cans were mysteriously leaking, so that Bjaaland was busy soldering to keep them tight.

The acceleration shows in the Norwegians' dates: on 8 November they reached 83°S, on 12 November they were at 84° and on 15 November at 85°. Initially Amundsen had planned a full day's rest for the dogs at every degree of latitude. 'But this proved superfluous; it looked as if they could no longer be tired. One or two had shown signs of bad feet, but were now perfectly well; instead of losing strength, the dogs seemed to become stronger and more active every day.' The Norwegians were not tired; most of them had ridden on the sledges most of the way with no more strain than having to wave a whip over the rippling backs of the dogs. They slept long and they had only excitement to make them dream.

The flowing progress made by the Norwegians should not disguise their boldness. They had far less emergency support than Scott's party, even if their bases were better marked. An accident or serious illness in any one of the five would have presented a great dilemma. In addition Amundsen now faced the most serious unknown in his way. He had no idea how easily the mountains could be ascended. By taking a new route he had trusted that he would be able to find some passage without too great a delay. It had also to be an ascent that the dogs could manage.

At the foot of the mountains Amundsen and his companions discussed their immediate plans. The result was a schedule of sixty days to get to the Pole and back; all surplus rations were left in a depot. They now had forty-two dogs – ten had been destroyed and consumed on the way – and Amundsen chose to take them all up the mountains; kill and depot twenty-four at the top and go to the Pole with the last eighteen, six of which could be sacrificed along the way. Thus the strongest twelve dogs would do all the journey; and, of course, the Norwegians had already taken care to estimate which were the strongest.

These calculations proved incorrect in only one detail. Whereas Amundsen had allowed ten days for the ascent, he accomplished it in four. The way was not simple, but the Norwegians had no trouble in finding it and had before them a rather shorter stretch of mountain than faced Scott, who was twelve days coming up the Beardmore Glacier. As in so many aspects of their work, the Norwegian performance improved: on the lower slopes they did eleven and a half miles and 2,000 feet, but in the end they managed nineteen and a quarter miles and 5,750 feet in a day. Amundsen was terse in his comments: 'it gives us some idea of what can be performed by dogs in good training ... it seems superfluous to give the animals any other testimonial than the bare fact'.

Every comparison of the two expeditions adopts the obvious difference of the dogs. But there are others to note. Amundsen did have kinder weather. He and his men were, in effect, better fed, simply because they made far fewer demands on themselves than the British. The Norwegian diet was not really different from Scott's; nor was it larger. Every day on the plateau they had 12·3 oz of pemmican, 1·4 oz of chocolate, 2·1 oz of milk powder and forty small biscuits. The ration on Scott's journey was as follows: 12 oz of pemmican, 16 oz of biscuit, 2 oz of butter, 3 oz of sugar and some tea and chocolate. What added to Norwegian health was the regular supplement of fresh dog meat. The

British did eat pony, though not as much and not consistently. When they did eat their animals, they could admit that it tasted good, but never with the relish that Amundsen felt:

They provided a feast for the survivors and for ourselves. We found that dog cutlets made a delicious dinner. These were not fried, as we had neither frying pan nor butter. We found it far easier and quicker to boil them, and in this way we got excellent soup besides. Wisting, who acted as chef, put into the soup all those parts of the pemmican that contained most vegetables, so that we had the rare treat of a fresh-meat soup with vegetables in it. After the soup was devoured, we ate the cutlets. All doubts that we had entertained about the quality of the meat vanished at the first taste. It was excellent – not quite as tender as one could have wished, if an appetite had been lacking, but to us perfectly delicious. I ate five cutlets at this first meal, and would have been glad if there had been more in the pot.

One other advantage of the Norwegians could be mentioned: their adeptness on ski. It is not always possible to know when the British were using or not using ski. In the last part of the journey all but Bowers were on ski, yet Bowers kept up. One doubts whether any man on foot could have kept pace with Norwegians on ski. Amundsen records that he and his companions had always been convinced that Antarctica would lend itself to those 'who were born and bred with ski on our feet'. He went so far as to say that ski were the most decisive element in the Norwegian journey, which may simply mean that real decisiveness lay in the Norwegians' lifelong familiarity with ski. Any novice skier knows how much more quickly an expert travels and with how much less fatigue.

On the plateau the Norwegians were at full tilt, and Amundsen noted that the dogs were becoming hungrier. The first great landmark was an incidental, but one that showed their respect for Shackleton – it was the farthest south anyone had reached. Hanssen had a silk flag on ski-sticks ready on his sledge, and Amundsen was the leading man, ahead on ski. His own account is charmingly ingenuous, for he pretends that he was daydreaming as he sped across the surface and oblivious of going farther south than any human being. Yet his men behind him may have been quite sure, in advance, as to who would lead that day. Amundsen says that his reverie was interrupted by a shout from Hanssen:

I find it impossible to express the feelings that possessed me at this moment. All the sledges had stopped, and from the foremost of them the Norwegian flag was flying. It shook itself out, waved and flapped so that the silk rustled; it looked wonderfully well in the pure, clear air and the shining white surroundings. 88°23′ was past; we were farther south than any human being had been. No other moment of the whole trip affected me like this. The tears forced their way to my eyes; by no effort of will could I keep them back. It was the flag yonder that conquered me and my will. Luckily I was some way in advance of the others, so that I had time to pull myself together and master my feelings before reaching my comrades. We all shook hands, with mutual congratulations; we had won our way far by holding together, and we would go farther yet – to the end.

One cannot resist Amundsen's pleasure. It is as direct and winning as a child's, as unnervingly solid and confident as his entire method. No matter that Scott and his men make the more engrossing study, there is a bracing relief in turning to Amundsen's streamlined glide. He loved and trusted human energy, and in that vigour he never seems to have found the doubts that afflict and hinder more compli-cated men. That Amundsen made things look easy does not mean that they were neither difficult nor dangerous. It suggests only that he had a genius for the simple, the facility of a great sportsman who does naturally things that tangle the coordination of most men. And such ease

in rare accomplishments is a real sort of human grace; no
suspicion or dislike of Amundsen must cheat the fact that
he travelled with comprehensive grace.

On the eve of the day that he knew he would claim the
Pole, he 'was awake several times during the night, and had
the same feeling that I can remember as a little boy on the
night before Christmas Eve – an intense expectation of what
was going to happen'.

They set out on 14 December, the celebration flag in
readiness. Again there was a kind manoeuvre among the
Norwegians to give Amundsen the primacy he needed, or
to temper the fierceness that would have seized it. Hanssen,
the leading sledge-driver, pretended that one of his dogs
had developed the odd neurosis of wanting a man beside
him; it is the first hint of emotion in these animals. Thus
Amundsen was called upon to ski ahead with this free-
running dog while the drivers behind him watched the
sledge distance meter intently. They had agreed that the
Pole was five miles away from their start and when the
moment came the drivers called a halt at one fixed spot in
the white expanse.

Amundsen insisted that all five men should plant the flag
together. 'This was the only way in which I could show my
gratitude to my comrades in this desolate spot. I could see
that they understood and accepted it in the spirit in which it
was offered. Five weather-beaten, frost-bitten fists they
were that grasped the pole, raised the waving flag in the air,
and planted it as the first at the geographical South Pole.'
They ceremonially named the plateau after King Haakon
VII of Norway and then made camp.

But the shyness and subtle absurdity of the South Pole
now made itself felt. The Norwegians had put one small
pole where they guessed the great, definitive Pole must be.
But there was no hole in the ground that a creator had left
for man to fill. There was even the risk that Pole hunters

might be a half mile short or a hundred yards to the right. To come so far and put the pole in the wrong place would be humiliating. What follows shows the first trace of worry in Amundsen and the deeper vacancy of going to the Pole.

They took more observations and found that they were still five miles away. Accordingly on 15 December they went five miles farther and then took another series of observations with two instruments over a period of twenty-seven hours. Now there seemed no doubt. But Amundsen would leave nothing to chance. He suggested that a set of flags should be put around the Pole at ten miles distance, and thus the bottom of the world become a network of Norwegian ski-trails. More observations gave further confirmation, but then Amundsen thought he would have one more flag 'five nautical miles out between the line to the left and the line straight ahead'. The South Pole was being made into a golf course, and some of the Norwegians may have been smiling. But Hanssen voiced their under-standing of Amundsen's nervousness: 'It may sound as if it was unnecessary work, but the Chief wanted it that way and so that was the way we wanted him to have it.'

On 17 December they had a special dinner in their tent with speeches and cigars. Then they set up, on the Pole itself they hoped, a small tent made of brown windproof gaberdine, the drab colour staring out of the bright snow. A Norwegian flag was run up the pole with a pennant from the *Fram*. Inside, the five men left their names, a letter for King Haakon and a note to Scott asking him to forward the letter to the king of Norway. Weeks later Scott was puzzled by this request. But it was typical of Amundsen's thorough-ness: if he had not got home, then Scott would have to carry news of Norwegian success. This suggests that Amundsen had little doubt that Scott's slow progress was at least safe. 'Scott will be here sooner or later,' he told his companions. 'If I know the British rightly, they will never give up once they have started, unless forced by something beyond their control; they are too tough and stubborn for that.' The Norwegians also left an assortment of equipment that they judged surplus – a sextant, some footbags and gloves and other odds and ends that the British picked among like children who had come to the Christmas party late.

The Norwegian return was indecently rapid, but still they detected a new, acute pitch of hunger, especially the three men who skied the distance. They travelled at night and set a first target of seventeen and a half miles, achieved in five hours. Amundsen noticed that the sledge-drivers were less ravenous than the other three and reasoned that that might be simply because they were less tired. But the Norwegian schedule had food in hand and Amundsen was able to increase the pemmican ration. All too soon the men became restless with the 'insufferably long' hours spent waiting in the tent. They also complained of the heat and sometimes slept out of their sleeping bags. This makes a grotesque contrast to the terrible cold that undermined Scott's last party six weeks later.

By 28 December they were going down the mountains and able to increase the pemmican ration to 16 oz a day. The surviving dogs were actually putting on weight and more eager than ever to run. The men on ski were hurried on by the dogs 'howling for joy' and there was never need for the whip. On one day the party willingly hurried past one depot, but two men then went back on a detour to it, thereby managing some fifty miles altogether. The leisurely rate of progress was amended to a scheme of seventeen and a half miles, six hours' rest and then another seventeen and a half miles. Thus, overnight, the daily distance was doubled. Scott died short of a depot by less than one such increase, too weak to move.

They were on the Barrier again by 6 January, when

Scott was still 100 miles from the Pole. Two days later they picked up their large depot at 85°S and doubled the dogs' rations: 'We had such masses of biscuits now that we could positively throw them about. Of course we might have left a large part of these provisions behind; but there was a great satisfaction in being so well supplied with food.' Of the sixty days Amundsen had estimated he might take between 85°, the Pole and back again, the journey had been done in thirty-eight. They needed only another seventeen days to return to Framheim, walking in out of the snow and asking if coffee was on the stove.

The *Fram* was loaded and away in another five days, on 30 January, the day on which Scott noticed for the first time that Edgar Evans was losing heart. On 7 March, as Oates's crisis drew near, the *Fram* reached Hobart, Tasmania and Amundsen went ashore brimming with news. It is a success to make anyone wince.

12
The Tragedy

I have suggested in the previous chapter that it would have been no disgrace, but the mark of insight, if Scott had turned back at the foot of the Beardmore Glacier. Some will object that for such a man in such circumstances that caution was impossible; to have turned back would have been to shirk the sense of duty that led directly to heroic suffering. I recognize that impossibility and the way it ties inflexibility to Scott's immortality. His fear of disgrace was so heavy as to exclude fine originality. But he was also a naval commander, unquestioningly followed by other men, and I believe that he failed to appreciate the risk he was running. It does not mar Scott's heroism to recognize the confusing strain of misguidedness; stubbornness can sometimes leave a man no other course than heroism, and self-sacrifice may turn on the capacity for losing sight of objective evidence. We can see in Scott the zeal to do noble things and the bitterness if thwarted. On the last stages of the Polar journey especially it is easy to forget the actuality of Antarctica and to respond to the men as figures in an allegorical epic, pilgrims again, walking in a wilderness so extreme and vacant as to preclude the worldliness that might have noticed so many warning signs as the men took up the full load of the sledges. What did they feel they had done to deserve such penance?

Three sledges went up the Glacier, and there were three

tents at night with four-men crews: Scott led the first sledge, with Wilson, Oates and Edgar Evans – significantly the core of the last party; Teddy Evans, Atkinson, Wright and Lashly came on the second; and, on the last, Bowers had Cherry-Garrard, Crean and Keohane as companions. Scott's intended method of man-hauling was for the men to go on skis with harness round their waists and shoulders. When four men pull in that fashion it only needs uneven surfaces for the momentum to fluctuate. Then every man will suffer the jolt of dead weight, of being pulled up short, and will feel it time and again in the same place so that rawness and bruising result. If he is hungry, the strain on his stomach will be particularly devastating.

The first two days going up the Glacier exposed several shortcomings in method and the terrible arduousness of such travel. The surface so deteriorated that they had to remove their skis: 'The pulling after this was extraordinarily fatiguing. We sank above our finnesko everywhere, and in places nearly to our knees. The runners of the sledges got coated with a thin film of ice from which we could not free them, and the sledges themselves sank to the crossbars in soft spots. All the time they were literally ploughing the snow.'

Very quickly this new strain told on Scott's temper. Teddy Evans's sledge was being pulled by men who had already lost their edge to man-hauling. Evans and Lashly had had five weeks of it, and both Atkinson and Wright had done some man-hauling as the ponies wilted. Apparently Atkinson had told Wilson that Lashly and Wright were both losing condition, and this verdict was passed on to Scott. Evans, of course, was upset at not keeping up and at being blamed for it when the reason was so evident. Scott somehow failed or refused to comprehend the cause and responded with fitful irritation that the larger purpose might be jeopardized. If the wonderfully robust Evans and

the very durable Lashly should be so affected by five weeks'
man-hauling, Scott might have reckoned the impact it
would have on a Polar party that had 1,000 miles to go.
Yet Scott only noticed the difference between one Evans
and another, between a man in his sixth week man-
hauling and another on his first day:

I have not felt satisfied about this party [Teddy Evans's
sledge] and very dissatisfied with its management. The finish of
the march to-day showed clearly that something was wrong.
They fell a long way behind, had to take off ski, and took
nearly half an hour to come up a few hundred yards. True, the
surface was awful and growing worse every moment. It is a very
serious business if the men are going to crock up. As for myself,
I never felt fitter and my party can easily hold its own. P. O.
Evans, of course, is a tower of strength, but Oates and Wilson
are doing splendidly also.

We may picture the men now, in and out of their skis,
losing some time in the changing and being so inexperienced with them that in difficult places they might feel more
encumbered than assisted. It is doubtful whether any of the
Norwegians changed theirs often. The next day ended with
similar difficulties and Scott lamented the soft snow: 'Ski
are the thing, and here are my tiresome fellow-countrymen
too prejudiced to have prepared themselves for the event.'
On the same day he ordered Meares and Demetri back with
the dogs, another sort of active prejudice and a mistake as
symptomatic as the belated realization that his men were
not comfortable on ski and had not used Gran's training as
well as they could have done. However, one wonders why
Gran, young, strong and easily the best skier, was not in
the southern party, both as a proven marcher and as a
source of advice for others.

Yet again Evans's sledge was last in, and Scott's diary
gave way to anguish and grumpiness, though much of this
was cut for publication:

Evans's party didn't get up till 10. They started quite well, but got into difficulties, did just the wrong thing by straining again and again, and so, tiring themselves, went from bad to worse. It is most awfully trying. I had expected failure from the animals but not from the men. I must blame little Evans much. He shows a terrible lack of judgement, instead of having his people trained & drilled he lets things go anyway.

The blizzard that had held them up four days had left great quantities of soft snow on the lower Glacier. For several days now they had abominable marches. These men were still strong, and after one day on which only four miles was achieved Scott was too full to finish his summit ration, but we must see such labour beginning to weaken them all and stimulate their need for food. No one sledge went better than another on that day; all seemed equally badly loaded. 'The toil was simply awful. We were soaked with perspiration and thoroughly breathless with our efforts. Again and again the sledge got one runner on harder snow than the other, canted on its side, and refused to move.' As a further problem, at about this time, several of the men were suffering from snow-blindness. What further addition to the purgatorial ordeal could there be than that some of these Samsons went blind? Bowers gives an account of this extra handicap, in which the reader begins to feel the obsession that alone protects and sustains such effort:

I was blind as a bat, and so was Keohane in my team. Cherry pulled alongside me, with Crean and Keohane behind. By sticking plaster over my glasses except one small central spot I shut off most light and could see the points of my ski, but the glasses were always fogged with perspiration and my eyes kept on streaming water which cannot be wiped off on the march as a ski stick is held in each hand; and so heavy were our weights that if any of the pair slacked a hand even, the sledge stopped. It was all we could do to keep the sledge moving for short spells of a few hundred yards . . . The starting was worse than pulling as it required from ten to fifteen desperate jerks on the harness to move the sledge at all.

Gradually the snow cleared, revealing blue ice beneath and much easier hauling. Scott admitted the pleasure of continuous, smooth going and the freedom from sickening 'involuntary stops'. By 16 December they were six days behind Shackleton's progress, but Scott also noted: 'As we advance we see that there is great & increasing error in the charting of the various points. Shackleton's watch must have greatly altered its rate which throws everything out including his variation.' Some of Scott's men observed that on these marches Shackleton was a more pressing rival than Amundsen. The above comment was made on 17 December, when the Norwegians were at the Pole and some of Scott's concentration lingered over old Geographical Society controversies. On that day the British did well enough for Scott to cheer up and utter on paper one of those encouraging remarks nearly the opposite of things he had written the day before: 'In spite of the hard work everyone is very fit and very cheerful, feeling well fed and eager for more toil.' That shows how far mood responded to performance and prepares one for the ruinous blow to the British state of mind when they found that Amundsen had forestalled them.

They reached their Upper Glacier Depot on 21 December, having made several good marches on the upper slope: on 20 December they did twenty-three miles and climbed 800 feet. They kept chasing Shackleton's progress and still disapproved of his reckoning. There were some falls, and Scott badly bruised his knee and thigh. Several of them had sore lips and all were very thirsty.

At the top of the Glacier four men were due to turn back. There may have been several hints about where Scott's choice would fall, but very often such decisions were pondered and awaited with real tension. It clearly weighed on Scott: 'I dreaded this necessity of choosing – nothing could be more heart-rending.' He decided that Atkinson, Wright, Cherry-Garrard and Keohane should go back and noted that Wright was 'rather bitterly' disappointed. The choice may have been sensible, though Scott acted chiefly on estimates of physical fitness, while Wilson consoled Cherry-Garrard's disappointment with another criterion: 'but it is right, because he is the youngest. He is not worn out in the least, though he had worked his utmost all the way.' At the same time Wilson said he expected to be in the next returning party while Scott 'was going to take on the strongest fellows, perhaps three seamen'.

Cherry-Garrard was very moved by being dropped off, but did not question his leader. His account of Scott's speaking to him is full of emotion. It shows us the pain Scott had in sending back someone so near to his own spirit; it hints at other plans that did not materialize and it is a reason for the ceaseless obligation Cherry-Garrard felt to those who went farther:

Scott was very put about, said he had been thinking a lot about it but had come to the conclusion that the seamen, with their special knowledge, would be needed: to rebuild the sledge, I suppose . . . I said all I could think of – he seemed so cut up about it, saying 'I think, somehow, it is specially hard on you'. I said I hoped I had not disappointed him, and he caught hold of me and said 'No – no – no,' so if that is the case all is well. He told me that at the bottom of the glacier he was hardly expecting to go on himself: I don't know what the trouble is, but his foot is troubling him, and also, I think, indigestion.

The last eight men went forward on the morning of 22 December: Scott, Wilson, Oates and Edgar Evans still together on one sledge; Teddy Evans, Bowers, Crean and Lashly pulling the other. They made such good progress that Scott felt sure 'we have weeded the weak spots'. Yet in the day they did only twelve miles, rather less than half the Norwegian distance on the summit. Although clear of the Glacier, they were still faced by inclines, and there was a wearing day when they struck treacherous surfaces and uncertainty as to whether or not they had found the plateau. Then, on 23 December, in ten minutes the surface hardened and 'our horizon levelled in every direction'. They could feel themselves on the base of the globe, as if it had once rested on God's palm. There was still enough of the optimist in Scott to be captivated by prospects: 'I am feeling very cheerful about everything to-night. . . . I trust this may prove the turning-point in our fortunes for which we have waited so patiently.'

They spent their Christmas Day on 'King Edward VII Plateau', unaware that it was now named after King Haakon VII. The cold was affecting them rather more, and Lashly – on his forty-fourth birthday – fell into a fifty-foot-deep crevasse, nearly dragging the others with him. Yet they did over seventeen miles and duly relaxed with their Christmas dinner. So removed from the paraphernalia of the middle-class Christmas, and so near to serious shortage in their rations, the eight men still had pemmican and horse meat stew, with onions, curry powder and biscuit; then a sweet hoosh of arrowroot, cocoa and biscuit; plum-pudding, rounded off with raisins, caramels and ginger. Afterwards, as they lay in their tent, Bowers murmured contentedly to Evans: 'Teddy, if all is well next Christmas we will get hold of all the poor children we can and just stuff them full of nice things, won't we?' Which suggests that Christmas happiness fosters pipe-dreams of charity tomorrow as easily at the ends of the earth as in Wimbledon, or Orange County, California.

Teddy Evans remembered the Christmas as being offset by increasing fatigue in the party. He and Lashly had man-hauled for over 600 miles, and Evans felt, in hindsight, that the men who exchanged 'Happy Christmas' in the morning 'soon lost their springy step, the sledges dragged more slowly, and we gazed ahead almost wistfully'. He also argued that 'a man trained to watch over men's health' would have seen that something was amiss. Wilson was such a man, yet he apparently noticed or reported very little.

There was seldom a sustained period in which Scott's men were free from variations of surface. It may be that the Norwegians had much better luck in this respect; equally their adeptness on ski and their sledging expertise may have made less difficulty out of similar terrain. But in another area of soft snow and a maze of crevasse disturbance Scott found it 'very worrying and tiring' to have to lead the party: 'one cannot allow one's thoughts to wander as others do', he wrote, with a trace of resentment. That swelled on 28 December when the 'second sledge once more loitered'. First he swapped himself for Teddy Evans, then Edgar Evans for Lashly, to see if it was simply a matter of 'staleness' in individuals. But in the afternoon the problem was located in the second sledge itself: 'talking it out, I found that all is due to want of seamanlike care. The runners run excellently, but the structure has been distorted by bad strapping, bad loading, &c. The party are not done, and I have told them plainly that they must wrestle with the trouble and get it right for themselves. There is no possible reason why they should not get along as easily as we do.'

There is prickly exasperation here, a frustration at mistakes, at the inability to detect them in advance, and even at his bewilderment over finding a remedy. The sledge was not the only problem; its crew was more tired than the other. But the mistakes in loading and strapping, the lack of 'seamanlike care' were occurring in a crew of men trained in the Navy. If sledge care was so vital, then surely there should have been no doubt anywhere about the proper procedures. We need only recall how extensively the Norwegians had revised their sledges to recognize another matter left too much to chance by the British.

On 31 December, with the second party 'certainly tiring', they made Three Degree Depot and knocked the sledges down to a ten-feet length. This was a task that had always been intended for Edgar Evans and Crean, and Scott was most gratified by 'a very remarkable piece of work'. But it took longer than expected and, while Evans, Crean and Lashly finished, the other five sat in the tent drinking tea. It was then that Evans badly cut his hand and did not report it to Scott or Wilson. That wound did not heal well – a sign of cold and his run-down condition – and thus began the decline of the Welsh seaman.

By 3 January Scott had made and announced his final selection. It suddenly veered away from his basic plan, and has been a matter of controversy ever since. It is one more outburst of character in Scott, disturbing his own wish for order. Yet, before looking at it, one should stress the un-likelihood that any other arrangement of the last eight men could have avoided death for the final party. The innova-tion was in abandoning the four-man unit. Scott took Bowers into his own tent and sent Teddy Evans back with Lashly and Crean. Cherry-Garrard, who was inclined to torture himself with the thought that disaster could have been prevented, once wrote that Scott should have kept a four-man party and taken Lashly with him – instead of Evans, presumably. Lashly had been hard-worked already and he was older than anyone else in the last five. But he was remarkably strong and phlegmatic and, with Crean, he helped carry Teddy Evans home as Evans succumbed to scurvy. It does seem certain that Scott was unaware of Evans's hand when he made the final choice; no doubt that is why the ambitious Evans kept silent. The wound should have excluded him and then Lashly or Crean would have filled the place that Scott had apparently earmarked for a seaman. Crean might have been the best choice. He was strong and less drained than Lashly. Indeed it was Crean who walked in the last thirty-four miles, on chocolate and biscuits, when Teddy Evans was too ill to be moved and was left in Lashly's care. Crean marched eighteen hours alone and without a break and arrived delirious, late in February. That performance has tended to be overlooked amid so much endurance and heroism. It is a tribute to Crean's strength and stability and hindsight support for choosing him as the seaman to reach the Pole.

The separation into two teams of five and three may have been more questionable than the choice of particular men. Scott's entire method was based on the quartet. Ponting filmed the tent routine and it is evident in these scenes that the tents would not easily take five men, just as the cooking and eating arrangements were for four. The last party must have been slowed and inconvenienced in tiny ways by this. Furthermore only the fortitude of Lashly and Crean prevented the last supporting party being lost. If Scott believed that Evans and Lashly were 'stale', he took a risk by sending them back a man short. There might easily have been eight deaths, and then Scott's leadership would have to be criticized severely.

It is interesting to wonder why Scott settled on the last four. Evans, I think, was the seaman who appealed to Scott and who may have been the most adroit in pressing his claims. Wilson, I would guess, was destined for the last stages out of deep friendship, no matter that Wilson himself was prepared to be sent back. Bowers – the actual addition to the last party – had earned a place through physical effort and thoroughness with pencil and paper. He is the best example of Scott's promoting a man just as he had made himself indispensable. Oates, I think, is as questionable a member of the last group as Evans. We know least about his response to the final stages, largely because his diary was destroyed, making him seem more taciturn than ever. But he does seem subdued and overawed by the ordeal, he did have an old wound and he did break down physically. There is even the suggestion that he was in pain and distress before the last supporting party returned and that he and Wilson kept silent about this. I must repeat that such speculation is probably academic. The last party, whatever the choice, were surely doomed. But the soundest choice might have been a foursome: Scott, Bowers, Lashly and Crean. This is a game, of course, and a grisly one, but it is a game Scott played before the result was known, and we should remember that Scott chose men not always for the most practical reasons, but to demonstrate his idea of a man.

Scott had asked Evans whether he could 'spare' Bowers, but the second-in-command was in no position to refuse. Evans claims that he knew he would never be in the Polar party, but Scott reported him as being 'terribly disappointed but has taken it very well and behaved like a man. Poor old Crean wept and even Lashly was affected.' The three went a little way with the five before turning and then watched the Polar party until they were 'a tiny black speck on the horizon'. Wilson sent a letter to his wife back with the three: 'Our five are all very nice together and we shall be a very happy party.' 'Nice together', or not, the decision to enlist Bowers was abrupt enough to have left Bowers's ski behind at Three Degree Depot, made only four days earlier. This meant that as the five men pulled on, Bowers had the extra handicap of being without ski: 'However, as long as I can do my share all day and keep fit it does not matter much one way or the other.'

They marched on, doing some twelve miles a day in sunny weather and counting the miles to Shackleton's mark. 'What lots of things we think of on these monotonous marches!' wrote Scott. 'What castles one builds now hopefully that the Pole is ours.' On the other hand Scott noted that cooking for five rather than four added half an hour's work to the routine: 'It is an item I had not considered when re-organizing,' he admitted lamely.

7 January was a day of bewildering vicissitudes. They began by depoting the ski but then had to go back and retrieve them as the sastrugi stopped. Scott also discovered Evans's 'nasty' cut and admitted 'if things remained as they are we could not keep up the strain of such marching for long'. The next day a blizzard held them up and Scott passed the time in writing praise of his companions. Wilson was an admirable doctor 'ever on the lookout to alleviate the small pains and troubles incidental to the work'; Bowers was a 'marvel' to whom Scott left all provision arrangement; Oates 'goes hard the whole time . . . and stands the hardship as well as any of us'. Greatest praise was kept for Evans who was given credit for every sledge, sledge-fitting and tent: 'a giant worker with a really remarkable headpiece. It is only now I realize how much has been due to him.' Scott's attachment to Evans is often sentimental, as if the Welshman's ease attracted him.

They passed Shackleton's farthest south on 10 January – 'All is new ahead' Scott responded. They were a week from the Pole, and it proved a week of great labour, deadened by feelings of monotony and dismay that signal tiredness. Scott's diary does not often seem excited: that speaks for the underlying worry of being forestalled and for the unfelt inroads of fatigue. The surfaces still clogged and dispirited them; yet stronger men might have gone through them more briskly: 'About 74 miles from the Pole – can we keep this up for seven days? It takes it out of us like anything. None of us ever had such hard work before.' The men were now in a most perilous condition, hardly able to appreciate the extent to which they had deteriorated. On 12 January they were surprised when the temperature read so high: 'It is most unaccountable why we should suddenly feel the cold in this manner; partly the exhaustion of the march, but partly some damp quality in the air, I think.'

There were hints of irrationality now in Scott. As they got slowly nearer, he wrote, 'If we don't get to it we shall be d—d close'. Yet did he really contemplate drawing back, as Shackleton had done? For the first time he is concerned over Oates, who seemed 'to be feeling the cold and fatigue more than the rest of us'. Quite simply the men were all now short of fuel and drawing on meagre reserves. How far did Scott forget the sustaining effect of anticipatory morale? Less than thirty miles from the Pole he thought 'it ought to be a certain thing now, and the only appalling possibility the sight of the Norwegian flag forestalling ours'. This is on the eve of the day of greatest pathos, and we must allow that Scott was himself too tired and too crowded with mixed feelings to measure that possibility or its impact realistically.

'The worst has happened,' he wrote the next day: 'or nearly the worst', grasping in that instant the darker future that failure horribly exposed. They marched on the morning of 16 January, and at about 2 p.m. Bowers saw what might be a cairn in the distance. They advanced, and it turned into a dark speck. They came up to it, and it was a black flag on a sledge bearer. It might as well have been a hotel or a railway station. 'Discovery' and 'civilization' are bestowed by the prior look of other men. 'It is a terrible disappointment,' Scott admitted, 'and I am very sorry for my loyal companions . . . All the day dreams must go; it will be a wearisome return.'

Next day they followed Norwegian tracks up to the Pole. They found the tent, the names inscribed there and the several things Amundsen had left. They had a 'fat Polar hoosh', and set up their own flags and posed for group

photographs, photographs that would be found, still undeveloped, on their dead bodies, like a last illness that had
taken away their vitality. The photographs are poignant.
Five men staring into the sun, one surreptitiously pulling
the string that will 'take' them. Bowers is huddled like
Uriah Heep in one; Wilson has his wrists resting on his
knees, like someone a little impatient at stopping for a snap
on a hard walk; Evans is still and awkward, unsure whether
to be at attention or not; Scott looks like a man standing
for the national anthem or a firing squad; Oates is drooping,
a puppet hanging in a cupboard.

In another picture Bowers is grinning, knowing the
camera can see him pulling the string. Evans is sitting
beside him, the patient set of his head the same. Oates is
still abject and Scott stands erect with one hand on a
flagpole. The easy Wilson is off to one side, legs astride,
hands on hips and a smile on his face. In both photographs
there is an inescapable humiliation in the five standing to be
pictured for a world that they will not see again. 'Great
God!' cried Scott in his diary, 'this is an awful place and
terrible enough for us to have laboured to it without the
reward of priority.' Bowers wrote to his mother like someone at Brighton – 'Well, here I actually am and very glad to
be here too' – and pleased that 'good British manhaulage
had done the journey'. Wilson said only that Amundsen
'has beaten us in so far as he made a race of it. We have
done what we came for all the same and as our programme
was made out.'

Scott adhered to his plan. He took sightings and marked
his own idea of where the Pole was:

We carried the Union Jack about ¾ of a mile north with us and
left it on a piece of stick as near as we could fix it. I fancy the
Norwegians arrived at the Pole on the 15th Dec. and left on the
17th. I think it quite evident they arrived to forestall a date
quoted by me in London as ideal, viz. Dec. 22. It looks as though

the Norwegian party expected colder weather on the summit than they got; it could scarcely be otherwise from Shackleton's overdrawn account. Well, we have turned our back now on the goal of our ambition with sore feelings and must face our 800 miles of solid dragging – and good-bye to most of the day-dreams!

In a little more than two months the five men were dead. Could they have survived? Most of them suffered injuries and frostbite in temperatures that were unexpectedly low. But every difficulty needs to be seen and felt as affecting men having to work too hard on too little food. Slow starvation made them more vulnerable to cold, frostbite, injury and depression. They found short measure of oil at several depots, but only because of the problem that the Norwegians had noticed and mended very early on. No, I think that they had no chance of surviving, and that Scott, at least, recognized that most of the time. Thus the return has no hopes of sanctuary, and it survives as an account of how men die. In Scott's description it is unexaggerated and never morbid. There is even a sort of calm and much less of the exasperation that had preyed on him going to the Pole.

On the summit things were not too bad, although the cold was now biting into worn clothes and thinner bodies. Despite the very lightly loaded sledge – for they usually carried no more than ten days' food at a time – the weight was onerous and enough to make them despair of the surfaces. Bowers was still labouring without ski, Oates gave further evidence of suffering from cold and, on 23 January, Evans's nose was found to be 'white and hard' from frostbite.

What follows with Evans is a strange, personal tragedy. In so many ways, the Welshman had been a centre of attention: a Polar veteran, a hero to the men, a favourite of the officers, a humorist who could get away with being drunk, a petty officer given more and more responsibility, a man with 'a remarkable headpiece'. It is not improper to suggest how much Evans might have gained with the Pole. As a lower-deck man he could have expected a major promotion, adulation from his fellows and perhaps a pub to manage and enthrall with stories. No doubt he trusted Scott implicitly and may have been the least prepared for Norwegians at the Pole first. Suppose he was demoralized by that loss and then his rapid crumbling becomes easier to understand. He may have been the most practical and least inspired of the five: that made him most vulnerable to disappointment.

Evans could not free himself from frostbite now: it stuck to his fingers like sugar. His large frame was thinning down dramatically and Scott realized for the first time that his spirit was gone: 'To add to the trouble Evans has dislodged two finger-nails to-night; his hands are really bad, and to my surprise he shows signs of losing heart over it which makes me much disappointed in him. He hasn't been cheerful since the accident.' On 4 February he fell in crevasses and was 'becoming rather stupid and incapable'. Wilson later guessed that Evans might have suffered a minor concussion, but Scott's attitude to him was always more moralizing, as if he felt that Evans's will had suddenly drained away. No one survived to speak directly, but the party are discreetly dismayed on paper by the seeming loss of character in Evans.

Coming down the Glacier, he was useless in camping work. Then he developed frostbite in a foot. On 16 February Evans twice stopped the march for trivial reasons and struck the others as 'nearly broken down in brain . . . He is absolutely changed from his normal self-reliant self.' The next day he worked his ski shoes lose as he marched and repeatedly fell behind. The other four were labouring over the sledge and realized that Evans was a long way back. They lunched and still he came no nearer:

By this time we were alarmed, and all four started back on ski. I was first to reach the poor man and shocked at his appearance; he was on his knees with clothing disarranged, hands uncovered and frost-bitten, and a wild look in his eyes. Asked what was the matter, he replied with a slow speech that he didn't know, but thought he must have fainted. We got him on his feet, but after two or three steps he sank down again. He showed every sign of complete collapse. Wilson, Bowers, and I went back for the sledge, whilst Oates remained with him. When we returned he was practically unconscious, and when we got him into the tent quite comatose. He died quietly at 12.30 a.m.

He was buried at the foot of the Glacier and the other four confessed what a desperate plight they had faced with a sick man on their hands. They took further heart at the Shambles Camp depot with a meal of pony meat: 'New life seems to come with greater food almost immediately, but I am anxious about the Barrier surfaces.'

The last month on the Barrier is a story of dwindling daily distances, the destructive cold – −40° sometimes at night – the shortage of oil at successive depots and the pitiful enfeeblement of the men. Scott was also realizing that it was late in the season to be out so far from home. As the days went by, a new certainty emerged, that the only question was where they would die. The loss of fuel meant that they had to eat some food warm and some unheated. The surface of snow and ice was like restlessness in their sleep-walking and Scott calmly recognized their fate as 'a race between the season and hard conditions and our fitness and good food'.

He began to dwell on the distance to the next depot and the days of marching and food that would entail. Their rate of marching was not much more than a mile an hour, so that they were compelled to go ten hours to stand any chance. But for that effort they needed more food, fat and fuel. The night temperature was down to $-37°$ and then $-40°$. Scott took the gamble of increasing the daily ration as the only way of producing the effort. The next depot always dominated them, but beyond that Scott saw only another touch-and-go ordeal. Then at the Middle Barrier Depot came three crushing blows: the temperature dropped below $-40°F$ and men needed one and a half hours to put on their footgear; the oil supply at the depot had evaporated to half; and Oates revealed that he had bad frostbite in his feet. 'We are in a *very* queer street since there is no doubt we cannot do the extra marches and feel the cold horribly.'

On 3, 4 and 5 March their situation became more stark: they did twenty-five miles in three days. One of Oates's feet swelled up, but the men gamely refused to abandon the show of cheerfulness. The sledge turned over twice and they did nine miles in ten hours. It is in such extremity that Scott comes tersely and limpidly to the point. The tragedy cannot be written about when these pencilled words survive:

Our fuel dreadfully low and the poor Soldier nearly done. It is pathetic enough because we can do nothing for him; more hot food might do a little, but only a little, I fear. We none of us expected these terribly low temperatures, and of the rest of us Wilson is feeling them most; mainly, I fear, from his self-sacrificing devotion in doctoring Oates's feet. We cannot help each other, each has enough to do to take care of himself. We get cold on the march when the trudging is heavy, and the wind pierces our worn garments. The others, all of them, are un-endingly cheerful when in the tent. We mean to see the game through with a proper spirit, but it's tough work to be pulling harder than we ever pulled in our lives for long hours, and to feel that the progress is so slow. One can only say 'God help us!' and plod on our weary way, cold and very miserable, though outwardly cheerful. We talk of all sorts of subjects in the tent, not much of food now, since we decided to take the risk of running a full ration. We simply couldn't go hungry at this time.

Oates was silent for long periods. On 10 March he asked Wilson if he had any chance, and Wilson said he didn't know. Oates was slowing them at every point, but Scott doubted if that made much difference to their prospects. The next day the laconic Oates tried to prompt the others to tell him what to do. How awkward and moving that discussion must have been for men pledged to bypass the intimate and the grave. They urged him to march, but the conversation ended with Wilson distributing opium tablets to every man.

That night Scott did a bleak sum: they were now capable of no more than six miles a day and had food for seven days – $6 \times 7 = 42$; but One Ton Camp was fifty-five miles away.

Now Scott's diary falters. He misses days and confuses dates. Oates asked to be left in his bag, but the others insisted that he come along on an awful march of a few miles. These men could not condone opium or the passive acceptance of death, though none of them can have been unwilling by then. Scott was now writing for history:

Should this be found I want these facts recorded. Oates' last thoughts were of his Mother, but immediately before he took pride in thinking that his regiment would be pleased with the bold way in which he met his death. We can testify to his bravery. He has borne intense suffering for weeks without complaint, and to the very last he was able and willing to discuss outside subjects. He did not – would not – give up hope till the very end. He was a brave soul. This was the end. He slept through the night before last, hoping not to wake; but he woke in the morning – yesterday. It was blowing a blizzard. He said, 'I am just going outside and may be sometime.' He went into the blizzard and we have not seen him since.

The horror of Oates's condition is now offset by the preservative fluid of heroism. Most English people know the example he set and respect it or look away sheepishly.

While writing this book, I heard a spokesman for legalized euthanasia enlist Oates as a consenting suicide trying to save others from suffering on his behalf. But time has made Oates very tidy. No one can or would take away his reputation, but who knows what mixture of delirium, helplessness and ecstasy prompted him? He was hardly a mature hero, but he may have guessed that the graceful exit would fix him securely in history.

On 18 March they were twenty-one miles from One Ton Depot, unable to face the weather. Scott's right foot had gone now. Next day they did five and a half miles and amputation of the foot was the best Scott could hope for. The end must come from his journal; nowhere else is that awesome gap of the final week made so clear. Scott was laid up, but it seems certain that he was the last to die, and therefore died alone:

Wednesday, March 21. – Got within 11 miles of depot Monday night; had to lay up all yesterday in severe blizzard. To-day forlorn hope, Wilson and Bowers going to depot for fuel.

Thursday, March 22 and 23. – Blizzard bad as ever – Wilson and Bowers unable to start – to-morrow last chance – no fuel and only one or two of food left – must be near the end. Have decided it shall be natural – we shall march for the depot with or without our effects and die in our tracks.

Thursday, March 29. – Since the 21st we have had a continuous gale from W.S.W. and S.W. We had fuel to make two cups of tea apiece and base food for two days on the 20th. Every day we have been ready to start for our depot *11 miles* away, but outside the door of the tent it remains a scene of whirling drift. I do not think we can hope for any better things now. We shall stick it out to the end, but we are getting weaker, of course, and the end cannot be far.

It seems a pity, but I do not think I can write more.

R. Scott

Last Entry
For Gods sake look after our people.

13
Aftermath

Lines of longitude surge round the Earth from the Pole like
a nervous system; the nexus leaves its imprint all over the
world, but a message travelled slowly in those days and it
took something like a year for the tragedy to sink in on the
civilized world. Sadness was the deeper knowing that it came
late. The great distance sometimes produced lurid coinci-
dences: Amundsen's success was admitted by the London
Times on the day that Scott did the sum, $6 \times 7 = 42$,
$55 - 42 = 13$, and cried out 'God help us!', like a
savage learning arithmetic and mortality in the same lesson.
Two days before Scott's last entry in his diary Kathleen
Scott, battered with the news of Amundsen's victory and
with so many reporters wondering what had happened to
her man, gave a party: 'There were one hundred and ten
people at it. It seems an odd moment to choose to give a
party but I went through with it rather on principle. I am
very glad I did. I was expecting your news hourly, but
determined to go through with the party anyhow.'

The first news had been tentative and problematic. On 8
March 1912 *The Times* reported a tight-lipped Amundsen in
Tasmania, perhaps waiting until he had informed King
Haakon by cable. It also carried a rumour to the effect that
Amundsen claimed Scott had been at the Pole. The London
papers beat on Kathleen Scott's door for confirmation 'but
I told them at once and with all the insistence I could that

those cables were worthless and unsigned, and that they would only make themselves and everybody else ridiculous by publishing them'. Some of the papers went ahead nevertheless, and the Scott house endured a day of pandemonium before Kathleen issued a resolute denial.

A day later and the news was official. *The Times* made a moderate gesture of qualified approval, and introduced the first note of British grievance and misunderstanding:

From the telegrams now received there is little room for doubt that Captain Amundsen has reached the South Pole. From the English point of view he may not have 'played the game'; we cannot forget the secrecy under which for months he shrouded his intention to steal a march on the man who had for years been making his preparations to attain the coveted goal. This was all the more unnecessary, for no one would have welcomed co-operation in the work of South Polar exploration more than Captain Scott. Unfortunately Captain Amundsen notified the latter of his intention too late for Captain Scott to get into communication with him. Still, no one who knows Captain Amundsen can have any doubt of his integrity, and since he states he has reached the Pole we are bound to believe him.

The emotional colour of such reporting was borne out in a fanciful leader that speculated over circumstances that might merely be disguising a victory for Scott:

We have still to hear the story of Captain Scott's expedition enduring the Antarctic summer; and it is by no means unlikely that he also succeeded in his chief endeavour, and, indeed, possible that he reached the Pole before December 14. The Pole is not as concrete or localized an object as the posts which mark the end of a given distance on a running track; and the flag or other signal of victory which one explorer set up to show that he had got there might easily be blown down and covered by snow, or hidden by bad weather from the next visitor to the same rather indeterminate spot. It is at present useless to discuss these varied possibilities; we must simply 'wait and see'. . .

In the civilized world, at least, it was possible to wait and see. For those members of the British party who remained in the south for another winter there was no alternative to regarding the Polar party as lost. Early in April 1912 Cherry-Garrard wrote: 'We have got to face it now. The Pole Party will not in all probability ever get back. And there is no more that we can do.' In that gloomy mood they had to sit out another winter before any chance of going south again to investigate what misadventure had befallen the last five.

But in London the Polar past was still open for anyone's thoughts or nightmares. Nansen sent a cable to Kathleen Scott saying how often he thought of her. She replied, wondering whether, in Norway, there was any inside knowledge of her husband. She ended bravely: 'Hurrah for Norway in spite of all', and the elderly explorer answered, 'Noble! no traces have been seen'. The Scotts' son, Peter, asked his mother, 'Mummy, is Amundsen a good man?' She said she thought he was, and the child responded: 'Amundsen and Daddy both got to the Pole. Daddy has stopped working now.' A few days later Nansen wrote to Kathleen Scott after more reflection, foreseeing that she would have some time yet to wait and giving her the consolation that King Haakon had said in private that he only wished it could have been Scott first.

Another busy correspondent was Sir Clements Markham. His view of Amundsen was always uncharitable – 'He has not had the decency to say a word about our expedition, which is most ungenerous unless he knows nothing, which is most unlikely.' As the press began to play upon the 'race' that Amundsen had won, so Markham wrote tetchily to *The Times* that Scott was above such things, while Amundsen was an interloper who 'merely wanted to make money by telling a good story. Scott's object was nothing of the kind, but scientific research. He, I hope, would not care whether

Amundsen was first, and there would be no question of racing, or conquering, or any claptrap of that sort.'

On 1 April 1912 the *Terra Nova* arrived off Lyttelton, having drawn out of Polar waters as slowly as it penetrated them. Pennell went ashore to discover the news and in his absence a small boat came out to the ship. One of two men in it called to anyone listening on the *Terra Nova*: 'Why didn't you get back sooner? Amundsen got the Pole in a sardine tin on 14 December.' When Pennell returned he confirmed this taunt and Griffith Taylor remembered that on 20 December 1911, while on a journey with Gran, the Norwegian had woken up with the certain intuition that Amundsen was at that moment turning back from the Pole.

Within days the latest instalment of Scott's report appeared in London, and Kathleen rejoiced at the vigorous account by a man already dead: 'The more one reads and weighs it,' she wrote to him in high delight, 'the more apparent the splendid achievement against awful odds appears, and the smaller the value of Amundsen's dash to beat you. I'm so glad, so very glad, you are staying another year. It would have been a thousand pities to return with such opportunities before you.' These passages are poignant, but they show us how Kathleen lived in marriage with Scott for nearly a year after his death, granted that bonus by the delayed communication. She read the private letters from her husband and admired his own wish to make no profit from the expedition. She worked on the diary for eventual publication and did all she could to temper Markham's well-intentioned wrath and 'prevent him publishing awful things about Amundsen and almost indecent eulogies of you'. Markham's letters to the press were an embarrassment, vibrant with the frustration and bitterness of the old man. Kathleen could persuade him to edit and cut, but not everything: 'I have left out the words "In the long run Britons can beat dogs" . . . I have said that dashes to the pole are outside my sphere of advocacy – but I really cannot say anything pleasant about Shackleton and Amundsen. The former is the worst, but they are both sneaking curs.'

Amundsen and Shackleton found themselves sharing an otherwise rather empty platform in November 1912 when the Norwegian came to London for a meeting of the Royal Geographical Society. Kathleen Scott was sent a ticket, but she returned it and went incognito in the top gallery: 'I wanted to avoid the Press and I do not feel sociable on the subject of Amundsen.' She noted that, apart from Shackleton, only Leonard Darwin and the then president of the Society, Lord Curzon, were on the platform. It was not an easy or affable evening, and the visit to London rankled with Amundsen long afterwards: a less brave or more modest man might not have gone.

Curzon opened the proceedings with the 'agreeable task' of making it clear that Englishmen did not begrudge 'a Norseman' his success. Nevertheless he did describe the Norwegian venture as essentially the result of a mild fate. With Scott's circumstances unknown, there was less pressing need to see or make a comparison between the two methods. Still, this is lordly and curt:

Our guest was attended throughout by a good fortune upon which we congratulate him: fine weather, sound health, a transport that never broke down, a commissariat that never failed. With these invaluable aids, he and his brave companions traversed the 750 miles that separated them from the South Pole and the same distance back with a speed that has never been equalled in the history of Polar exploration; and on 14 December 1911 he planted the flag of his country upon the Pole itself. I have seen the results of his scientific observations, which have been carefully worked out by the learned Professor Alexander, of Christiania, and there cannot be a doubt that, though the Pole itself is not a spike or spot in the ground visible to the naked eye, Amundsen and his men crossed and recrossed the actual site. . . .

There are so many subtle condescensions in that – the opinion that good luck most characterized the expedition; the trimming of the actual distance that Amundsen travelled; the belief in the necessity for objective scrutiny before the deed could be accepted; the emphasis on the dogged back and forth employed by the Norwegians to trample the Pole into submission. Nothing is said of the planning, the skill, the daring or the professional understanding of the conditions. Yet, as he introduced Amundsen, Curzon had the cheek to make this lavish reference to Scott:

. . . and even while we are honouring Amundsen this evening, I am convinced that his thoughts, no less than ours, are turning to our brave countryman, Captain Scott, still shrouded in the glimmering half-light of the Antarctic, whose footsteps reached the same Pole, doubtless only a few weeks later than Amundsen, and who with unostentatious persistence, and in the true spirit of scientific devotion, is gathering in, during an absence of three years, a harvest of scientific spoil, which when he returns will be found to render his expedition the most notable of modern times.

Thus chastened, and handicapped by his accent, Amundsen gave a speech that struck Kathleen Scott as plucky, modest and dull – 'and of a dullness!'. Shackleton had the vote of thanks, and he was brief with it 'because time is getting late'. For someone so close to Amundsen's temperament, it was a tepid thanks, remarking on good organization and the soundness of teamwork. Much fuller tribute came from Wilfred Bruce. Then Curzon rounded off the evening with a sly dart for the Norwegian's back. 'I almost wish', he said, 'that in our tribute of admiration we could include those wonderful, good-tempered, fascinating dogs, the true friends of man, without whom Captain Amundsen would never have got to the Pole.' Snideness and affectations of superiority were not unknown in English Polar gentlemen, and Curzon's magnificence was often rooted in arrogance, just as Scott's nobility owes something to intolerance.

In the south thirteen men had stayed on at Cape Evans. Atkinson was in command of Cherry-Garrard, Wright, Debenham, Gran, Nelson, Lashly, Crean, Keohane, Geroff, Hooper, Williamson and Archer. He was the last naval officer left in the main party and Wright has said that he could not imagine a better leader for maintaining morale in the small group. We have seen that men and gentlemen mixed more freely than in the previous winter. Because of the shortage of men, Atkinson had no option but to add the petty officers to the roll of men trusted with taking scientific observations. Not too much of the scientific record was sacrificed, while Crean and Lashly were accepted by everyone as respected Polar heroes who had earned a voice in any discussion. Their dedication and resolution in bringing the terribly reduced Teddy Evans to safety had helped to nudge on the advance of democracy in the expedition.

The feeling of an indistinct tragedy, waiting to be discerned, may have gently consolidated the party. Atkinson made several thoughtful efforts to occupy the men: he had the thirteen live as a single group and dispensed with many of the demarcations of the winter before. There were long scallywag competitions in which everyone was expected to take part. Nevertheless gaps of awareness remained, if nothing else. Cherry-Garrard was sure that the last five were dead by 1 April, yet Petty Officer Williamson came to that realization more slowly. He returned from a trip on 23 April, fully expecting to find the southern party home. But there was no news and Williamson admitted: 'I do not know what to think. I am half afraid that a great disaster has happened poor fellows.'

There were renewed lectures, so strong was the influence of Scott's taste for adult education, the *South Polar Times* reappeared and the men exercised the remaining dogs and seven mules sent by the Indian Government. These creatures had been requested by Scott, on Oates's suggestion, as a means of transport for a second attempt on the Pole, should it be necessary. The mules did well enough at Cape Evans, and had been carefully trained, but it is a moot point as to how effective they would have been nearer the Pole. The mules were sent south by the commander-in-chief in India, Sir Douglas Haig, a man who would direct the greater part of British destruction in the coming war.

The most serious dilemma that faced the thirteen men was whether to devote the coming spring and summer to journeys that would learn the fate of the Polar party or perhaps rescue Campbell's eastern party, who might still be alive, though certainly threatened and at risk. Their reasoning on the subject is very interesting. When Atkinson – whose decision it would be – first raised the alternatives, Cherry-Garrard felt it 'unthinkable that we would leave live men to search for those who were dead'. Every 'military' estimate would have shared that instinct: no one could believe that Scott was alive, or guess where he had died. For all they knew, he might be dead at the Pole, at the bottom of a deep crevasse on the Beardmore or dead of scurvy in a tent far from any predictable course. Whereas there was a real chance that Campbell's party were alive but in urgent need of assistance.

Yet the final decision was romantic, impractical and nearly unanimous. In the middle of June Atkinson assembled the company and put both sides of the argument to them. He concluded with his own feeling, that they should go south. Eleven supported this plan, and one person abstained. Cherry-Garrard's revised opinion was affected by a sense of original purpose and posterity. That it carried can best be explained by the nagging vacancy of not knowing the terrible details. To have tolerated doubt about Scott and his last men would have left a mournful empty place in British history: 'The first object of the expedition had been the Pole. If some record was not found, their success or failure would for ever remain uncertain. Was it due not only to the men and their relatives, but also to the expedition, to ascertain their fate if possible?' Just as, in the 1840s, Britain had been restless to know Franklin's fate, so the pressure to understand Scott's end proved crucial.

Thus, on 29 October 1912, eleven men set out to discover what had happened to Scott. Archer, the cook, was left in the hut with Debenham who had a leg injury too bad for further sledging. On 11 November they reached One Ton Depot: Cherry-Garrard was panicked by the black outline of ponies and thought it was a tent. 'It would be too terrible to find that, though one knew that we had done all that we could, if we had done something different we could have saved them.' The depot also disclosed considerable loss of paraffin which had somehow leaked from insecure cans on to provisions. This was early fulfilment of a complaint that ran through Scott's last weeks.

Their plan was to follow the line of depots as far as necessary. The very next day Wright noticed something off to the right of the march. Some thought it was a cairn from the previous year, but Wright had a curious conviction that the bamboos sticking out of the snow were tent poles. The rest of the party waited for Wright to investigate and report. 'It is the tent,' he said, and some of the others went up to it with him. There are several accounts of what followed, full of little inconsistencies, as if men had been too moved to observe exactly or as if that day had swelled with emotion in their memories. Williamson wept and, with others, 'did not touch anything but just stood off guaging [sic] & wondering what awful secrets the tent held for us on opening it'. Someone brushed snow away and they all saw the green cloth of an expedition tent.

Atkinson was a little behind with the dogs, and the others waited for him to arrive. Then the tent was dug out and he and Lashly went in. The three men were lying there, dead more than seven months but lividly preserved. Scott was in the middle; his left hand was stretched across the body of Wilson; Bowers lay on his right. Scott was in a bag with open flaps, as if he had meant to let the cold in and life out, but Wilson and Bowers were both done up. The two followers who had died first were prone and at peace. Wilson had his hands folded over his chest – perhaps the fond tidying of Scott – and his face was 'wonderful to look at'. Bowers had 'gone away in a kind of happy dream'. But Scott was half sitting up. His diaries, tobacco and a bag of tea were around him, final companions. His face was agonized and pinched and his skin reminded Williamson of old alabaster.

The sorrowful men dug deeper and found skis, the sledge and all the geological specimens. Little by little they restored the tent to the way it must have been when put up for the last time. None of the bodies was moved, though one of Scott's arms had been broken in freeing things from his garments.

It was Atkinson's task to sit down and read Scott's journal, beginning at the end and going backwards. Then he called the men together and read and explained what had happened. This cannot have been a thorough report, but it included the deaths of Evans and Oates, the final ordeal and Scott's Message to the Public. This was an attempt to explain 'the causes of the disaster': early loss of the ponies; bad weather on the way out; poor surfaces on the glacier.

Scott also referred to the shock of Evans's death, the temperatures and the shortage of fuel. The Message is frank, but not understanding; it is the more moving in that Scott died with only a sketchy notion of his mistakes. Overwhelming this, however, and both daunting and inspiring for the eleven men who found the diary and listened to it there on the Barrier was the soaring patriotism of its conclusion, one of the last unalloyed cries of love of country, only years before most countries disappointed their patriots:

> We are weak, writing is difficult, but for my own sake I do not regret this journey, which has shown that Englishmen can endure hardships, help one another, and meet death with as great a fortitude as ever in the past. We took risks, we knew we took them; things have come out against us, and therefore we have no cause for complaint, but bow to the will of Providence, determined still to do our best to the last. But if we have been willing to give our lives to this enterprise, which is for the honour of our country, I appeal to our countrymen to see that those who depend on us are properly cared for.
>
> Had we lived, I should have had a tale to tell of the hardihood, endurance, and courage of my companions which would have stirred the heart of every Englishman. These rough notes and our dead bodies must tell the tale, but surely, surely, a great rich country like ours will see that those who are dependent on us are properly provided for.

Scott had always been a shy man. Before his expeditions he was ill-at-ease and abrupt when called upon to speak to the people of his country. Yet his Message to the Public is one of his least inhibited achievements and shows how great an urge there was in Scott to represent a noble country. Near death he felt no reticence, and the message has the freedom that comes with release and abandon. It may overlook actual causes of failure; it may gloss true motives. But the sentiment of the plea is uncontrived and the prose – written *in extremis* – is fit to end an epic. Very soon after Scott's death England and the rest of the world became sceptical of epic and rhetorical conviction. Yet, surely, surely, the invocation of 'a great rich country' still waits to be realized by Englishmen. In that country there has always been an aspiration to altruism and nobility. Too often it has taken forms that struck observers as sanctimonious, arrogant or fraudulent. But Scott's extremity and his response make an unflawed example of the English hero, so that the message still moves ears unused to its forthrightness. In J. B. Priestley's *Eden End*, set in the disillusion of the years between the wars, a character says that he wishes he had gone south with Scott. And many still respond to the message, whether mountain-climbers, round-the-world sailors or those eccentrics striving to perform some daft feat undone by others but likely to find a place in the *Guinness Book of Records*. To go where no one else has gone may look absurdly precarious, vain and wasteful; but the impulse behind it is still capable of producing 'a tale to tell'.

The discoverers withdrew the bamboo poles and the green tent fell upon the bodies. Then they built a cairn over the tomb and set a cross on top of it, made by Gran from Lashly's skis. Atkinson read the burial service and the men left a note, 'a slight token to perpetuate their gallant and successful attempt to reach the Pole'. Every one of the finding party signed the note. On the night of the 12 November Cherry-Garrard mulled over the suffering there must have been, and began to wonder whether the disaster could have been averted: 'It is all too terrible – I am almost afraid to go to sleep now.'

They went on to look for Oates's body, but it has never been found. Instead they built another cairn and left this note on it, a last message speaking to the power and impenetrability of wilderness:

Hereabouts died a very gallant gentleman, Captain L. E. G. Oates of the Inniskilling Dragoons. In March 1912, returning from the Pole, he walked willingly to his death in a blizzard to try and save his comrades, beset by hardship. This note is left by the Relief Expedition, 1912.

When the *Terra Nova* went south again, the recovered Teddy Evans was once more in command. His convalescence had been slow. In New Zealand, with his wife's family, he had had to wear his jackets unbuttoned until the swelling in his body went down. Amundsen visited him there and marvelled that the British had made such half-hearted use of dogs. Evans went back to England, was kissed by Kathleen Scott at Charing Cross Station and did what he could to raise funds. He met the king in June 1912, and was made commander, even as Scott's last journals and letters were frozen in the snow along with a message to Kinsey that included 'Teddy Evans is not to be trusted over much though he means well'.

Still, Pennell gracefully yielded command of the *Terra Nova* to Evans. Late in January 1913 the ship came back to Cape Evans, and Teddy saw Campbell on the shore. He was upset at having to tell the shore parties that Amundsen had won, but the burden from the shore was graver. Campbell shouted the bare facts across the water and Evans remembered, 'a moment of hush and overwhelming sorrow – a great stillness ran through the ship's little company and through the party on shore'.

In the book he wrote years later, Evans was still haunted by that suspension: 'I have been reminded of it particularly on the anniversaries of Armistice Day.'

The remains of the expedition put up a memorial cross on Observation Hill, and on 23 January they went north. By 10 February they were off New Zealand, evading questions until they reached Lyttelton. There the harbour-master came on board and broke down when Atkinson told him the news. Cherry-Garrard already growing into the role of seer, noted:

we had been too long away, and the whole thing was so personal to us, and our perceptions had been blunted: we never realized. We landed to find the Empire – almost the civilized world – in mourning. It was as though they had lost great friends.

Kathleen Scott was still on her way to New Zealand with the intention of meeting her husband; she had debated over selling stock to pay the fare, but decided there was no need. On 19 February she was sitting on the deck of her steamer when the captain asked her if she would come down to his cabin.

'I've got some news for you, but I don't see how I can tell you,' he said.

'The Expedition?'

'Yes.'

'Well, let's have it.'

He showed her the message that had come over the ship's radio and Kathleen said: 'Oh well, never mind. I expected that. Thanks very much. I will go and think about it.'

She took the Spanish lesson that was already scheduled and talked about American politics with some other passengers. But there were not enough anodyne hiding places on the ship. She read a book on the loss of the *Titanic* – in the following years she would sculpt memorials to its captain and her husband – and stayed on deck till evening, fearful of the stuffiness below:

My god is godly. I need not touch him to know that. Let me maintain a high, adoring exaltation, and not let the contamination of sorrow touch me. Within I shall be exultant. My god is glorious and could never become less so. Loneliness is a fear that

I have never known. Had he died before I had known his gloriousness, or before he had been the father of my son, I might have felt a loss. Now I have felt none for myself. Won't anybody understand that? – probably nobody. So I must go on with the tedious business of discretion. Must even the greatest visions of the heart be blurred by discretions?

The passengers learned of the news and so decorously walked around tragedy that Kathleen sought privacy in the radio room. Between midnight and three in the morning she sat there watching the wireless operator transcribe letters of condolence, further news reports and, finally, passages from Scott's diary:

We were alone, the wireless operator and I. I had come back after undressing, just to see if anything was coming. It was my first knowledge that it was starvation that had killed them. I thought it was exposure. The operator is an Irishman; we have never had any conversation. He just hands me the papers as he has finished writing them. I took my papers and went to bed; I didn't want to hear any more.

Human tragedy in public events sometimes helps us remember moments from our own life. Many of this generation recall where they were when they heard of the shooting of President Kennedy in Dallas. Scott's death riveted people in similar ways; it was immediately recognized as both a private and a universal tragedy. But the world was then informed by telegraph and newspaper, so most people learned of the disaster on the same morning when they came face to face with the cold calm of newsprint. Disaster today trembles with the need to interrupt other programmes and the anxiety invading a voice that is usually bland and script-bound. The impact in Britain was as acute as it must be when a man has aimed his message as directly as Scott had done.

On the day the news was received in London, 10 February, the Royal Geographical Society had a meeting planned that was due to hear a paper on the Balkans and welcome its first female members, including Gertrude Bell. These things were put aside and a vice-president, Douglas Freshfield, addressed the members. He wondered whether any Polar expedition had ever been better equipped or more armed with gallantry and experience. Yet Polar travel would not be 'a training ground for the highest qualities of the British race', were its dangers not extreme and incalculable. Especially blizzard. Only the previous summer, Mr Freshfield added, he had lost a friend in the Alps in such a storm. One of Freshfield's predecessors, Sir Clements Markham, was wintering at Estoril in Portugal. He organized a memorial service in that resort, attended by the German and English ministers in Portugal, as well as many British residents. It seemed to Markham more soothing and moving than the service held in St Paul's on 14 February, which he did not attend.

At this point, to the substantial debts of the expedition there was added the bereavement of relatives and the need to make some recompense. Several funds were opened within a few days, and the variety confused the public. When all the funds were consolidated in the Lord Mayor's Mansion House Fund, the people responded as willingly as Amundsen's dogs. £30,000 was donated in three days and suddenly the grinding slowness of fund-raising gave way to a flood of generosity. In all, over £74,000 was subscribed, enough to test the ingenuity of the trustees.

On 24 February the Royal Geographical Society met again for a florid speech by Curzon, which also contained a shrewd evaluation of why the British had failed, which unwittingly clashed with this solemn valediction on the leader:

Captain Scott has shown in the last hours and in the latest words of his life, what his whole life had conclusively proved to his friends. Simple-minded, high-souled, earnest, indomitable, a wonderful organizer, a natural leader of men – his main characteristic was his utter disregard of self. His last thoughts were for his comrades, his last praise for them, his dying wish to impute no human blame, but to accept without a murmur the inscrutable decrees of Providence.

It was May before all the documents and photographs were in Britain, and then the press brought out special memorial issues, just as the solemn *Geographical Journal* for March had had twenty-one pages boxed in heavy mourning. The *Daily Mirror* had a photograph of the burial cairn on its cover and, inside, pictures of many of the men, of widows and children, full reports, biographies of some of the men and extracts from diaries. A leader quoted Carlyle on hero-worship and the impetus it gave to emulation:

And, indeed, there must be, in all who have it in them sincerely to admire brave men and sincerely to love brave doings, a spark of generosity and good feeling that any day may enable them to imitate that which they admire, and, imitating it, to make it part of themselves and to grow like it.

It is for this reason that we find, in the warmth of love and admiration called up in all Englishmen by the manner in which Captain Scott and his friends met their end, something only a little less encouraging than that end itself.

A little less encouraging was the way the memorial edition was packed around with advertisements for materials and goods used in the south. Oxo had a picture of men on the *Terra Nova* with hot drinks and Scott's own moderate tribute to the beverage. Cerebos Salt had a photograph of shore party stores with one or two of its own boxes prominent. Catesby's Linola owned up to having been on the floor of the hut, and the *Children's Magazine* reminded readers that its own account of the tragedy, in March, had left 'undying memories in the minds of the boys and girls who read the Magazine'.

Among the photographs in the *Mirror* were pictures of women and children now without support: a portrait of Kathleen Scott and family snapshots of Peter Scott; a picture of Oriana Wilson, in a wide-brimmed hat secured by a bow; Mrs Bowers, plump and white-haired; Edgar Evans's wife – dark, severe and pretty; and Evans's three children, awkwardly arm-in-arm on the doorstep of their house, scrubbed urchins suspicious of a London cameraman. All of these, and others, had to be provided for. Only Oates's mother declined any charity. £34,000 was given to relatives: which included £8,500 to Kathleen (now Lady) Scott, and £1,500 to Evans's widow. Even in death and kindness, British officialdom observed hierarchies. £3,500 was set up in trust for Peter Scott to be his at the age of twenty-five, while his education was assisted by an Admiralty grant of £25 a year. Whereas Mrs Evans's pension was £48 a year, Lady Scott had £300.

The Lord Mayor's Committee then turned to the proper publication of the expedition's records. A subcommittee of three was set up: Leonard Darwin on behalf of the Geographical Society; Archibald Geikie from the Royal Society; and Atkinson as representative of the staff. This trio was to advise the unpaid editor of the proceedings, Captain H. G. Lyons. Clements Markham disapproved of the choice and would have preferred Teddy Evans to Geikie. Lord Curzon, who was active on the Lord Mayor's Committee, told Darwin that they had 'tried to soothe everything down with Cmdr Evans (who is a very silly person) & hope all will go well'. Apart from Markham, Evans had few supporters; yet he was the uncontested senior survivor. Whenever a major lecture was called for, Evans was the obvious spokesman. When the remains of the party marched from the Victoria Street office to Buckingham Palace in July 1913, Evans was at their head and introduced the men to the king. He was not on warm terms with the Scott family and must have been deeply distressed by Scott's last verdict on him or by the efforts of other men to conceal it from him. Worse than that, Evans had suffered a personal tragedy that may have been overlooked amid so much famous loss. He and his wife Hilda had sailed back from New Zealand on the P. & O. liner, *Otranto*. But in the eastern Mediterranean she fell ill with peritonitis, and by Naples she was dead. Teddy took the body ashore at Toulon and saw it buried. The strain on him must have been cruel, for he would have felt compelled to carry his own mourning lightly as he rose to introduce Ponting's film or lecture to eager suburbanites. Perhaps the man deserved kinder soothing than he got.

The publication sub-committee was allowed £17,500, an adequate sum considering that the Trustees of the British Museum had undertaken to pay for the publication of all the biological material. But war interrupted the work of the various scientists who had to compile reports, and tripled the costs of publishing. Thus, after the war, earlier plans were modified and Debenham, for instance, had to work long hours on scant pay to finish his task. The figures of some of Evans's surveying did not work out when scrutinized, and there was more embarrassment over the flatness of Atkinson's narrative. It was the early 1920s before publication was done with, and by then some of the scientific data was a little faded. The volumes were large and impressive, and because of their expense they only found their way into institutional libraries. They are thorough and conscientious, as one would expect, but no one has strenuously claimed that the *Terra Nova* expedition made much more of a contribution to science than fill several feet of library shelves.

The deficit of the expedition – over £5,000 – was paid off, and there were grants made to individuals for special services. This left some £18,000 for memorials. The Lord

Mayor's Committee proposed three possible ways of using this sum: a bronze plaque in St Paul's Cathedral; a large statue for some site in London 'by a sculptor of approved eminence to be hereafter selected'; and the balance, some £10,000, to form 'an Endowment Fund in aid of future Polar Research'. The statue was entrusted to Lady Scott and unveiled in Waterloo Place in November 1915. The balance led gradually to the establishment of the Scott Polar Research Institute at Cambridge, now a part of the Geography Department at the university. Debenham played a leading role in its founding and was its first director. By today, the Polar Research Institute has settled into several functions. It has a small museum of Polar relics that schoolchildren are taken to in the afternoon. It houses an archive that holds the originals of many diaries written in the Arctic and Antarctic and all manner of documents and manuscripts pertaining to Polar travel. But the Institute is also a delightful and hospitable gathering place for anyone interested in the various sciences that Scott explored in the south. Those who have researched this subject are fond of the Institute, very grateful to its expert staff and likely to remember afternoon tea signalled by the ringing of the ship's bell from the *Terra Nova*.

Scott's diaries were published by Smith, Elder in 1913 with a preface by Clements Markham that concluded with this tribute and its undiminished sense of responsibility:

From all aspects Scott was among the most remarkable men of our time, and the vast number of readers of his journal will be deeply impressed with the beauty of his character. The chief traits which shone forth through his life were conspicuous in the hour of death. There are few events in history to be compared, for grandeur and pathos, with the last closing scene in that silent wilderness of snow. The great leader, with the bodies of his dearest friends beside him, wrote and wrote until the pencil dropped from his dying grasp. There was no thought of himself, only the earnest desire to give comfort and consolation to others in their sorrow. His very last lines were written lest he who induced him to enter upon Antarctic work should now feel regret for what he had done.

'If I cannot write to Sir Clements, tell him I thought much of him, and never regretted his putting me in command of the *Discovery*.'

The Antarctic often served as a club. People who had lived there together were reluctant to abandon one another. Very deep ties formed amid so much hardship. 'ust as Wilson had wondered whether the Cape Crozier ,arty could go straight inside the hut, some of those who :ame back were never as easy again in comfortable circumstances. Nevertheless Scott's men dispersed all over the world, they went into different walks of life and met their mixed fates.

Tom Crean was awarded the Albert Medal (with Lashly) for saving Teddy Evans. He stayed in Britain only a year and then, as war materialized, he set out with Shackleton on the *Endurance* in an attempted trans-Antarctic journey. No expedition matched it for spectacular adventure, as if Shackleton came into his element once the purposelessness of Antarctic travel had been made clear. The *Endurance* was trapped and crushed in the ice, forcing the company to abandon the ship in the area of South Georgia and camp on an ice floe. Shackleton then took three rowing boats the 100 miles to Sea Elephant Island, with Crean in command of one of the boats. They made that island but were still in such danger that Shackleton decided to row one of the boats the 800 miles to South Georgia. He took five men with him, including Crean, in a twenty-two-foot open boat. They were sixteen days in tumultuous seas and arrived exhausted on a desolate coast. There remained a seventeen-mile walk across mountains to the nearest whaling station. Shackleton took Crean and one other with him on a journey

that lasted thirty-six hours. Only then did Shackleton begin
the reverse process of recovering the men he had left
behind at different points.

The *Endurance* expedition is blatantly heroic and sense-
less. It follows the ideal of adventurous travel for its own
sake, and evidently Crean impressed Shackleton as one of
the most hardy and reliable of men. When Shackleton
returned,* Crean had a year of war in the Navy and was
promoted to warrant officer. Then the Irishman went home,
married and in 1920 retired and settled in Annascaul at the
South Pole Inn where he died peacefully in 1938. A
prodigious traveller, he suddenly became a man who
seldom went far from his village.

His one-time companion, William Lashly, served as ship-
keeper on the *Terra Nova* until late in 1913 and was then
pensioned off at the age of forty-five. But war recalled him
and he served on the *Irresistible* – which was sunk in the
Dardanelles campaign – and on *Amethyst*, and only
demobilized in 1919. He then worked in Cardiff for the
Board of Trade and retired in 1932 to Hambledon, in
Hampshire, the place of his birth. Like Crean, he lived
quietly, an old vessel in a backwater reflecting on great
adventures. He wrote often to former comrades and read
anything published on Antarctica. He died in 1940 in a

* Shackleton could not resist the draw to one end of the earth or the
other. Even in the altered mood after the War, he put together an
expedition to go to the Arctic and the Beaufort Sea, known still as 'the
zone of inaccessibility'. Late in the day these plans were thwarted and
so, like Amundsen before him, he went south instead and died there,
suddenly, on 5 January 1922, in the cabin of his last ship, *Quest*. The
party then came under the command of his old subordinate, Frank
Wild. Wild wrote the account of *Shackleton's Last Voyage* (London,
1923), which includes this poignant admission: 'Though I was his
companion on every one of his expeditions, I know little of his life at
home. It is a curious thing that men thrown so closely together as
those engaged in Polar work should never seek to know anything of
each other's "inside" affairs.'

house he had built himself and called Minna Bluff after a mountain in the south.

There was never a becalmed retirement for Teddy Evans, the wreck of a man that Lashly and Crean had brought to safety. The unhappiness that gathered round Evans after the expedition had made him think of giving up the Navy for farming. But war averted that and made him the youngest commander at sea. He saw active service in the Dover Patrol, married again – a Norwegian girl – and then in April 1917 won swashbuckling fame as commander of the *Broke* in an engagement that involved Evans refusing to rescue Germans from the sea and roaring out to them 'Remember the *Lusitania*!'.

He was made captain, awarded the D.S.O. and became a newspaper hero – 'Evans of the *Broke*'. He was still boisterous and robust, still unaware of the way he disturbed quieter men. After the war he served in the east and while commanding the *Carlisle* supervised a mass rescue of coolies from a sinking steamer. He went into the water himself to scoop up the last Chinese and was thereafter immensely popular in Hong Kong.

Evans was also writing now; *South with Scott* was published in 1921, and he wrote cheery, jingoistic pieces for the *Daily Express* and the *Strand* magazine as well as rousing stories for roused boys. At one time he even planned a play, 'a comedy about Navy life'. The middle-aged man could still overwhelm any lieutenant at feats of strength, and was likely to demonstrate them at the dinner table. He was made commander-in-chief of the Royal Australian Squadron and, while living in Sydney, caught a house thief. Rather than call the police, Evans took off his coat and gave the man first a thrashing and then a ten shilling note – the ingredients of imperial benevolence.

In 1932 he was made vice-admiral and commander-in-chief of the Africa Station and in 1935 he was knighted and appointed commander of the Nore. As war again drew nearer and Evans was forcibly reminded of the silence that joined shore and ship when the *Terra Nova* went south for the last time, he urged the example of Scott and Oates on young men – 'Oates and his companions dying in the blizzard left what was virtually a message to youth, a dying appeal to play the game and play it like men'. But the second war, more than ever, would mock the 'game' in Evans's mind and denude the players. He also visited sea cadets and did spectacular exercises on deck if ever their interest in Polar heroes waned.

Just before the war he declined the opportunity of a Tory seat in Parliament and became a regional commissioner for civil defence in London. In that capacity he flustered civil servants but appealed to the public; he went on morale-raising tours of the provinces where his good humour apparently overcame massive ignorance of local facts and issues; he almost led an invasion of Norway; he was seconded to the Ministry of Aircraft Production; and then he turned into a whimsical socialist. At the 1945 election he declared, 'I'm Labour, honest-to-God Labour,' and in October of that year he was one of the new Labour peers, Lord Mountevans. He returned to Norway and died in 1957, a man who always illustrated the limitations of burnished purity and zeal. Scott thought him shallow and unsound; how far then might Scott have risen in the world? Or did his scepticism about Evans signify a lack of the ability to mix with many men and tolerate misunderstanding? Evans enjoyed his life, and it is no real disservice to see him as an unwittingly comic figure, a character that Evelyn Waugh might have relished, and a man who survives Scott's grim distaste.

Others of Scott's men had a less jolly war, made no headlines and were as helpless as Edgar Evans coming down the Beardmore Glacier. The industrious and always tactful Pennell was drowned at Jutland when the *Queen Mary* sank. Rennick went down with his ship, the *Hogue*. Alf Cheetham, a boatswain who served on *Discovery*, *Nimrod*, *Terra Nova* and *Endurance*, survived the hazards of all those journeys and died in 1918 in the North Sea when his trawler was torpedoed. Atkinson served in Flanders with siege-gun crews. He was awarded the D.S.O. and then the Albert Medal when he did rescue work on the burning *Glatton* in Dover harbour. It was during this incident that he lost an eye. Atkinson had been widely liked in Antarctica, and commander of those who found Scott. But he was modest, nearly as reticent as Oates, and neither prepared nor able to assert himself. What we know suggests that his life tapered away to an early death in 1929 – he was only forty-seven. In the early 1920s his illness delayed publication of an official narrative. In 1928 his wife died and, after an appendicitis operation, he went in to the Royal Naval Hospital at Chatham where he had a break-down. His distressed sister, Hazell, wrote to Cherry-Garrard, wondering if he could not visit Atkinson and comfort him. This is a sad picture of a forgotten and demoralized hero:

> My very great fear is that, should he leave the navy (his one interest) he will go to pieces & drink himself to death, as he mentions in his letter that he 'hopes to join his dead wife soon'. I mention this in confidence, to show you the state into which he has got, & the help he will need.

Many of the scientists had notable careers. George Simpson became director of the Meteorological Office. Debenham made a life at Cambridge. Griffith Taylor wrote several books and became professor of geography at the University of Chicago. After the war Wright spent ten years working for the Admiralty on Scientific Research and Experiment, and from 1929 to 1934 he superintended the

Admiralty Research Laboratory. Then from 1934 to 1946 he was director of Admiralty Scientific Research. He retired to his native land, Canada, and lived in British Columbia until his death in 1975, cheerfully and kindly assisting anyone inquiring about the history of Scott's travels. He married the sister of Raymond Priestley, who was a Fellow at Clare College, Cambridge, from 1923 to 1934, from 1935 to 1938 the vice-chancellor of Melbourne University and from 1938 to 1952 vice-chancellor of Birmingham University. Priestley died only in 1975. An odd amalgam took place among the scientists, further evidence of the Antarctic Club. Not only Wright, but Griffith Taylor too married one of Priestley's sisters, while Priestley himself married a relative of Debenham. These four men were especially close, all Wilson's young men, and they inaugurate the breed of scientists who have been in and out of Antarctic research establishments ever since. Griffith Taylor wrote in 1916 encouraging other men to take up that work:

> I shall, in all probability, never again see the Antarctic; but my advice to any volunteer, who has that opportunity offered him, is to take it. Especially is this the case if he be a scientist or writer, for the present tendencies of modern life are all opposed to the multiplication of such experiences. Only in Polar lands is to be found the joy of a 'real return to the primitive', in association with the best types of strenuous youth. There, if anywhere, is life worth while, and effort sure of recognition. To few explorers is it given to serve under a leader with Scott's kindly sympathy for every detail of his work; but after each and every expedition, the heavy cloud of discomforts, dangers, and disasters gradually fades from memory, and nought remains but the brightness of the silver lining.

Kathleen Scott bore the year 1913 with flamboyant dignity, but she was worn out and, typically, went off alone to the

Sahara to recover herself. In one way there is not much difference between 'the lone and level sands' of the desert and the wrinkled white glare of Antarctica. No doubt the solitary experience intensified the mystical feeling for all the vital courage she had gained from her husband.

Thereafter she was a famous lady, a respected sculptress and the confidante of celebrities as different as Nansen and Asquith. She was often visited by old *Terra Nova* men, and she had her favourites as well as a terse, manly way of endorsing them:

I found Victor Campbell waiting at home. He had the flag-ship on both the Zeebrugge and Ostend stunts. The back of his ship, H. M. S. *Warwick*, a destroyer, was broken; but he talked of it as though it were a rather good game of tennis. Nice things, sailors!

Her devotion to Scott could reduce her to tears years after his death, and it put her in great torment whenever others wrote of him at all critically or, in 1929, when Stephen Gwynn published a biography of Scott that was allowed to quote from private letters:

I don't know how I am going to bear having that published. I'm told he is not my property, that he is public property, that I have no right to withold anything that throws light on his character, that I must subject my own susceptibilities to what-ever is best to sustain his name at the highest. All that may be so, nay – is so; and yet when I come to see letters that have made me weep and will make me weep every time I think of them till I die, when I come to see these letters laid bare for my chauffeur, my grocer, and small boys at my son's school to read, my skin shrinks round me tight and hard.

Something like that tightening distaste for being intruded upon was voiced by Mrs Caroline Oates, the mother of Scott's companion. She had the diary that Oates had left behind when he walked out into the blizzard. It may not have been inhibited or extensive, since Oates was a reluctant letter-writer who often had to be bullied by his companions to send a note to his mother. At the same time those letters from Oates that are now viewable are often critical of the expedition. Oates's diary, destroyed upon his mother's instructions, may have contained some material to justify the mother's unconcealed dislike of Scott. When Gwynn's book appeared, Mrs Oates was disdainful of the indiscretion that had permitted the letters to be made public.

But Kathleen Scott was always impetuous and emotional, quick to feel and eager for fame. Not many widows would have gone all the way to Berlin in 1930 to see a stage play based on the race between Amundsen and Scott. Without fuss, Kathleen went and quite enjoyed the beginning, despite the fact that Scott was portrayed as 'a puny little man'. But by the end she was distraught and appalled at the vulgarity:

> The last act sends the whole play to damnation. So far it has been bearable. Back in the snows, Scott's party are weakening. There is a long, unhistoric, and intensely melodramatic scene of the failing of Oates, in which they all howl and shriek like demented Latins – a sorry affair indeed. They are made to leave Oates behind and lose him, and Bowers goes out to look for him, whilst Wilson and Scott go to sleep in the tent. A likely happening! There is no attempt at truth. There is no blizzard. They all sit about outside as though enjoying a sunny picnic. They rant and shriek and finally die; and then the fine chorus returns. This act was not only bad but unspeakably dull. But it is undoubtedly meant to be a tribute, prompted perhaps by the Germans' wish to show that defeat may be more noble than success.

Kathleen married again, to the Labour M.P. Hilton Young, later Lord Kennet, and they had a son, Wayland Young. As for Peter Scott, he has lived very much in the way his father had hoped. In several of his last letters Scott asked friends to look after the young Peter, and in one he wrote: 'Make the boy interested in natural history if you can; it is better than games; they encourage it at some schools. I know you will keep him in the open air.

'Above all, he must guard and you must guard him against indolence. Make him a strenuous man. I had to force myself into being strenuous, as you know – had always an inclination to be idle.'

That cannot have been the easiest instruction for a boy or man to follow, especially if he has ever suspected indolence in himself. Perhaps Peter Scott took more inspiration from Edward Wilson; indeed Scott's wish must have been affected by the impression Wilson had made on him. Still, in the spirit of Scott's hope, and yet in his own fashion, Peter Scott has been a dedicated popularizer of natural history and a defender of threatened wildlife. In his writing, his paintings – as naturalistic and mild as Wilson's – his work on nature reserves and in that earnest, kindly voice he has been a fine educator in a world gradually losing familiarity with nature.

I have left Cherry-Garrard till last, because no one else so insists on the deep impression left in him by being one of Scott's men. It would have been very dangerous to write a book about those men that had as its motive the determination to make them appear as the last English gentlemen, trudging honourably but meekly towards receding white horizons and the wasteland of war, depression and alienation. The story of Scott's men must be, simply, that of ill-advised and not always very critical humans going out in the great cold, without complaint, for a purpose that bewilders many practical people. I have tried to tell that story clearly and accurately, while allowing the reader to see where English heroism was aided and abetted by mistakes. The drama of the walk, of the south itself, and of the tragedy surely remains. But, as we look back on it now, it is difficult not to interpret the tragedy, not to see Scott's men as pilgrims, knights or First World War donkeys gone away from a distressing world to seek a grail. Now that we are indifferent to the South Pole, as we are to the Moon, we have to respond to the imaginative impact of that journey and to the way in which it embodies ideals and a sensibility about what life might have been. 'Going south' is all the more poetic a concept to us because of the matter-of-fact way in which Scott's men set about it. However faithful one is to this material, it lends itself to the framework of epic and legend. As an incident it now seems more momentous than it was, and that can only be because it is a gesture of a sort of gentlemanly valour and altruism which we tend to think flourished before the First World War. It may never have been real in a general sense; thus it is important to see how far Scott was a prickly, inhibited bungler; equally we must recognize that many of the survivors lived through all the changes of this century, adapting to them as well or as awkwardly as anyone else.

But I think we are all now uneasy about what a man could or should be. Scott's men chose or were trapped into being heroes of a rare sort: commonplace men, perhaps, who stir any imagination that reflects on how they spent their time in the south. Their going so far for so little only reveals more of the obsessive lure and obscure purpose of human inquiry. Cherry-Garrard more than anyone else lived in the shadow of Scott's men. He could not come to terms with the tragedy until the exhausted calm of his old age. But the effect was not merely personal. He was a thoughtful, dogmatic man, not always possessed of great insight or tolerance. But he held firm notions of how men should behave; he had seen piercing examples of it in the south; and for the rest of his life he felt the world scuttling farther away from that code. It is easy to detect the conservative in Cherry-Garrard. One cannot have too much faith in the flexibility of his thoughts on, or his own capacity for, bending ideals round a world turbulent with so many released and conflicting energies. In other words his view of the gentleman depends too much on the economic, social, psychological and intellectual stability that a gentleman enjoyed before 1914.

Not every one of Scott's men would have shared all of Cherry-Garrard's emotional ideas. One can hear Oates sniffing at them, Bowers fending them away with a joke. Evans could only have stood at attention for them in silence. But Scott and Wilson, I think, would have been moved by them and proud to have expressed them in the abrupt but quivering style that Cherry-Garrard dug out of himself. *The Worst Journey in the World*, published in 1922, and written in the long and never complete convalescence after Cherry-Garrard had been invalided home from the Western Front, is more than a history of journeys. It is a record of a state of mind, and an urgent if pessimistic address to the 1920s. The original preface began with these words:

This post-war business is inartistic, for it is seldom that any one does anything well for the sake of doing it well; and it is un-Christian, if you value Christianity, for men are out to hurt and not to help – can you wonder, when the Ten Commandments were hurled straight from the pulpit through good stained glass. It is all very interesting and uncomfortable, and it has been a great relief to wander back in one's thoughts and correspondence and personal dealings to an age in geological time, so many hundred years ago, when we were artistic Christians, doing our jobs as well as we were able just because we wished to do them well, helping one another with all our strength, and (I speak with personal humility) living a life of co-operation, in the face of hardships and dangers, which has seldom been surpassed.

The mutual conquest of difficulties is the cement of friendship, as it is the only lasting cement of matrimony. We had plenty of difficulties; we sometimes failed, we sometimes won; we always faced them – we had to. Consequently we have some friends who are better than all the wives in Mahomet's paradise, and when I have asked for help in the making of this book I have never never asked in vain. Talk of ex-soldiers: give me ex-antarctics, unsoured and with their ideals intact: they could sweep the world.

The trouble is that they are inclined to lose their ideals in this complicated atmosphere of civilization.

Sour changes threatened Cherry-Garrard; his country house was encroached upon by developers and his innate conservatism flinched at frivolity and radicalism alike. He was not a well man, and he did not need to work. Anger and dismay can gather in such a marooned figure, and he passed his time in friendships with George Bernard Shaw, T. E. Lawrence and the mountaineer, Mallory; in pursuing kindness for other people, especially men who had been with Scott; and with attempts to make Macquarie Island a sanctuary for seals and penguins. He slowly agonized over some of the smaller failings that had contributed to Scott's tragedy: the loss of oil in the depots and the chance that if he had taken the dogs beyond One Ton Depot in the spring of 1912 he might have saved Scott. Like any sick man who has once been energetic, he brooded at his own physical decline.

We can catch something of the obsessed, universal anxiety growing out of personal distress in an Introduction he wrote for George Seaver's biography of Edward Wilson in 1933. Wilson was the paramount 'artistic Christian' in Cherry-Garrard's eyes, and Antarctica had been the fittingly austere setting for such men – even if the description could hardly have weathered scrutiny anywhere else. The reference to a monastery shows us the appeal of the great white south, and one way in which its cleanliness was a saving virtue for strong men not always robust enough to deal with the compromises and confusion of civilization:

If this book succeeds in showing what kind of man Bill was, it will give you courage; and this is what the world has wanted since he died, and never perhaps so much as now. When things for which men have worked for centuries are being destroyed; when those who have done most for the longest time are being sacrificed; when no one who has any intelligence and does not live in a monastery can but be deeply stirred by the chaos which threatens, you will read here the story of a man who, however appalling the conditions, and whatever the dangers, in the face of starvation and more than once of inevitable death, just went on doing his job.

The second war forced him in upon himself and introspection led to something near breakdown in the first shabby years of peace. He was nursed back to better health and in the early 1950s followed the hobbies of book-buying and travelling. But he broke down again in 1953 – the year Everest was climbed for the first time – and made another slow recovery. His last years were more peaceful and he died in 1959, as men made ready for the Moon. In 1951, chronically upset by the thought that Scott might have been saved, he had privately printed a postscript to *The Worst Journey in the World* that includes a touching lament and celebration of man's inquiring spirit. It is resolute, profound but also brittle and simplistic. It speaks of Cherry-Garrard's troubles, and I think it reproduces some of the ardent confusion in a man like Scott. Above all, it captures the way in which the journey in the snow was not just a physical but a spiritual and imaginary journey. The view of the world is jaundiced. The will and means to remedy its pain are not very convincing. It is distressing to see the disenchantment with man extend to a scepticism of government or any of the ways that might reform them.

But the feeling of the need to do some extravagant, clean thing to show one's readiness is moving and persuasive, and here I think that Cherry-Garrard speaks for Scott, just as he concludes with the subject I have tried to examine in this book:

We cannot stop knowledge: we must use it well or perish. And we must do our tiny scrap to see that those who do use it are sound in mind and body, especially in mind, or good education, with a background of tradition, a knowledge of human nature and of history: with a certain standard of decency which inspires trust: with disinterestedness and self-control. Plato said the good ruler is a reluctant man. The really wise man knows what an awful thing it is to govern, and keeps away from it. Our problems are not new: they are as old as the men who hunted the prehistoric hills. When *they* hit one another on the head with stones the matter was confined to a few caves: now it shakes a crowded world more complicated than any watch. Human nature does not change: it becomes more dangerous. Those who guide the world now may think they are doing quite well: so perhaps did the dodo.

Man, having destroyed the whales, may end by destroying himself. The penguins may end like the prehistoric reptiles from which they sprang. All may follow the mammoths and dinosaurs into fossilized oblivion, like the ferns which grew at the South Pole two hundred million years ago, found by the Polar Party on the Beardmore and carried on their sledge to the end at Wilson's special request: museum pieces of life in time.

Any age, new or old, wants courage and faith. To me, and perhaps to you, the interest of this story is the men, and it is the spirit of the men, 'the response of the spirit', which is interesting rather than what they did or failed to do: except in a superficial sense they never failed. That is how I see it, and I knew them pretty well. It is a story about human minds with all kinds of ideas and questions involved, which stretch beyond the furthest horizons.

Note on Sources

The most immediate sources are the published works by men who went south or by friends and relatives whose thoughts went with them.

Robert Falcon Scott, *The Voyage of the 'Discovery'* (London, 1905) *Scott's Last Expedition* (London, 1913): this is, in large part, the journals kept on the second expedition; they were edited by Leonard Darwin, possibly after consultation with Lady Scott and others, and many passages from the original were not printed; the journals are in the British Museum and a facsimile edition was published (Penn, Buckinghamshire, 1968) which also includes his Sledging Orders and those editions of the *South Polar Times* published during the *Terra Nova* expedition

Roald Amundsen, *The South Pole: An Account of the Norwegian Antarctic Expedition in the 'Fram'* (London, 1912) *My Life as an Explorer* (London, 1927)

Apsley Cherry-Garrard, *The Worst Journey in the World* (London, 1922); in 1951, Cherry-Garrard had privately printed a *Postscript to the Worst Journey in the World*

Frederick A. Cook, *Through the First Antarctic Night 1898–1899* (London, 1900)

Edward Evans, *South with Scott* (London, 1921) *The Desolate Antarctic* (London, 1950)

Tryggve Gran, *Hvor Sydlyset Flammer* (Christiania, 1915) *Kampen om Sydpolen* (Oslo, 1961)

Thomas Griffith Taylor, *With Scott: The Silver Lining* (London, 1916) *Antarctic Adventure and Research* (New York, 1930)

Helmer Hanssen, *Voyages of a Modern Viking* (London, 1936)

William Lashly, *Under Scott's Command: Lashly's Antarctic Diaries*, ed. A. R. Ellis (London, 1969)

Sir Clements Markham, *The Lands of Silence, a History of Arctic and Antarctic Exploration* (Cambridge, 1921)

Herbert G. Ponting, *The Great White South* (London, 1924)

Raymond E. Priestley, *Antarctic Adventure: Scott's Northern Party* (London, 1914)

Kathleen Scott, *Self-Portrait of an Artist* (London, 1949)

Ernest Shackleton, *The Heart of the Antarctic: Being the Story of the British Antarctic Expedition 1907–1909* (London, 1909)

Edward Wilson, *Diary of the 'Terra Nova' Expedition to the Antarctic 1910–1912*, ed. H. G. R. King (London, 1972)

There are also several valuable studies of explorers and exploration.

Margery and James Fisher, *Shackleton* (London, 1957)

Stephen Gwynn, *Captain Scott* (London, 1929)

J. Gordon Hayes, *Antarctica, a Treatise on the Southern Continent* (London, 1928)

Admiral Sir Albert H. Markham, *The Life of Sir Clements R. Markham* (London, 1917)

Reginald Pound, *Evans of the 'Broke'* (London, 1963) *Scott of the Antarctic* (London, 1966)

George Seaver, *Edward Wilson of the Antarctic* (London, 1933) *'Birdie' Bowers of the Antarctic* (London, 1938)

The Scott Polar Research Institute in Cambridge has a large archive of unpublished manuscript material, out of which the following were of special value (figures in brackets refer to the SPRI catalogue):

assorted papers accumulated from the *Terra Nova* expedition, 7 volumes (280/28/1–7)

Note on Sources

statement of account sent to Sir Edgar Speyer by auditors
(761/8/12)

diary of Frank Browning, 1910–11 (870)

journal of Bernard Day, 1910–11 (660/1)

letter from C. Reginald Ford to Reginald Pound, 1965 (761/4)

journal of Patrick Keohane, 1911–12 (825/1)

letters from Robert Falcon Scott to Joseph Kinsey, 1909–12
(761/8/13–34)

letters from Stanley Richards to Reginald Pound, 1964 (761/16/
1–6)

address book of Robert Falcon Scott (352/7)

journal of George Simpson, 4 volumes (704/1–4)

journal of T. Griffith Taylor (718)

diary of Thomas Williamson, 1912–13 (774/2)

a collection of letters from L. E. G. Oates to his mother, 1899–
1910 (1016/1–339)

the notebook of Sir Clements Markham (715/9)

letters from Edward Atkinson to A. Mead, 1910 (1023/1–2)

letters from George Simpson to Arthur Schuster and Hugh
Mill, 1909–20 (1122/3/1–29; 100/120/1–2)

letters from Albert Armitage to Hugh Mill, 1922 (100/11/1–7)

letters from Clements Markham to Kathleen Scott, 1911–15 (8)

letters from Kathleen Scott to Sir Lewis Beaumont and Apsley
Cherry-Garrard, 1913–19 (16; 559/111/1–32)

letters from Hazell Atkinson to Apsley Cherry-Garrard, 1928
(559/26/1–4)

letters from Caroline Oates to Hugh Mill and Apsley Cherry-
Garrard, 1918–30 (559/166/1–2; 100/88)

Acknowledgements

It may be that Captain Scott's most useful legacy is the Polar Research Institute at Cambridge. Anyone concerned with examining Polar history and science must benefit from its services. I am deeply appreciative of their collection of manuscript materials, from full diaries to one-page letters, that bear upon Scott's life and work. The staff of the Institute could not have been more helpful or more ready to discuss all matters arising. I am especially grateful to the librarian, Harry King, and his assistant, Kristen Hollick.

Elsewhere I was lucky enough to enjoy correspondence with Sir Charles Wright, who willingly responded to many questions about the expedition of which he was one of the last survivors. I must also thank Eva Scott-Hanssen, who provided me with translations of parts of Tryggve Gran's books; the office of the Royal Norwegian Consulate in Madeira; the National Film Archive, who were able to show me Herbert Ponting's film, *Ninety Degrees South*; the staff and resources of the London Library, the West Sussex County Library and the library of New England College; and Miss Edith Oates, cousin of the explorer, who talked about her family with me.

Index

Index

Index

Index

Index

Index